IMAGES
of America

ABERDEEN GARDENS

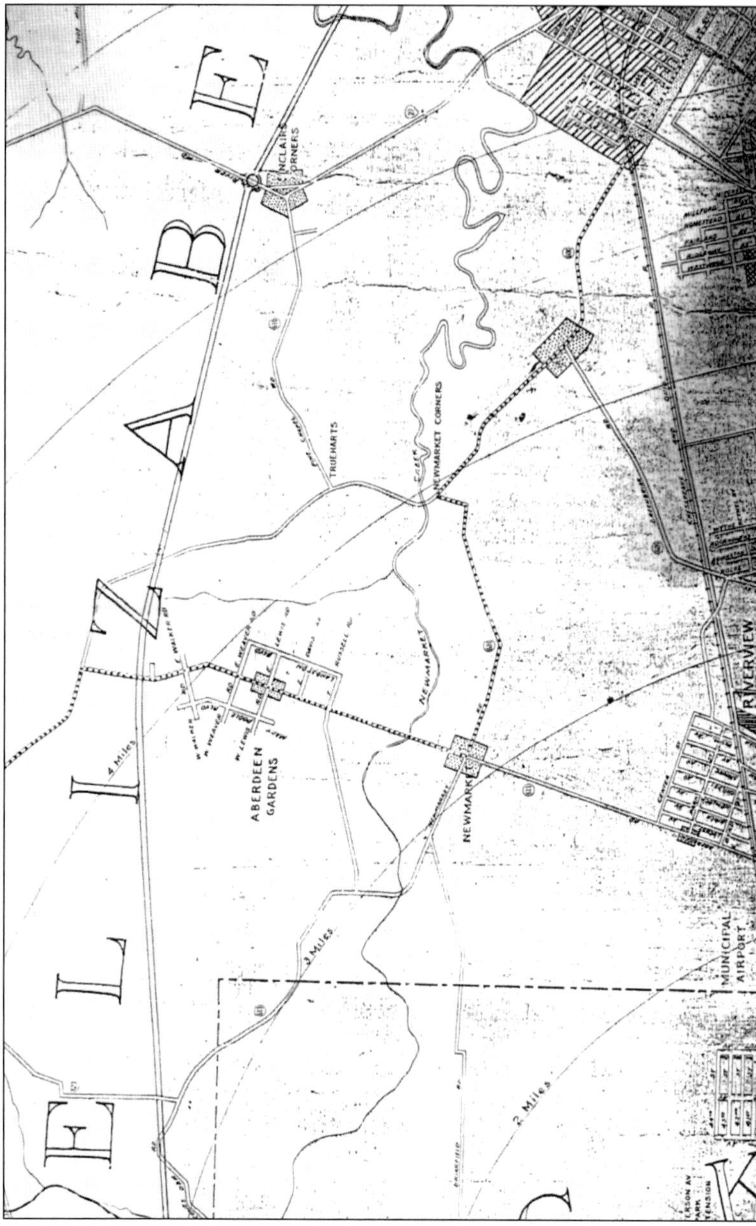

R. F. Bower's map of Newport News and Environs, Elizabeth City County, Hampton, Phoebus, and Buckroe Beach is a graphic outline representation of Aberdeen Gardens' layout with street names in the 1940s. The Newmarket Creek tributary engulfs the Aberdeen neighborhood in a horseshoe shape from the bridged area crossing Aberdeen Road. Note the misspelling of Mary Peake Boulevard as Mary Poole Boulevard on the map. (Courtesy of Hampton Library.)

ON THE COVER: This multi-purpose building unit, pictured in 1947, was a part of the original 1936 plans. The commercial occupants were the Aberdeen Gardens Management Office, Co-op Food Store, and Toy's Tavern. William Roscoe Walker Jr. (standing left), the housing agent, is pictured along with office staff. (Courtesy of Claude Vann Jr.)

IMAGES
of America

ABERDEEN GARDENS

Aberdeen Gardens Heritage Committee

ARCADIA
PUBLISHING

ISBN 978-0-7385-5292-7

Published by Arcadia Publishing
Charleston, South Carolina

Printed in the United States of America

Library of Congress Control Number: 2007928069

For all general information contact Arcadia Publishing at:
Telephone 843-853-2070
Fax 843-853-0044
E-mail sales@arcadiapublishing.com
For customer service and orders:
Toll-Free 1-888-313-2665

Visit us on the Internet at www.arcadiapublishing.com

To the residents of the Aberdeen neighborhoods on behalf of the Heritage Committee of Aberdeen Gardens Historic and Civic Association, Inc.

CONTENTS

ACKNOWLEDGMENTS

The Heritage Committee of the Aberdeen Gardens Historic and Civic Association, Inc., thanks a number of people who have helped in the preparation and support of this book. Special thanks to Pres. Joseph Holland, Historic Foundation of Aberdeen Gardens, for bridging the gap of resources. Thanks to the Virginia government, the Virginia Department of Historic Resources, and Preservation Alliance of Virginia's officers and directors for their research support. All departments of the City of Hampton, especially the neighborhood office, parks and recreation, and the fire and police department, have been supportive with resources. Thanks to Liz Wilson, librarian supervisor in Hampton Library's Virginia Room, and to Donzella Maupin and the graphic technician for Hampton University's archival research and photographs. Thanks to Walter P. Calahan Photography, "Doc" at Camera City, and Heck Production Company for processing images. Claude Vann Jr. has been an extremely valuable, detailed historian. Jacqueline Arrington helped with captions and showed patience in organizing the photographs collected. Jacqueline Roundtree provided the book with historical photographs. Photographer Catherine Howard captured the images in the Aberdeen Who's Who chapter. Margaret Jones Wilson has been very supportive in photograph preparation. Thanks to Harmon Stokes for his dedicated support. Thanks to partnered neighborhood members and Aberdeen families that shared photographs for this awesome task.

Thanks to authors Colita Fairfax, Reginald Johns, and Alfreda Drummond for their guidance and support.

Thanks to Rev. Hallie Richardson, Lillian Dalton, and Little Zion Baptist Church's administrative staff for providing research support and to Mark Hudson, principal of Aberdeen School, for providing library and technological resources.

Thanks to District 10's elementary and middle schools for their support. Pres. Roosevelt Wilson of Aberdeen Gardens Historic and Civic Association, Inc., and Pres. Linwood Harper of Aberdeen Athletic Association were supportive.

A special thanks to Shellae Blackwell, Hampton Neighborhood Office District 10 facilitator, for patience and guidance in providing archived photographs and resources.

Thanks to publisher Lauren Bobier and editor Maggie Bullwinkel at Arcadia for their patience and guidance throughout this project.

Finally, we would like to thank our families and friends for their patience and support during the past few months. Thanks be to God for His love and mercies.

INTRODUCTION

Aberdeen Gardens began as a New Deal settlement community offered by Pres. Franklin Delano Roosevelt in the early 1930s following the Great Depression, initiated by Hampton Institute (now Hampton University), and designed specifically for the resettlement of African American workers in Newport News and Hampton, especially the workers at Newport News Shipbuilding and Dry Dock Company. Aberdeen Gardens was the only Resettlement Administration community for blacks in Virginia. Even though there were 55 New Deal communities, Aberdeen Gardens had the only homes built of brick by blacks for blacks. The lead architect was Hilyard R. Robinson (1899–1986) in Washington, D.C. The civil engineer was Charles Sumner Duke (1879–1952). Duke was the first black engineer to have been awarded such a large responsibility in the area of housing.

Aberdeen Gardens was, from 1934 to 1952, a part of Elizabeth City County, Hampton, Virginia. Elizabeth City County is now extinct. Hampton, Virginia, is the oldest, continuously settled English community in the United States. The town of Hampton, established in 1680, became the largest town in Elizabeth City County and was the county seat. In 1908, Hampton was incorporated as an independent city. In 1952, the county and the former town of Phoebus in the county were merged into the independent city of Hampton.

Aberdeen Gardens is named for Aberdeen Road, the principal transportation corridor that linked the worker-residents with Newport News and its shipbuilding facilities. The Aberdeen Gardens Historic District was begun in 1934 and was finished in 1937 with 158 single-family homes, one school, and a vital commercial structure compared to a small mini-mall. President Roosevelt wanted to ensure that black workers had a decent place to live. On April 21, 1938, Eleanor Roosevelt, who had always been a supporter of subsistence homesteads, visited the neighborhood when she spoke at Hampton Institute's 70th-anniversary ceremony. The federal government purchased a 440-acre land tract made up of five farms—J. G. Curtis, E. Todd, L. B. Todd, H. Todd, and Old Dominion Land Company. All homes had electricity, indoor plumbing, a furnace, living/dining rooms, kitchen, closets or hang-up areas, a bathroom, second-level bedrooms, a front stoop or porch and/or a breezeway side-entry porch, an attached garage, and spacious front and back yards for gardens, fruit trees, and chicken coops. Some residents had mules for plowing, pigs, and cows. Two residents were grandfathered in for raising chickens and pigs as late as 2000.

The streets in the historic district were alphabetically named. On December 9, 1937, the federal government recommended that Hampton Institute replace the alphabetically named streets with names of well-respected African Americans of the era, such as: Lewis Road (A Street), named for Matt N. Lewis, pioneer Negro journalist, founder, and publisher of the *Newport News Star*; Weaver Road (B Street), named for W. B. Weaver, founder and director of Weaver Home for Negro Orphan Children in Hampton; Walker Road (C Street), named for Maggie Lena Walker, founder and president of St. Luke's Bank in Richmond; Mary Peake Boulevard (D Street), named for Mary Peake, who taught the first school for contraband children by the Emancipation Oak on the grounds of Hampton Institute; Davis Road (E street), named for Daniel Webster Davis, minister, teacher, lecturer, and poet from Richmond; Russell Road (F Street), named for Archdeacon James S. Russell, founder and president of St. Paul's Normal and Industrial School in Lawrenceville; and Langston Boulevard (G Street), named for John Mercer Langston, first president of Virginia State College and one-time U.S. congressman from Virginia. These names remain today.

The first Aberdeen Elementary School graduating class was in 1942. The Aberdeen Elementary School had large rooms, indoor restrooms, indoor plumbing, heat, and electricity. Children attending Aberdeen were from near and far neighborhoods. Busing started in 1939 and brought students from Father's Height, Park Place, Back River, and Semple Farms Roads. Aberdeen Elementary School's first five principals were Claude Anderson, Mrs. Johnson, Mr. Swain, James A. Hill, and Calvin Owens. There have been many principals since the early years; as of 2007, Mark Hudson is the current principal.

In 1946, the Aberdeen Rattlers fast-pitch softball team was formed. They took their name because so many rattlesnakes were found in the Aberdeen Gardens greenbelt. Many team members or their families continue to live in Aberdeen. In 1988, the old team members united and began to reminisce about their old neighborhood, including their family members and new neighbors from adjoining neighborhoods. From the reunion, the discussion was to make Aberdeen Gardens a historic neighborhood. In 1992, the Aberdeen Rattlers formed the Aberdeen Gardens Historic Group, and from this, the Aberdeen Historic and Civic Association, Inc., came into existence in 1994. Aberdeen Gardens was listed as a historic district on the Virginia State Register of Historic Landmarks, as well as on the National Register of Historic Places in 1994. In 1998, the Historic Foundation of Aberdeen Gardens was organized.

Twenty-two committees were formed in the Aberdeen Gardens Historic and Civic Association to meet the needs of the community, interact with various departments of the City of Hampton, and be in communication with other neighborhood districts. A few of the committees include awards and certificates, beautification, contract and procurement, education, family services, government affairs, heritage, historian, hospitality, library, mature adults, museum, neighborhood development, neighborhood watch, newsletter, safety, storm water, youth in action, and wetlands.

The two churches in the area in 1938 were Mount Olive Baptist, built around 1872 on Big Bethel Road with Rev. W. Randolph Rylander as pastor, and Little Zion Baptist Church, established in 1885 on West Queen Street with Rev. Hallie Richardson Jr. as pastor. The churches and their parishioners are thriving today in new edifices at the same locations.

The Aberdeen Gardens Historic and Civic Association spelled success for the community and all of its partners, surrounding neighborhoods, and businesses. Many awards have been won for collaborative projects with partnered business, local and state governments, and adjoining neighbors. Two awards from Neighborhoods of the United States of America (NUSA) were presented to the Aberdeen Gardens Historic and Civic Association: first-place and overall winners as Neighborhood of the Year 2002 for remodeling a 1936 Aberdeen Gardens home into the Historic Aberdeen Gardens Museum and first place in 2005 for neighborhood commitment in bringing about the construction of the West Hampton Community Center. The Aberdeen Gardens Historic District was featured on the Homes and Gardens television network (HGTV) twice: in 1999, Bob Villa's Restore America showcased the neighborhood, and in 2006, HGTV featured Aberdeen Gardens as a winner (with a $50,000 grant) in *Parade* magazine's "Tell America's Story" contest.

The Aberdeen Gardens Historic and Civic Association motto is "In Unity there Is Strength, and with Commitment and Work, We Can Achieve."

One

Aberdeen Gardens
The Early Years

Construction took place on the Colonial Revival–style houses of Aberdeen Gardens from 1934 through 1937. The area was truly a greenbelt. Newmarket Creek snaked its way throughout the Aberdeen greenbelt into Newport News. Rattlesnakes, black and green snakes, and moccasins were prevalent in the early years. Many families were beginning to move in, and renting was done first in East Russell Road homes. Small families with one child weren't allowed to rent large houses of three bedrooms. Families lived harmoniously, raised their children, and maintained their home and community. Large families with 6 to 15 members, including parents, lived in Aberdeen Gardens Historic District. Discovering twins and getting to know them were the talk of the day. Three sets of twin were identified in the early years: Ruben and Ruby Daniels, Erma and Eilene Taylor, and Leon and Mignon Kerry. Many Aberdeeners were identifying their heritage. Some found their families to be descendants of American Indians and Africans and others Europeans. There was nothing like Aberdeen hospitality. Aberdeen residents cared for one another and shared tools, telephones, farm animals, meals, and garden vegetables. As late as 1965, avid gardeners such as Duprat and Evangeline Ricks, and Troy and Oliva Smith Sr. continued to give neighbors vegetables. The Aberdeen Gardens neighborhood's next challenge was to be placed in history.

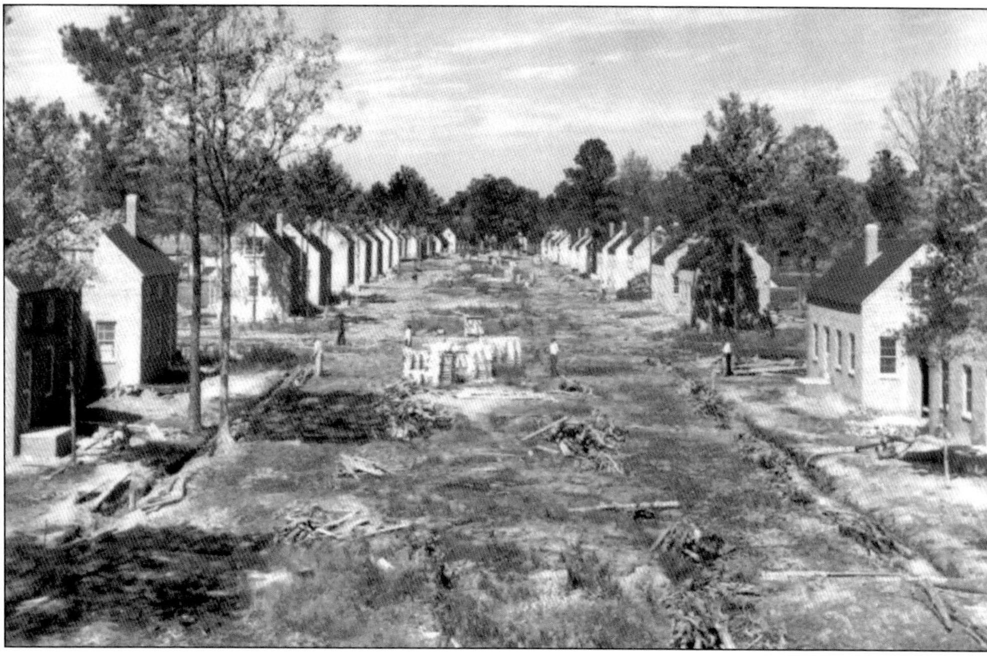

The framed houses are mostly completed with the windows in place, incomplete front steps, driveways, electric lights, and so forth. Tree branches are being cleared from the yard onto Mary Peake Boulevard in front of this house for easy removal. Extra wood is piled in neat stacks for use inside and out in garage doors and side-porch screen doors. (Courtesy of Hampton University Archives.)

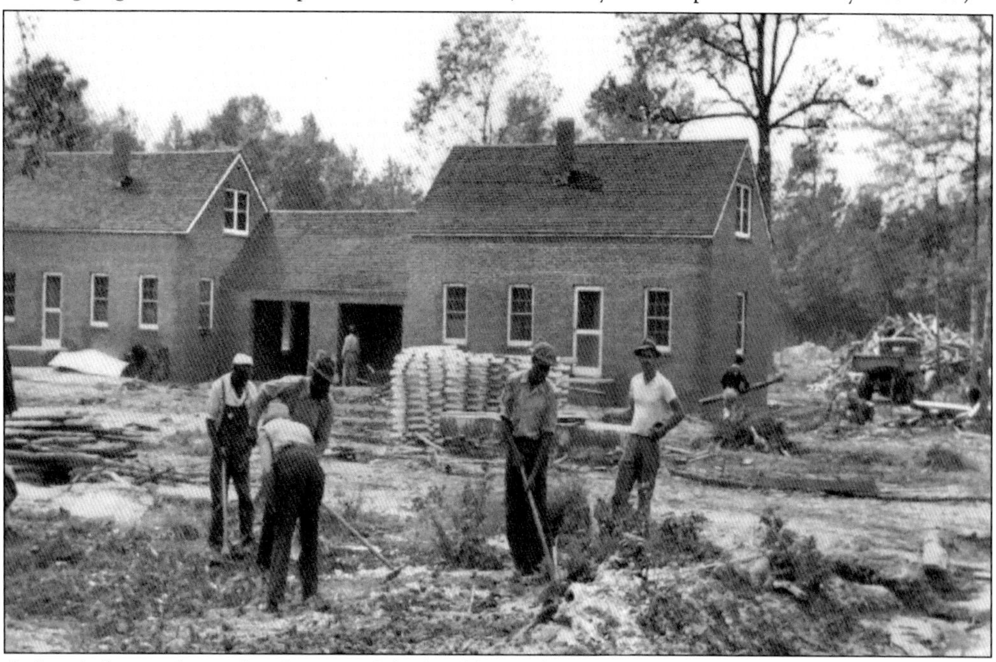

A detailed view shows the clearing of the land by workers. The area seen is dry, and the Aberdeen greenbelt area consisted of trees, untamed bushes, and thick ground foliage. After a rain, when the Newmarket Creek tributary overflowed, the Aberdeen elders reported that water was knee-deep. (Courtesy of Hampton University Archives.)

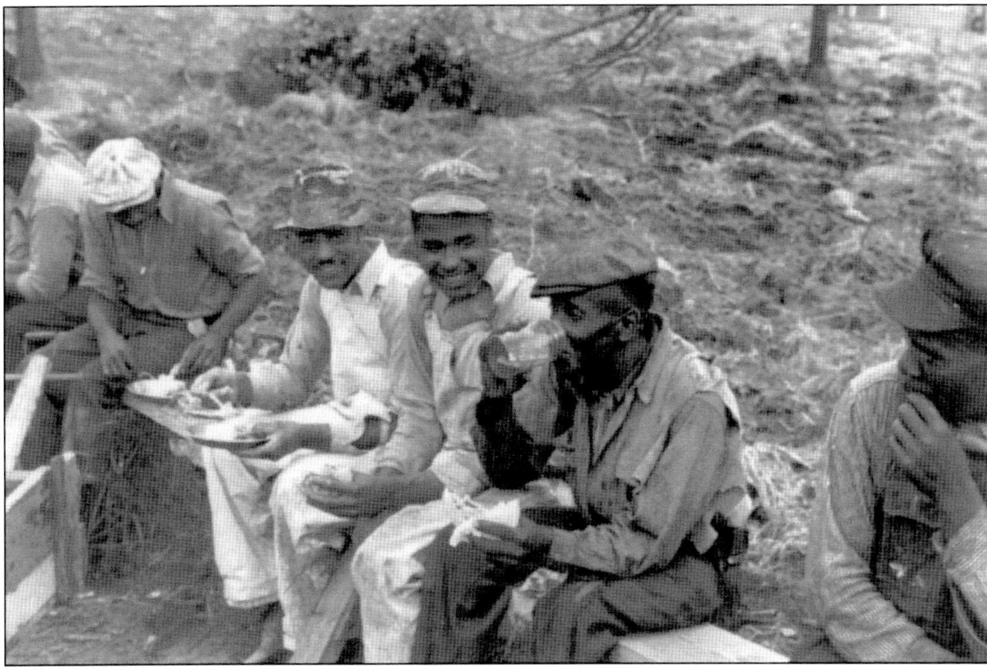

The workers are taking a break. Eating lunch and talking were the social events of the day. Looking at the undergrowth in the background, physical labor could prove to be exhausting. Two of the men in white were painters. A wooded 6-inch-by-4-inch bench was the outdoor seating during this midday break. (Courtesy of Hampton University Archives.)

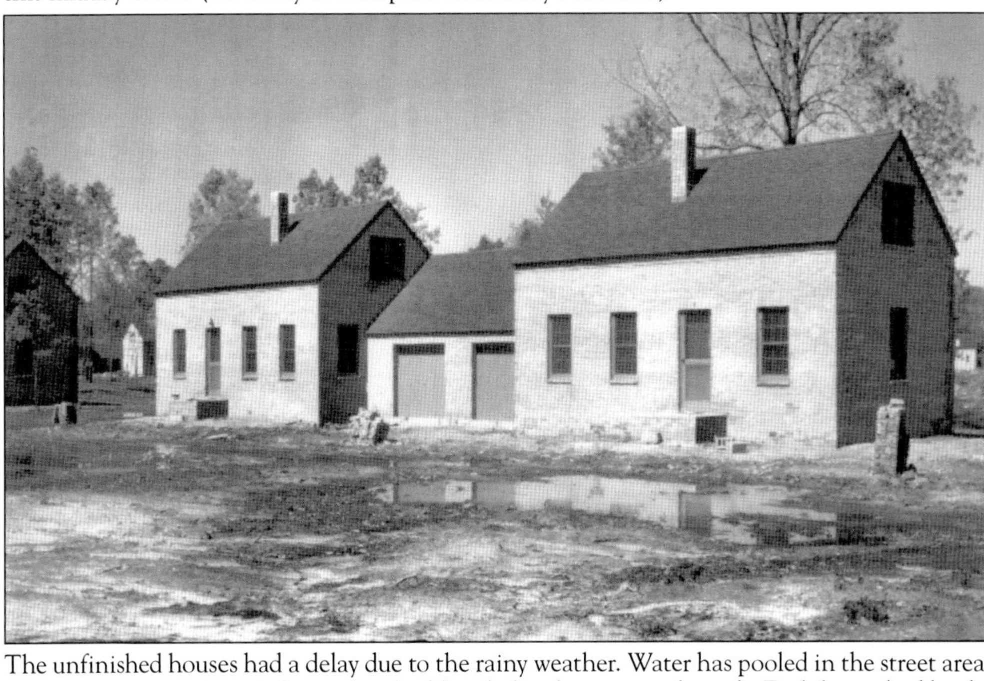

The unfinished houses had a delay due to the rainy weather. Water has pooled in the street area. The workers have cleared the street of wild underbrush, trees, and weeds. Each house had bricks supplied according to the blueprint. The surplus at each house is stacked accordingly. (Courtesy of Heck Production Company.)

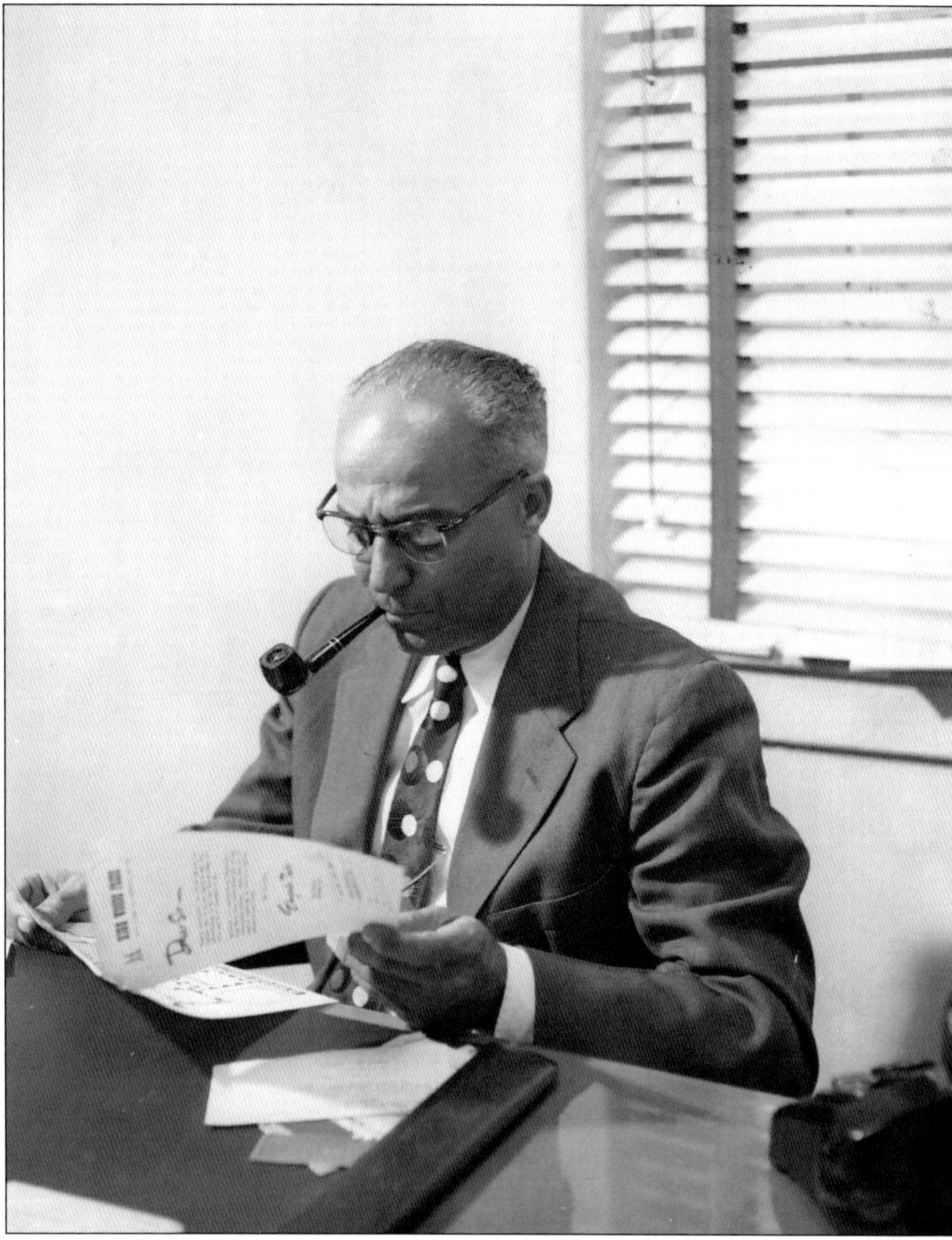

William Roscoe Walker Jr. was the first and only resident Farm Security Administration (FSA) manager of the Aberdeen Gardens' housing project for blacks. Upon completion, many of the 158 homes were rentals. Renting residents paid $11 to $15 a month. Built on 110 of the 440 acres purchased by the government, the furnished homes on East Russell Road were the first to be rented in 1936. Walker moved into 2 East Russell Road in 1937, and on April 21, 1938, Eleanor Roosevelt visited his home, which was also partly his office. In 1945, Walker moved the Aberdeen Gardens management office to the commercial building, resembling a small mini-mall. In 1946, Walker recommended to the federal government that homes be sold to those who could afford to buy them. Walker cared much about his neighborhood. (Courtesy of Claude Vann Jr.)

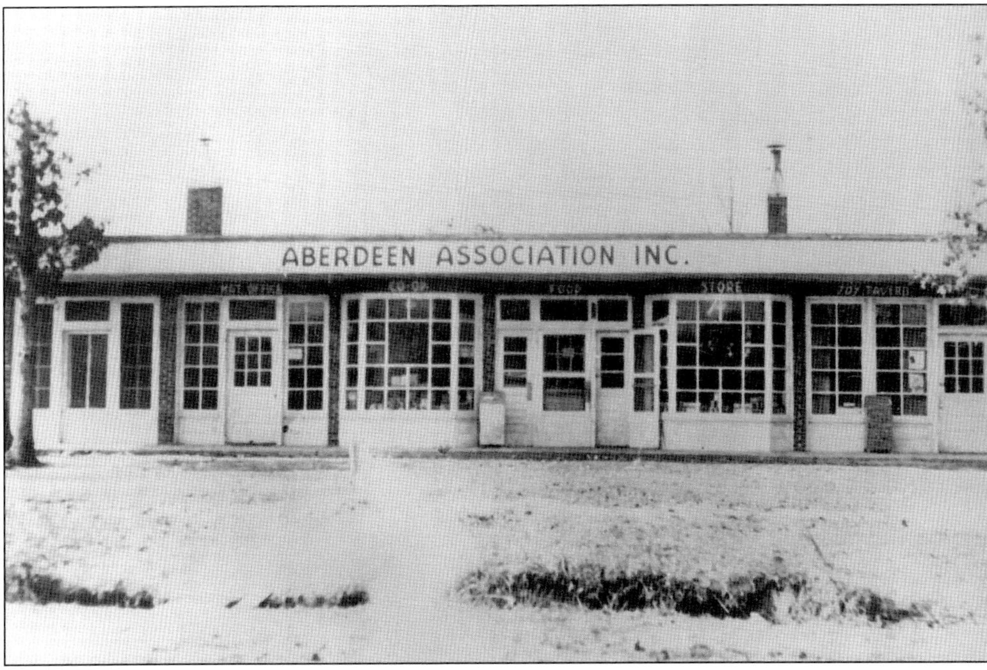

Pictured in 1947, the Aberdeen Association, Inc., looked the same for the next 21 years. This was called a commercial center in the original 1936 plans. Three spaces were available: the barbershop (later the manager's rental office), Brown's Grocery Store, and Toy's Tavern. Sidney J. Wyche's Co-op Grocery Store was located between East Weaver and East Lewis Roads. (Courtesy of Mamie Batchelor.)

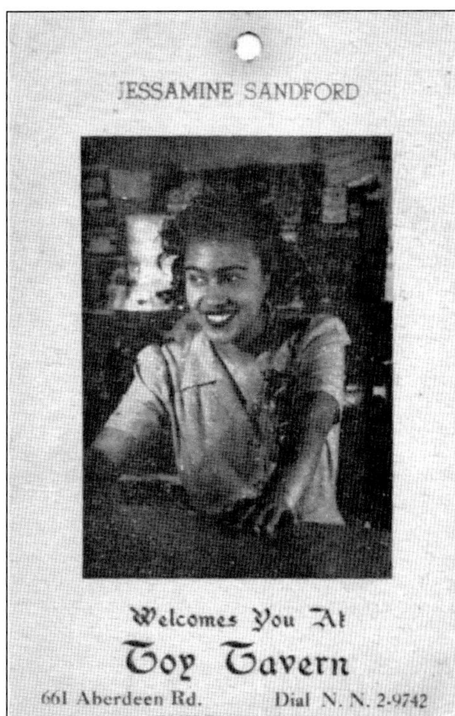

Jasmine Sandford was the first African American female to own and operate a tavern; she ran Toy's Tavern from the early 1940s to the late 1950s. Toy's Tavern was located in the Aberdeen Association mini-mall. Many Aberdeeners gathered in and socialized at this quiet yet friendly bar where everyone was known. (Courtesy of Carol Gordon.)

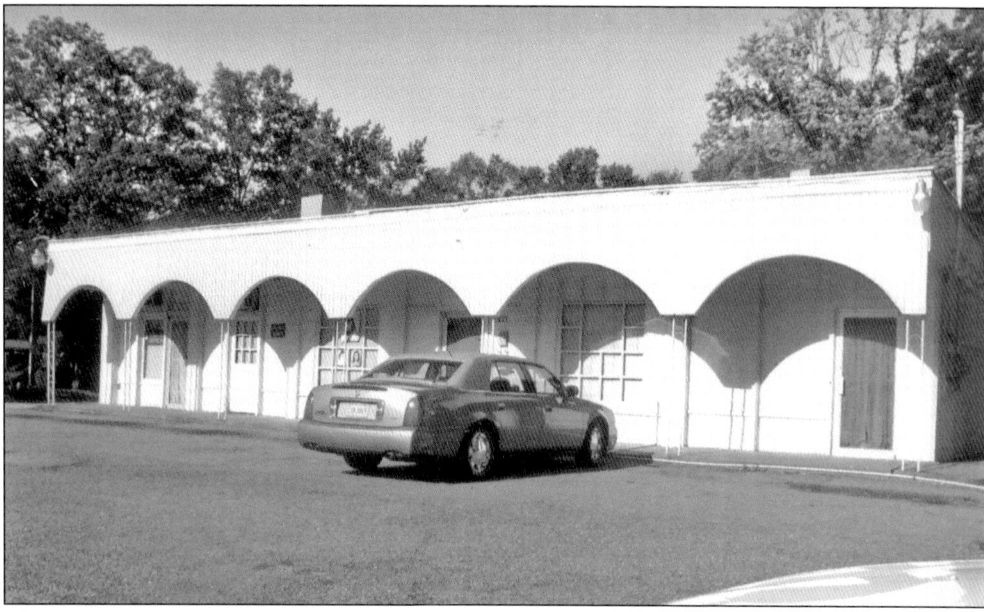

The Aberdeen Association mini-mall was renovated by Mamie A. Batchelor in 1968 while she was renting from Byrum Walker, who lived in the Aberdeen Gardens Historic District. It now has its second licensed barbershop, operated by Lin Irwin Batchelor, the son of Mamie Batchelor. (Courtesy of Mamie Batchelor.)

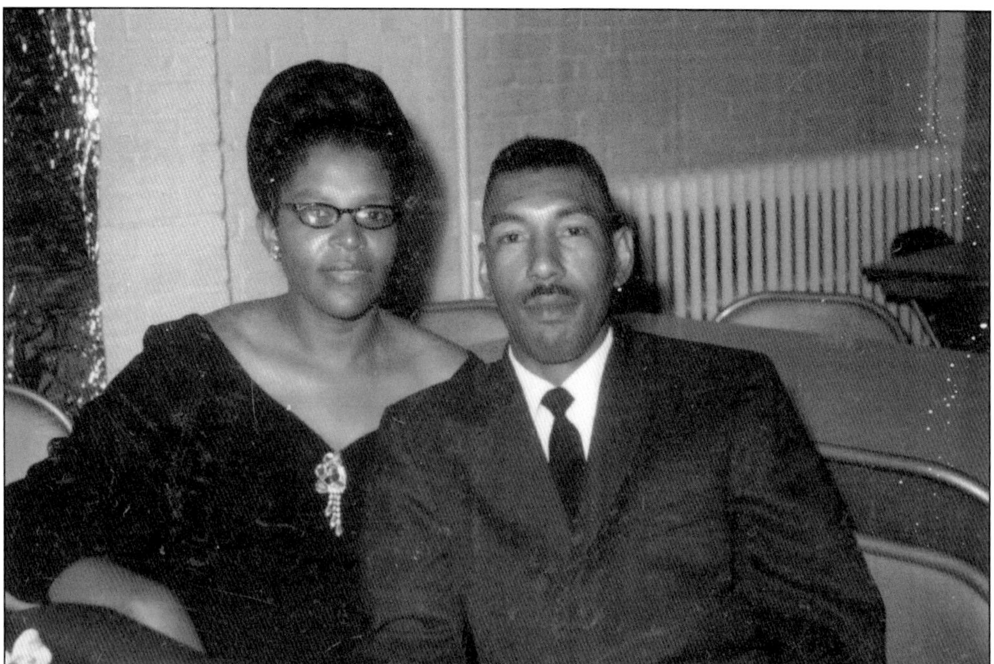

In 1964, Linwood H. and Mamie A Batchelor moved to the Granger Court East neighborhood, south of the Aberdeen Gardens Historic District, not far from their future business venture. In 1976, Mamie purchased the mini-mall and renamed it Aberdeen Fashion Flair and Hair Clinic. (Courtesy of Mamie Batchelor.)

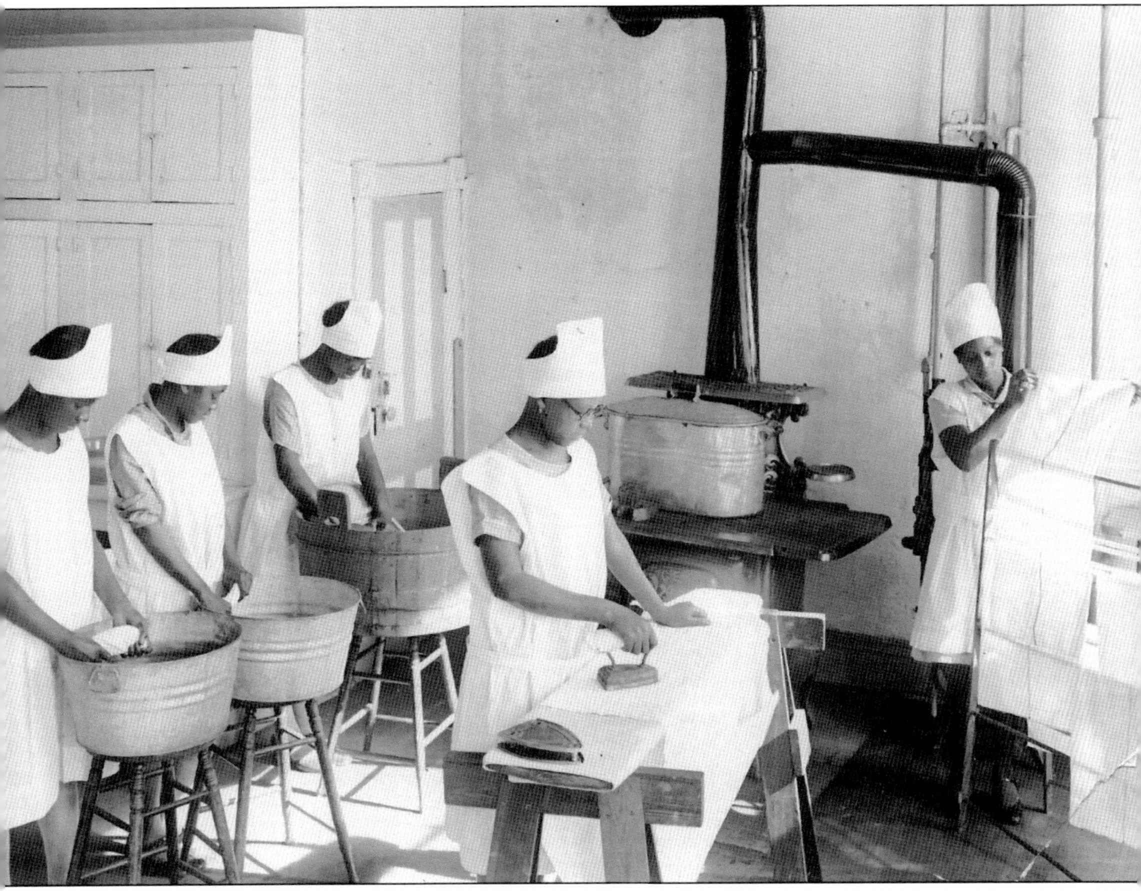

In 1939, the National Youth Administration of Virginia was a work-experience project to train needy and capable young black women for household employment in Virginia. The project was sponsored by Hampton Institute with the assistance of the FSA and Negro Women's Clubs of Hampton and Newport News. The young women were drawn from the Hampton Roads area and were chosen on the basis of intelligence, industry, and character. The girls lived cooperatively in eight housing units and devoted 90 hours a month to project work. The program included planning, preparation, and service of meals; house care and cleaning; house management; childcare; maid service; laundering; food preservation; gardening; and sewing for personal and household use. The training program was directed by a full-time resident home economist from Hampton Institute and assisted by the resident FSA home economist. The instructor gave individualized instruction in the field of household employment. (Courtesy of Lenrow Milo.)

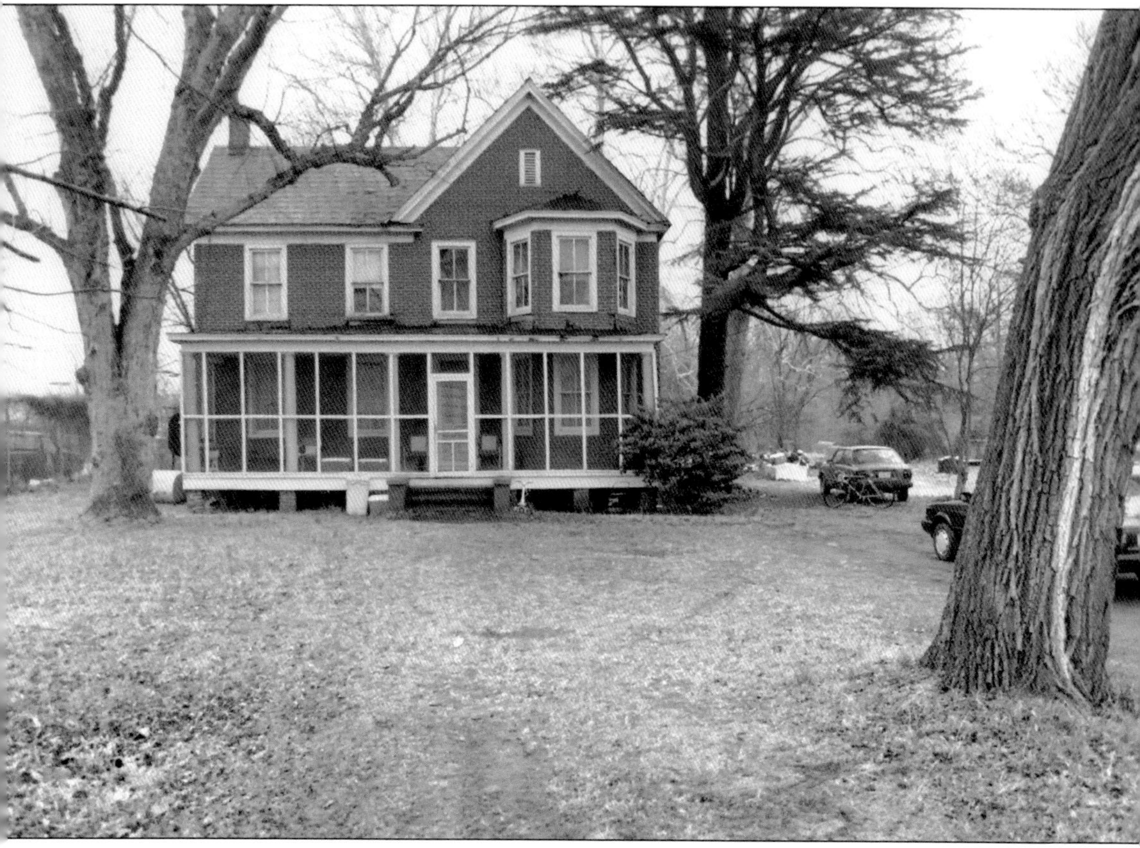

The Todd farmhouse, a Queen Anne vernacular-style home built around 1890, was included in the Aberdeen Gardens Historic District. With their large family, Wesley and Daisy Johnson took over the farm and sold produce locally. This last original farmhouse was referred to as the Johnson Farm. On the Johnson property was a well and a very large windmill. In 1968, the Johnson children donated the windmill to Blue Bird Gap Farm, located off Pine Chapel Road in Hampton. Wesley Johnson was a railroad porter and a Newport News Shipbuilding and Dry Dock worker. He also prepared income taxes. The 10 children are Ollie Johnson of San Bernardino, California; Rosa Bassin of Cherry Hill, New Jersey; Wesley Johnson Jr. of Philadelphia; Clarence Johnson of Newport News; Edith Johns, Daisy, Otis, and James Johnson, all of Hampton, Virginia; Ruth and Bertha Johnson are deceased. Family members were occupants until 2001. In 2007, the Johnson home was removed from the historic listing, the home demolished, and the land sold. (Courtesy of Walter P. Calahan.)

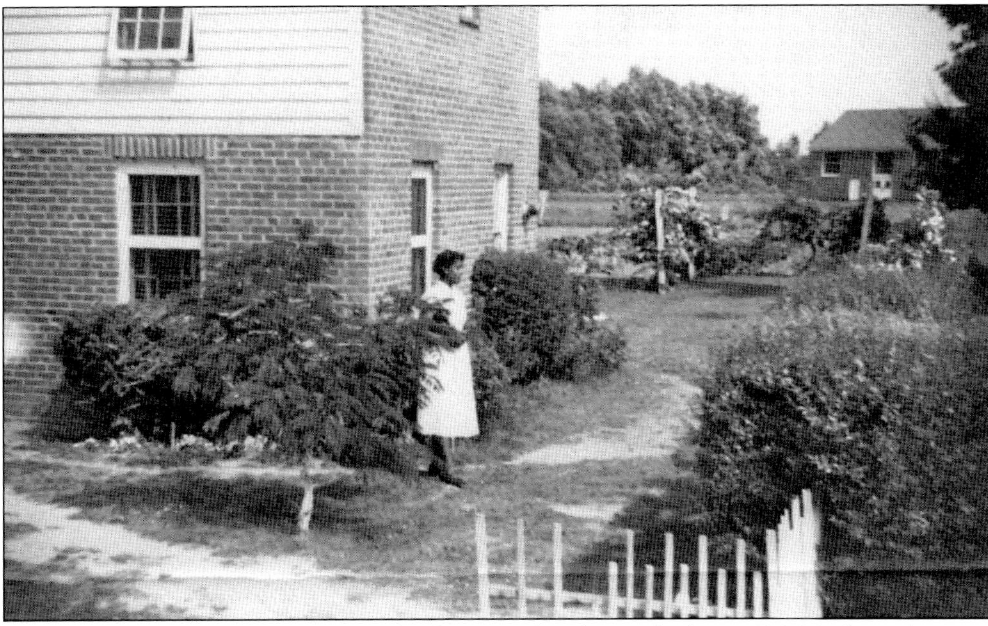

Large gardens were a feature of the Aberdeen Gardens homes built in 1936. Much produce was harvested from gardens for the family and shared with neighbors. From the Sturdivants' Walker Road home, the left side of Aberdeen Elementary School is seen in the background. Pictured here is Joyce Sturdivant Brown. Hedges or trees separated the yards of many homes. (Courtesy of Joyce Sturdivant Brown.)

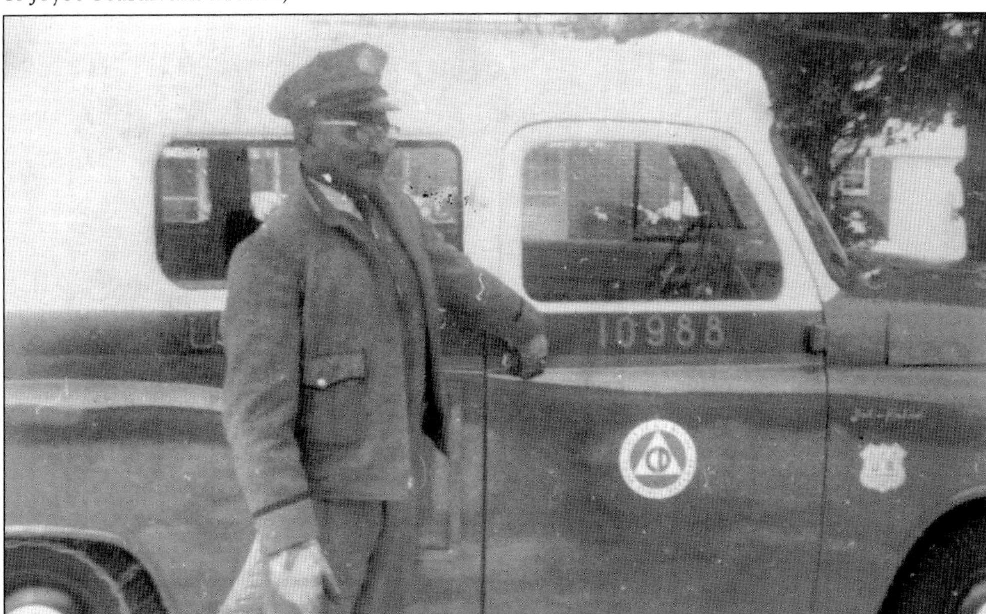

In 1937, Ashland Dickerson Sturdivant Sr. was the first postman assigned to Aberdeen Gardens. Ashland and Ethel Sturdivant lived in Aberdeen Gardens on East Walker Road with their family of eight—two daughters and six sons. Sunday school was conducted in their home in the 1940s and 1950s. He was one of the organizers in the Aberdeen community. He retired from the postal service in 1968. (Courtesy of Joyce Sturdivant Brown.)

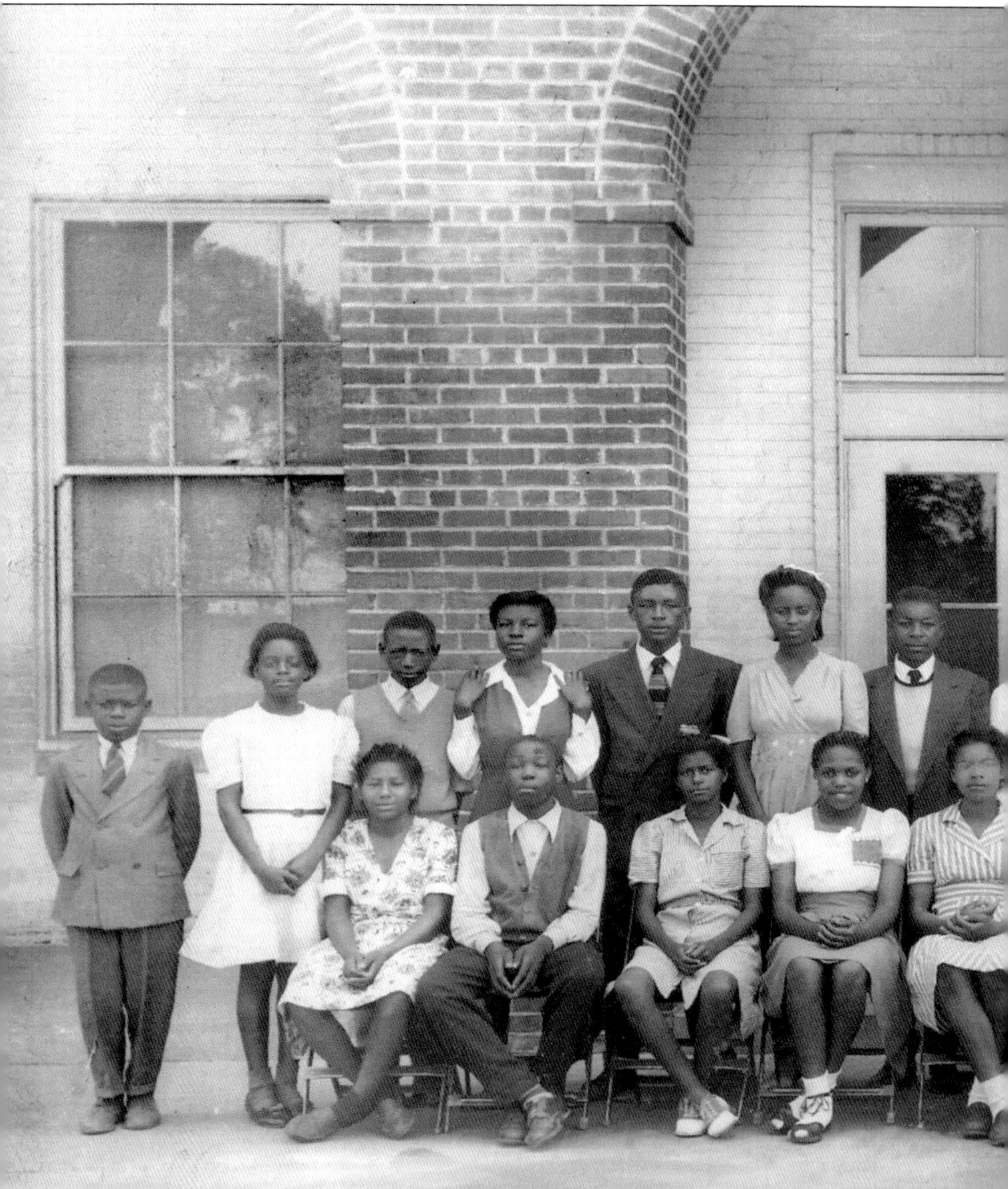

The 1938 Aberdeen School, which was part of the original construction plan for the neighborhood, was completely renovated in 1973. It was a one-story building with large windows. Each classroom held 25 or more students. Grades ranged from first through seventh. The first class graduated in 1942. This is the 1944 graduating class. Schooling involved discipline in the early years. No chaos was tolerated. Teachers would spank the hands of students with a ruler or bolo bat, and some students were made to stand in the corner. Detention was for those students who misbehaved

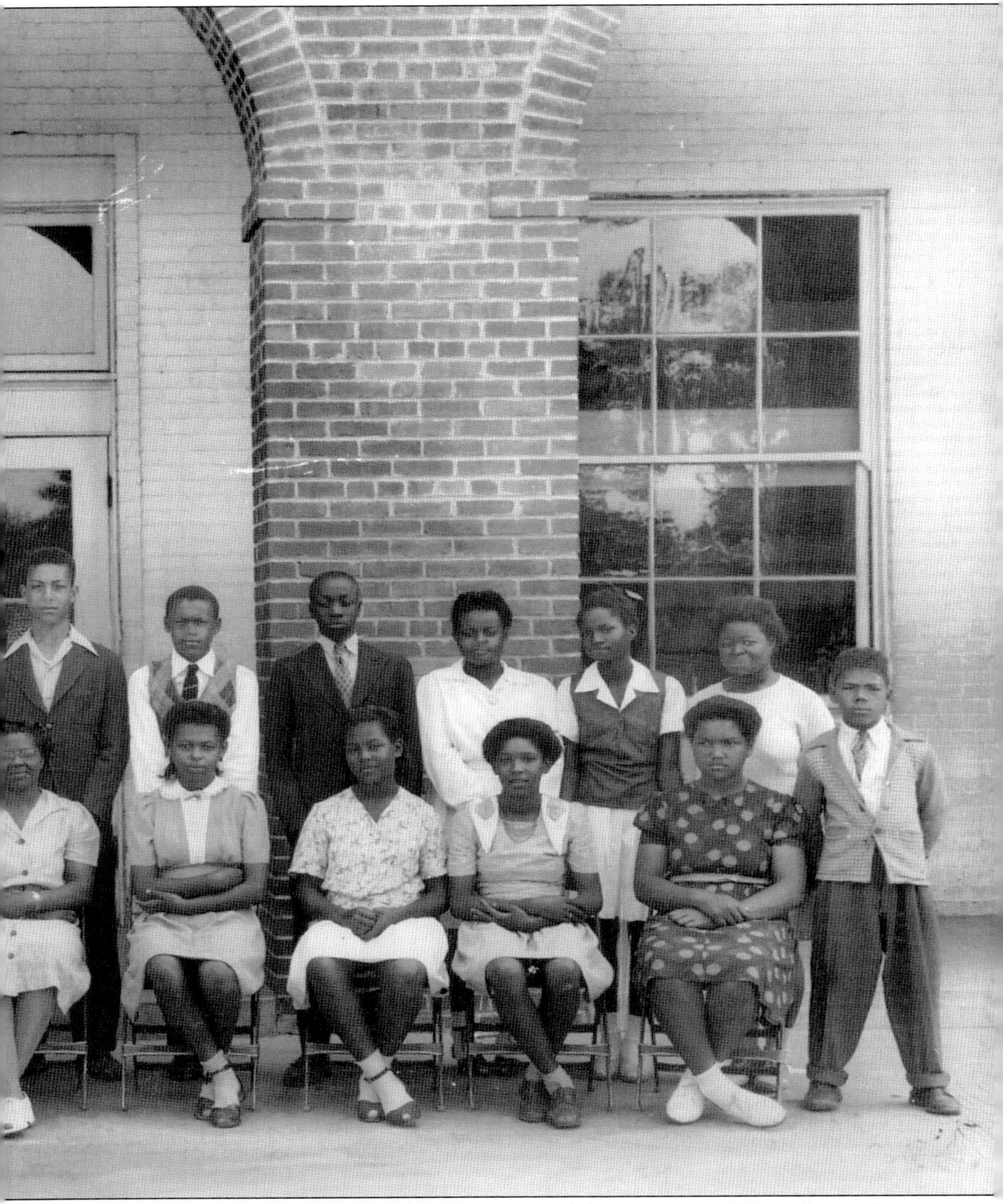

more than once and were resistant to hand spanks and dunce corners. When the teacher informed the parents of students' naughty behavior, the students would also be reprimanded by their parents. This photograph shows students attired in suits, jackets, or vests, and the ladies are all wearing dresses. They are in front of the original Aberdeen Elementary School. (Courtesy of Walter Jackson.)

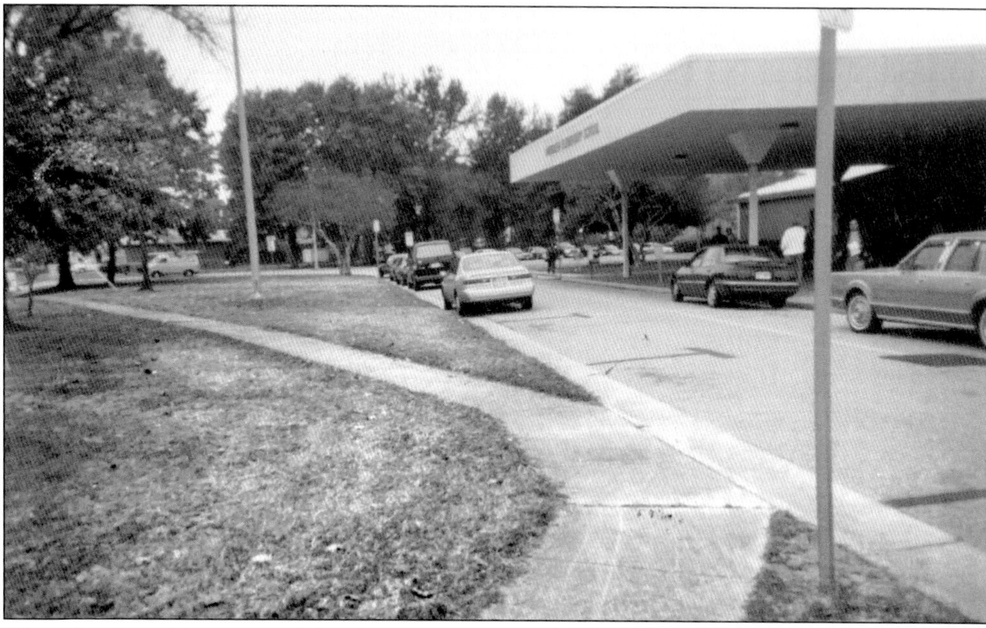

The Aberdeen Elementary School was a one-story, brick, Colonial Revival structure that has been remodel approximately five times to reach its present appearance. The school serves as a meeting place for the Aberdeen Gardens Historic and Civic Association, as well as social functions involving community and youth activities. It is a historical structure of Aberdeen Gardens Historic District. (Courtesy of Aberdeen Gardens Historic and Civic Association, Inc.)

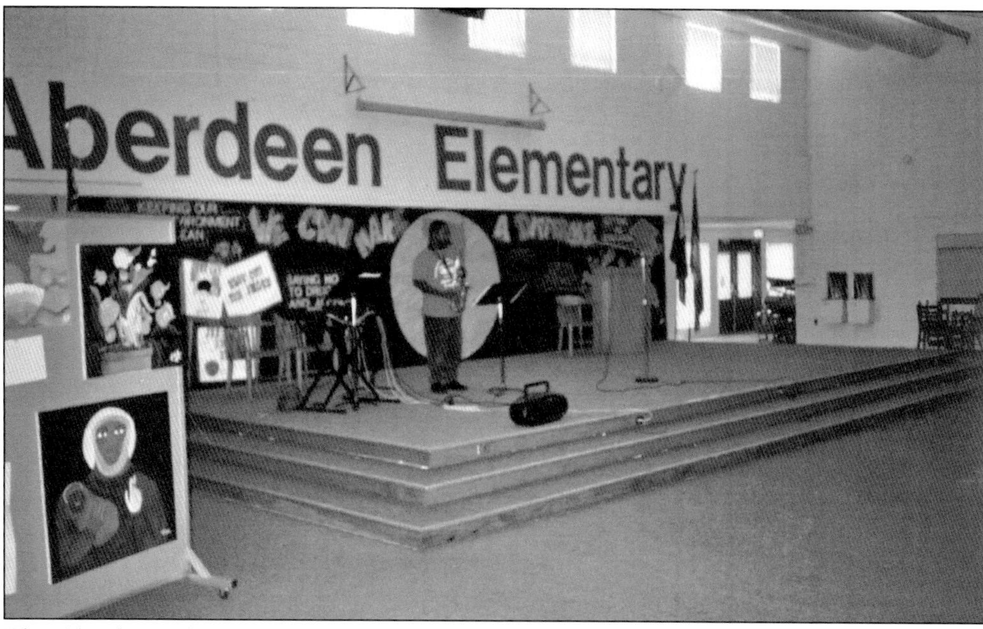

The Aberdeen Elementary School auditorium/dining hall is utilized for many student and community activities. Here Fellip Fields, a progressive gospel instrumentalist, performs for the Aberdeen Gardens Historic and Civic Association and residents after the neighborhood achieved historic recognition as the Aberdeen Gardens Historic District. (Courtesy of Aberdeen Gardens Historic and Civic Association, Inc.)

On November 1, 1937, Charlie and Maggie Jones were the first couple to move into their East Russell Road Aberdeen Gardens home. While Maggie was a stay-at-home mother, Charlie was employed by the Newport News Shipbuilding and Dry Dock Company. They had four children. (Courtesy of Mannan Zakia Amin and Margaret Jones Wilson.)

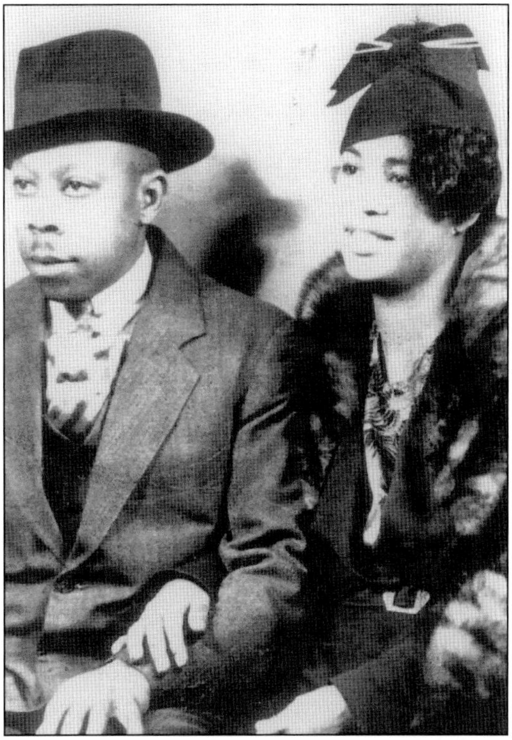

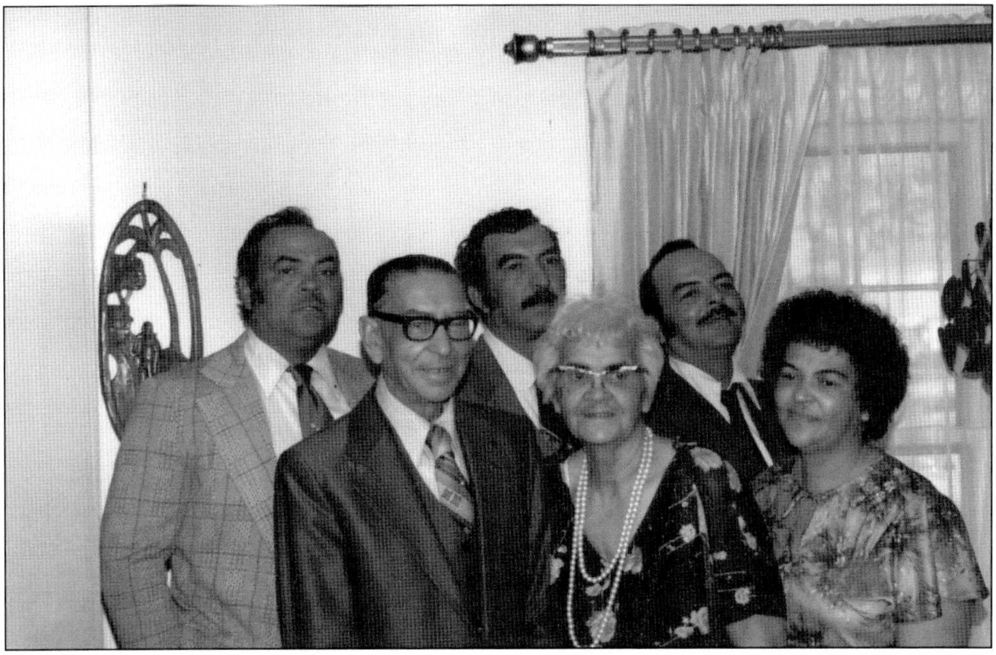

The Vann family is, from left to right, (first row) Claude Vann Sr.; his wife, Doris Vann; and Thelma Vann Lattimore; (second row) Claude Vann Jr., the Aberdeen paperboy shortly after the move to Aberdeen Gardens; John "Pete" Vann; and Andre "Monk" Vann Sr. Claude Vann Sr. moved his family to Aberdeen Gardens when his children were six years of age and younger. (Courtesy of Claude Vann Jr.)

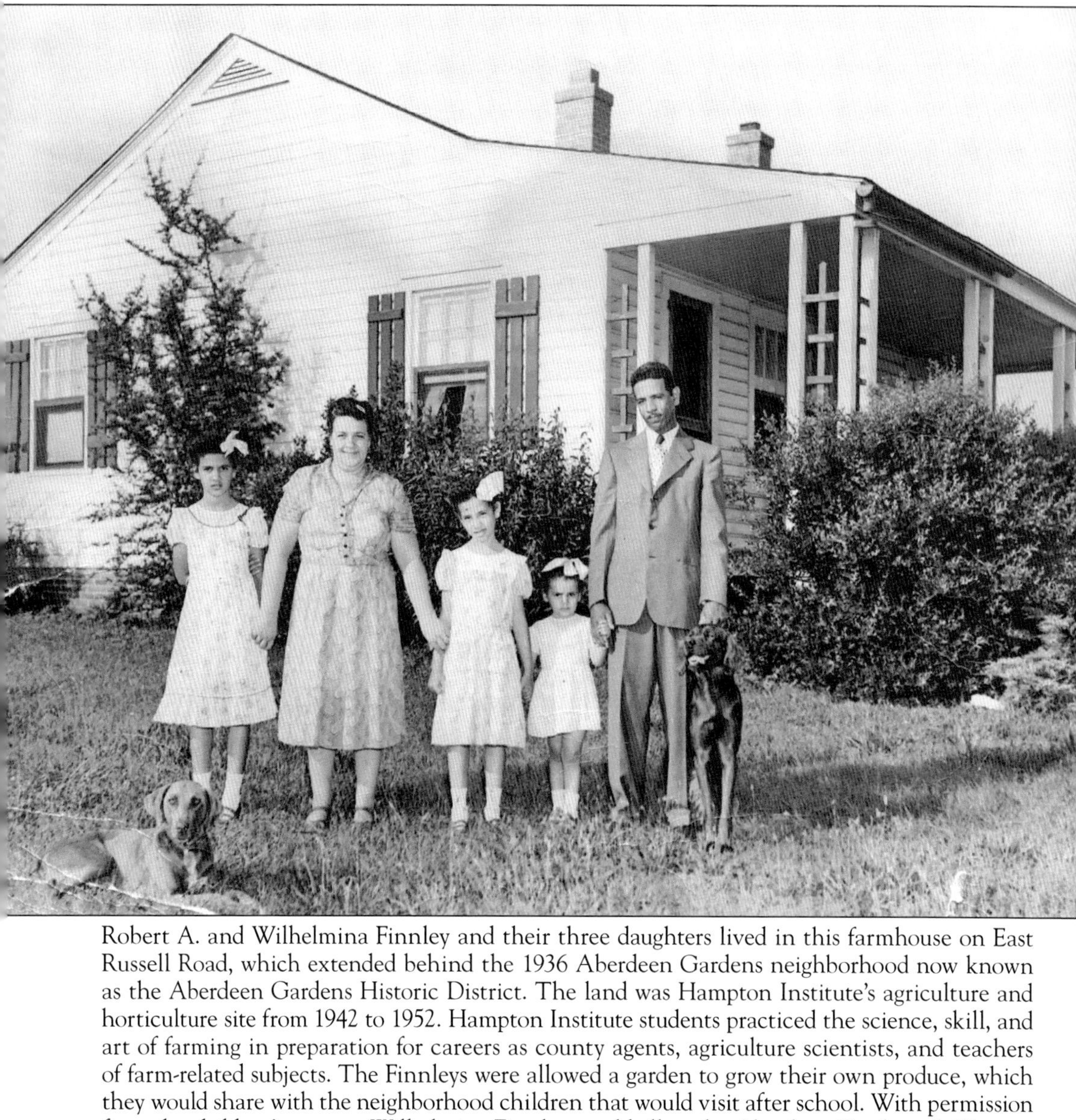

Robert A. and Wilhelmina Finnley and their three daughters lived in this farmhouse on East Russell Road, which extended behind the 1936 Aberdeen Gardens neighborhood now known as the Aberdeen Gardens Historic District. The land was Hampton Institute's agriculture and horticulture site from 1942 to 1952. Hampton Institute students practiced the science, skill, and art of farming in preparation for careers as county agents, agriculture scientists, and teachers of farm-related subjects. The Finnleys were allowed a garden to grow their own produce, which they would share with the neighborhood children that would visit after school. With permission from the children's parents, Wilhelmina Finnley would allow the Aberdeen Gardens children to observe animal birthing and milking cows. In the mid-1950s, the land was redeveloped as Granger Court East and now has beautiful homes. The photograph shows the Finnleys standing in the front yard. (Courtesy of Carol Gordon and Roberta Finnley Atkinson.)

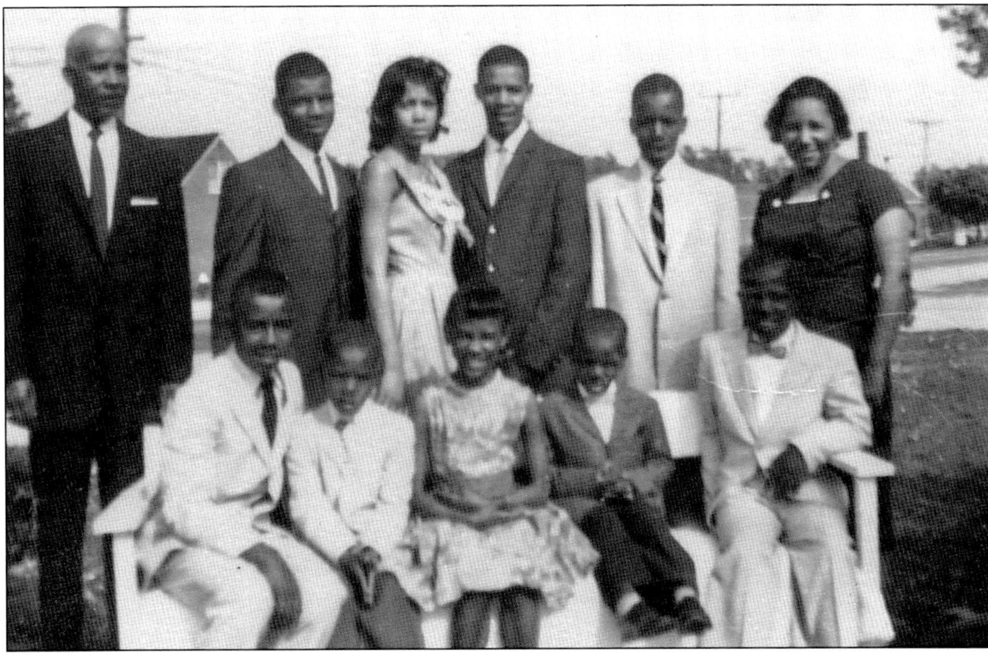

Many large families lived in the 1937 Aberdeen Gardens neighborhood: the Washingtons, Stokeses, Sturdivants, Danielses, Gillises, Clayton-Gilchrists, and Burwells, to name a few. Eleven Burwell family members are pictured in their West Walker Road backyard, and the 12th person, the photographer, is the oldest daughter. (Courtesy of Clarice Burwell Hughes.)

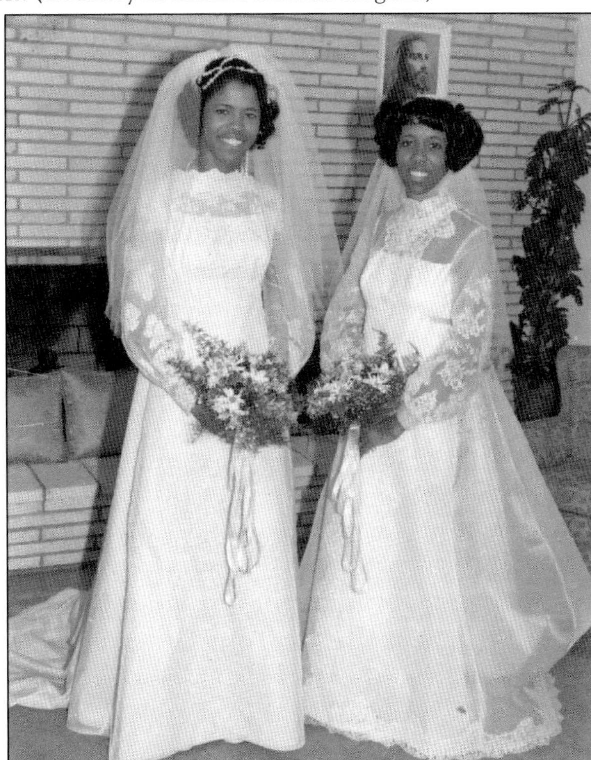

Eileen (left) and Erma (right) Taylor, who lived on Mary Peake Boulevard, were one of three sets of twins in the early years of Aberdeen Gardens. They attended Aberdeen Elementary, Y. H. Thomas Junior High School, and George P. Phenix High School. They were graduates of Hampton University, and their double wedding took place at Hampton University Memorial Chapel. (Courtesy of Shirley Morgan.)

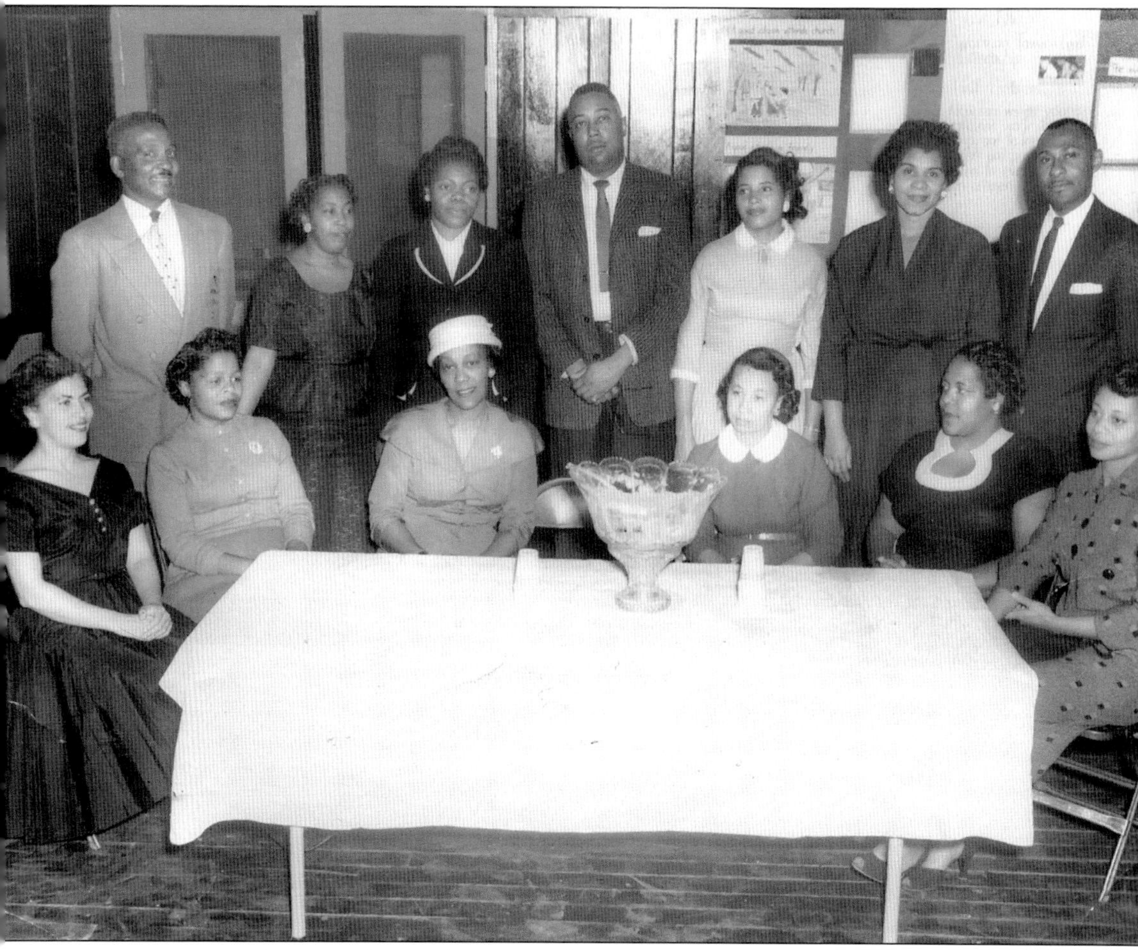

Many community groups featured parents and teachers, principals, and business entrepreneurs of Aberdeen Gardens and involved neighborhoods. They met to emphasize neighborhood safety, the well-being of the children's education, social activities that would engage community awareness and economic security, and fund-raising events to support charities and after-school projects. The PTA kept the neighborhood informed of imperative information on vaccinations and health care, charitable food programs, gymnastic exercise programs, and transportation issues. The Chandler family of Armstead Avenue in Hampton provided buses to transport students and teachers to many activities. Timothy Chandler even provided bus service for Aberdeen Gardens residents to get to church services on Sunday. Standing at the far right is Calvin Owens, the principal of Aberdeen Elementary School in the 1950s. (Courtesy of Linda Smith Good.)

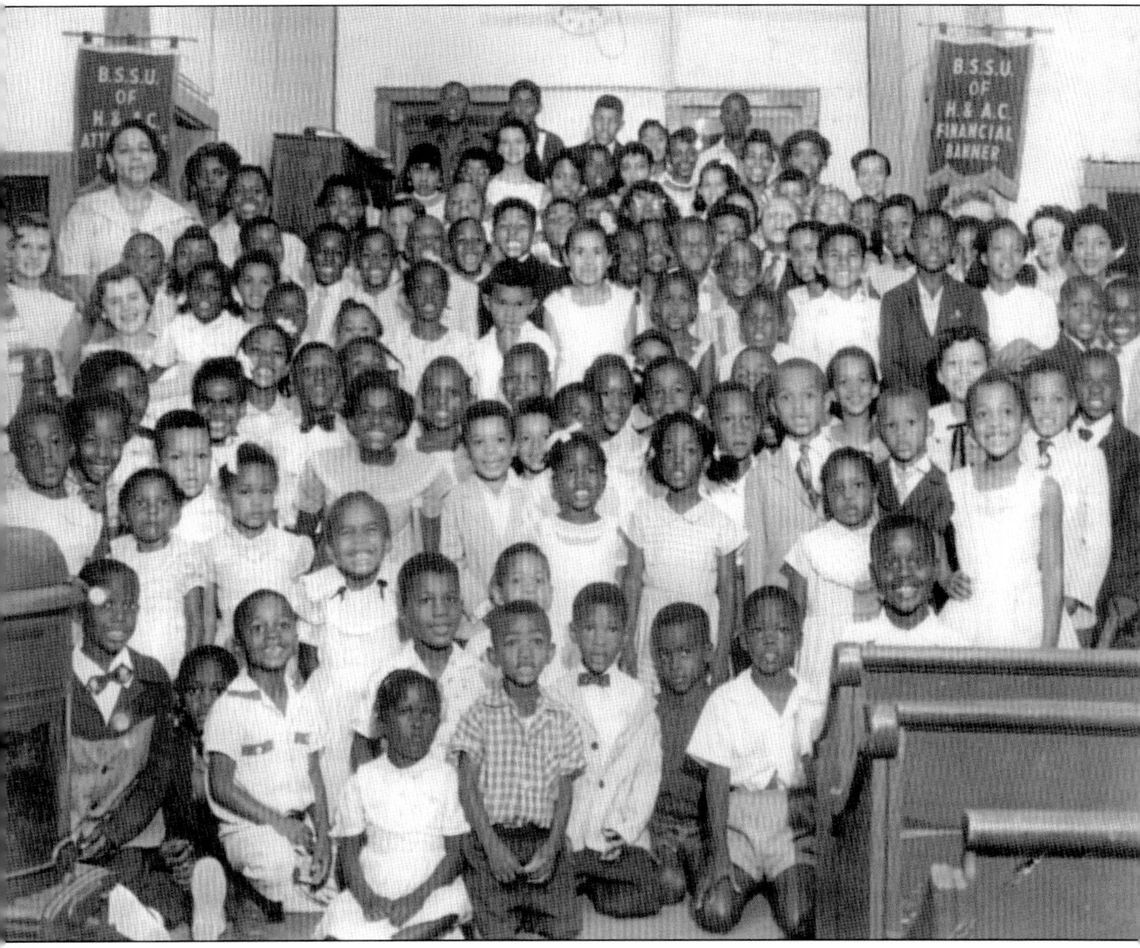

Various neighborhood children are gathered for Bible study and a student union summer conference in 1958. Little Zion Baptist Church of Queen Street, adjacent to Weaver Road in the East Aberdeen neighborhood, is one of two historical churches in the Aberdeen greenbelt. The students are in the interior of the original Little Zion Baptist Church, which was built in 1880 and renovated in 1962. It was a one-story building that lacked sufficient indoor plumbing until 1962. The neighborhood provided meals and opened homes for rest and bathroom breaks. The Baptist Training Union of Virginia was founded by one of the early leaders of Little Zion Baptist Church, Deacon Cornelius Jones, and the leaders of various other churches in Virginia. The Sunday school was organized by Deacon Jones and Deacon W. Nettles. (Courtesy of Eunice Peele.)

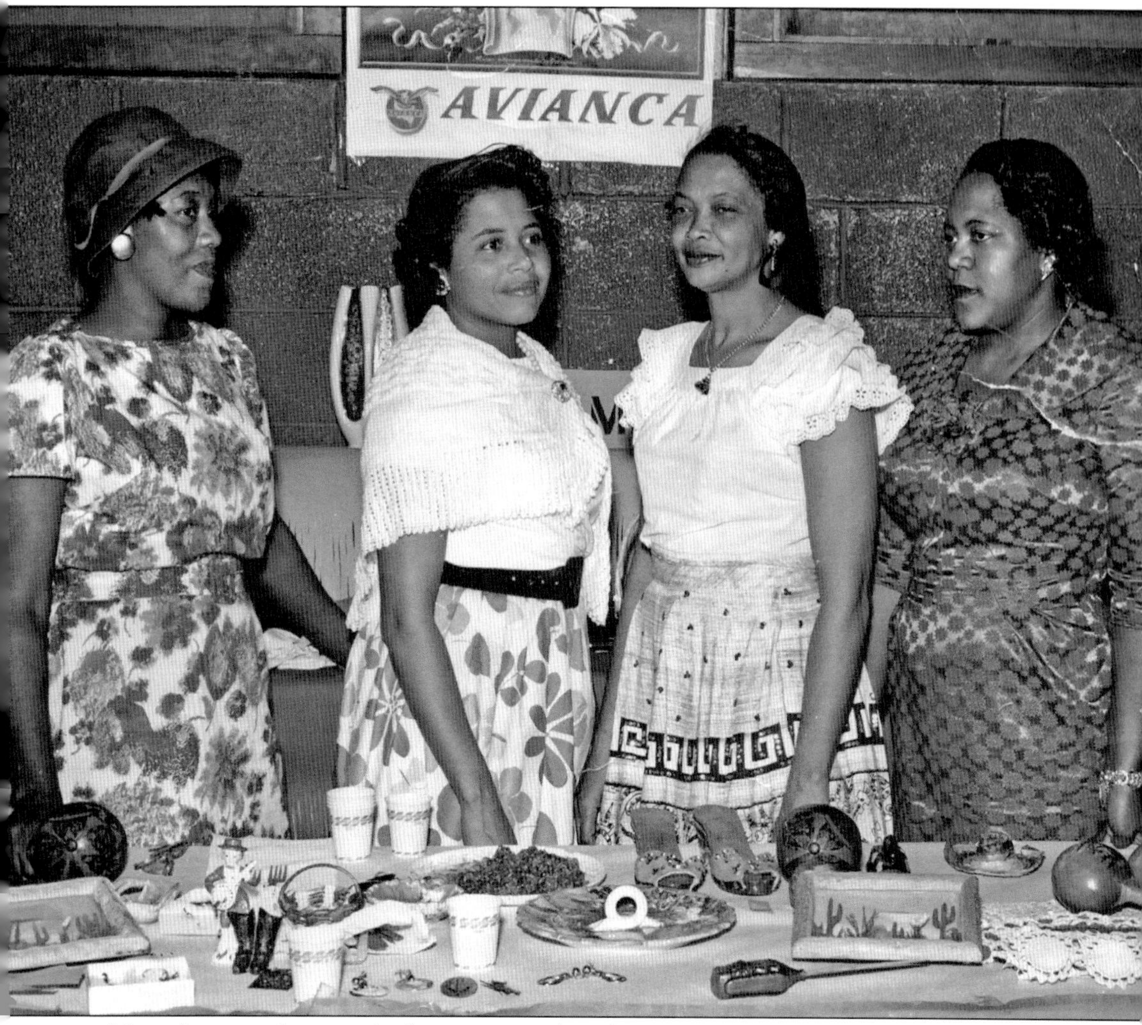

Many American heritage displays were prevalent during PTA meetings and school study programs held within Aberdeen Elementary School. Community events like this were used for fund-raisers. Many Aberdeen residents have traced their heritage to American Indian tribes, others to Hispanic and European cultures. Ancestral artifacts on display in the school's auditorium were shared by, from left to right, Ethel Sturdivant, Olivia Smith, Lillian Frazier, and Beatrice Jennings. Jennings was inducted into the Aberdeen Gardens Historic and Civic Association Council of Elders in 2005 and received an engraved medallion. Her daughter, Carol Jennings, accepted the award due to her mother's health. The Hunt for Hampton's History event, held in January 2007, allowed second-generation Aberdeen residents to share their heritage once more. Aberdeen Gardens' history continues to thrive thanks to the tradition established by these first-generation ladies of Aberdeen Gardens in 1958. (Courtesy of Linda Smith Good.)

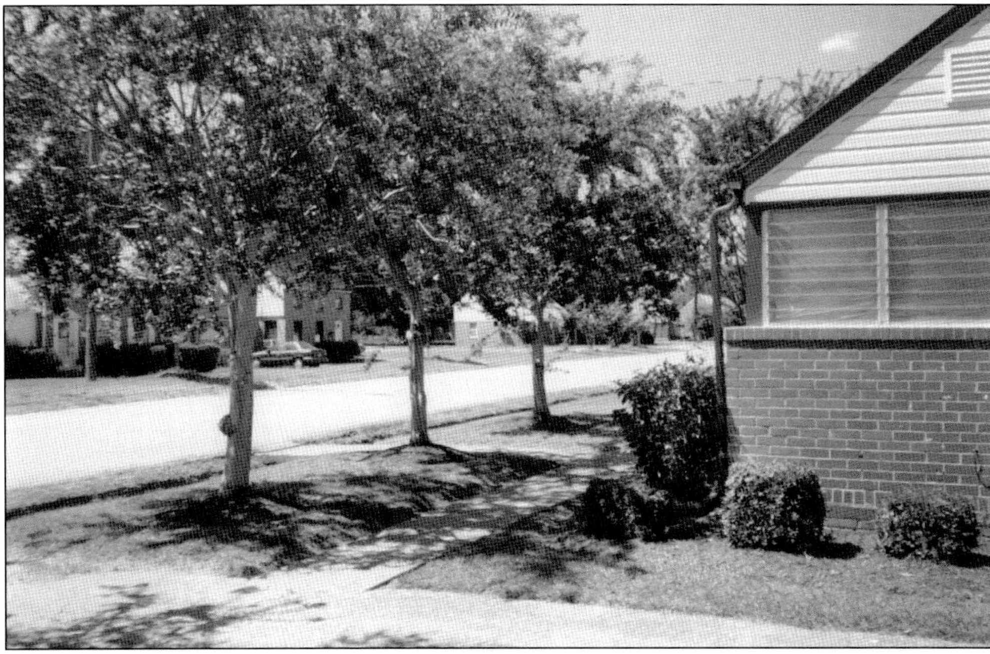

Crepe myrtles were planted throughout the completed neighborhood of Aberdeen Gardens in 1938. Yards, streets, and medians were simply beautiful under the pink blossoms, as seen along this Aberdeen Gardens Historic District home on Langston Boulevard where six crepe myrtles bloom in the Arringtons' front yard. (Courtesy of Jacqueline Arrington.)

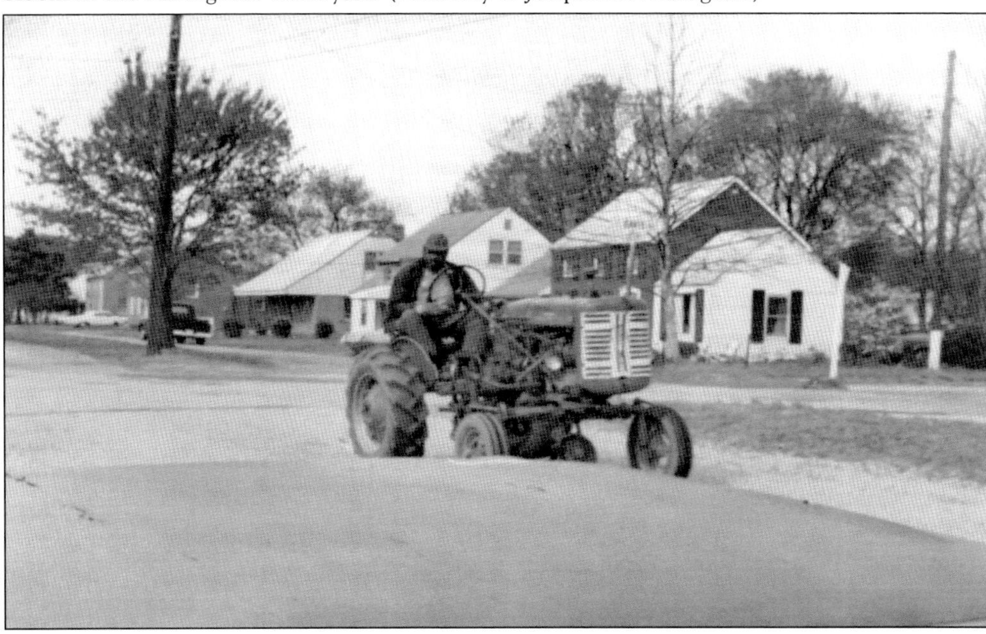

Farm animals pulled the plow in the early years of Aberdeen Gardens. In the mid-1950s, not everyone in Aberdeen Gardens had a tractor to till their gardens. Here Herman Baker is on Langston Boulevard traveling to a home to cultivate the land. His cost was very reasonable—he was paid in cash, took no checks, and sometimes used the barter system. (Courtesy Jacqueline Baker Roundtree.)

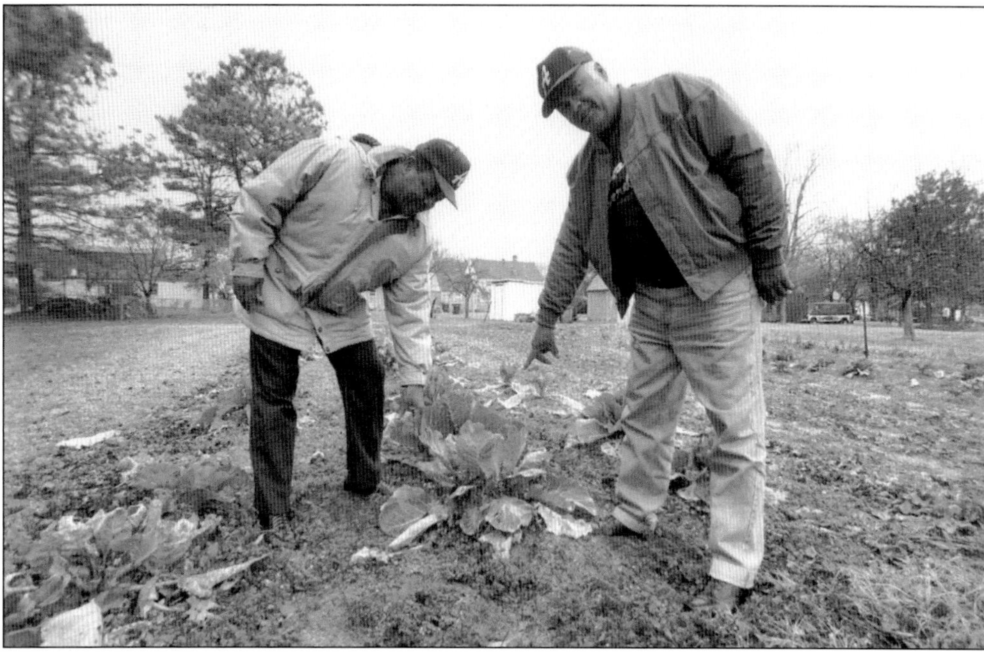

Walter Jackson (left) and Claude Vann Jr. are looking at the size of the cabbage in the garden. Apple, pear, and peach trees were provided for an orchard area, as well as strawberry and blackberry plants for Aberdeen Gardens residents in 1937. Many gardens were prevalent until the late 1950s. Only a few first-generation residents have gardens today. (Courtesy of Walter P. Calahan.)

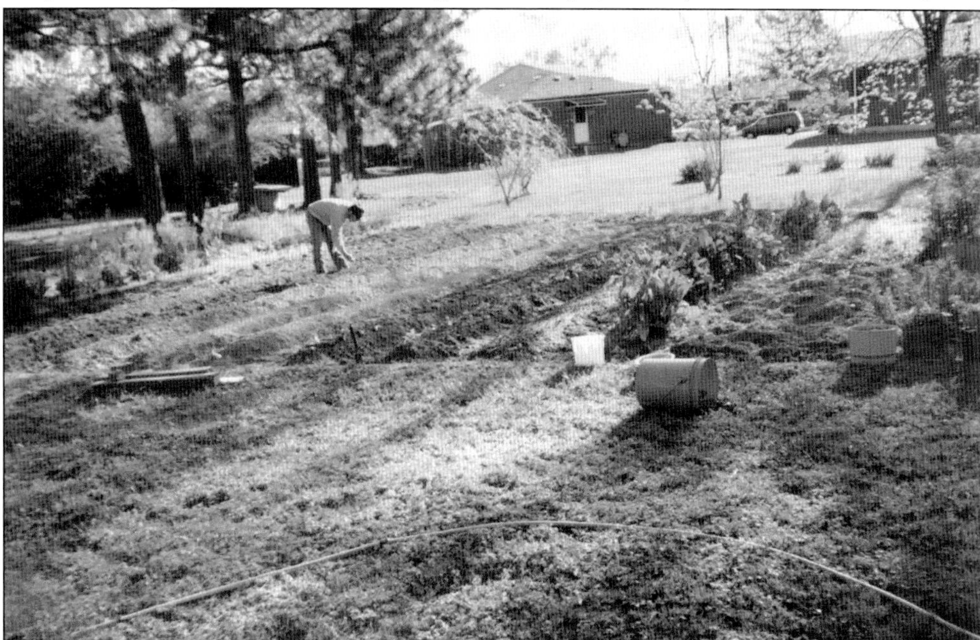

Theodore O. Howard is a resident of Granger Court East, south of Aberdeen Gardens Historic District. He is preparing his rows for seeding to grow vegetables. His flowers are ready to be planted. Theodore O. and Catherine Howard enjoy sharing their harvest with neighbors, thus continuing the Aberdeen Gardens residents' tradition going back to 1936. (Courtesy of Catherine Howard.)

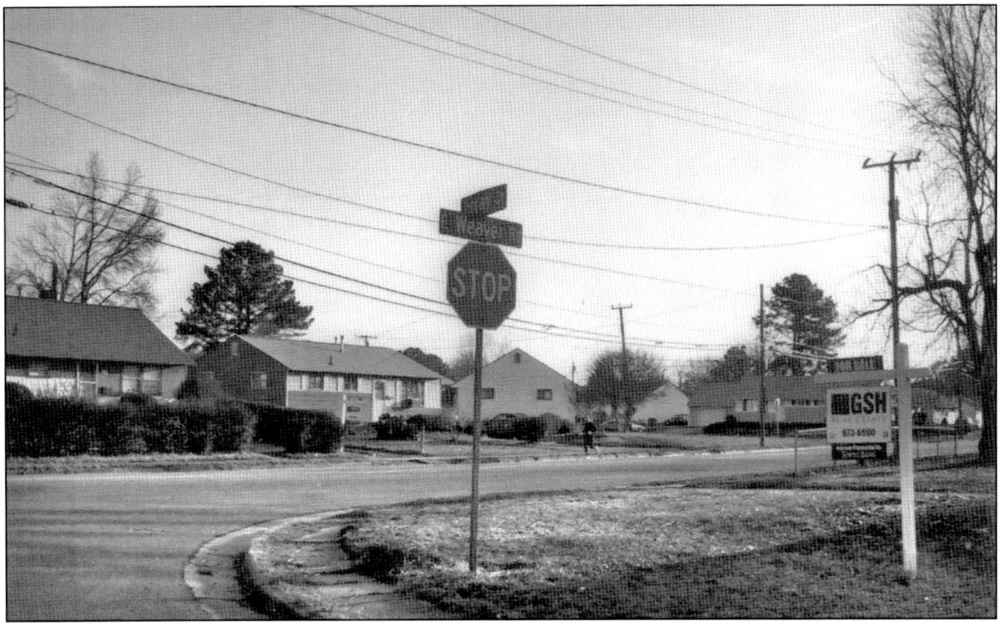

East Aberdeen is a partner neighborhood of the Aberdeen Gardens Historic and Civic Association; it is located east of the Aberdeen Gardens Historic District and is accessed along East Weaver Road, continuing through to Queen Street. It is located behind the Aberdeen Gardens Historic District section of Langston Boulevard and Aberdeen Elementary School. The one-story, single-family homes were built between 1954 and 1957. (Aberdeen Gardens Historic and Civic Association, Inc.)

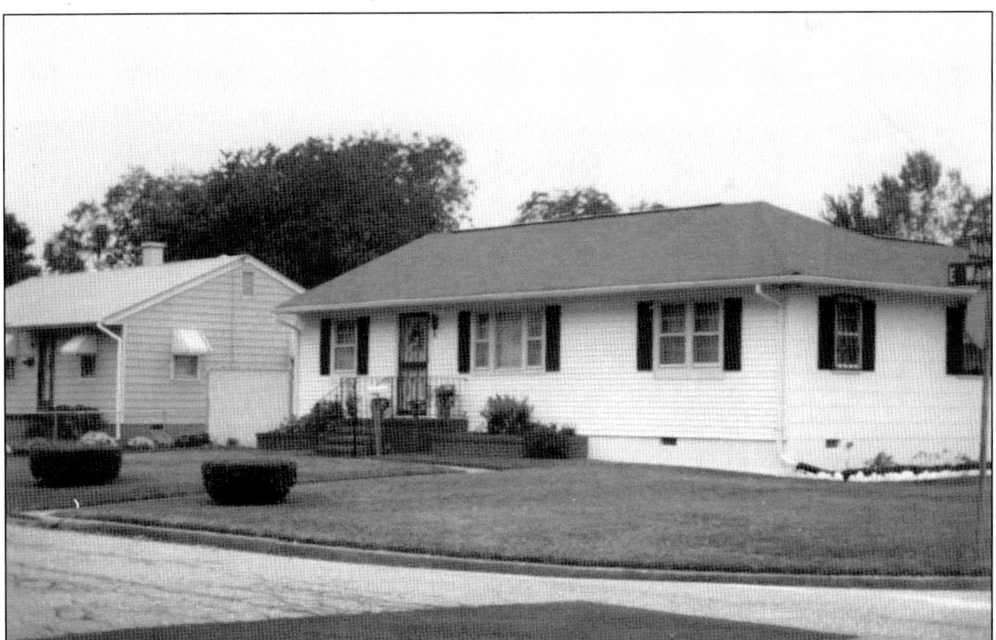

North Aberdeen, a part of the original 440 acres that was purchased in 1936 by the federal government under Pres. Franklin Delano Roosevelt, was built in the 1950s and accessed through Aberdeen Gardens Historic District by way of East Walker Road. The homes shown are typical in this neighborhood of approximately 41 houses. (Courtesy of Charles and Annie Cook.)

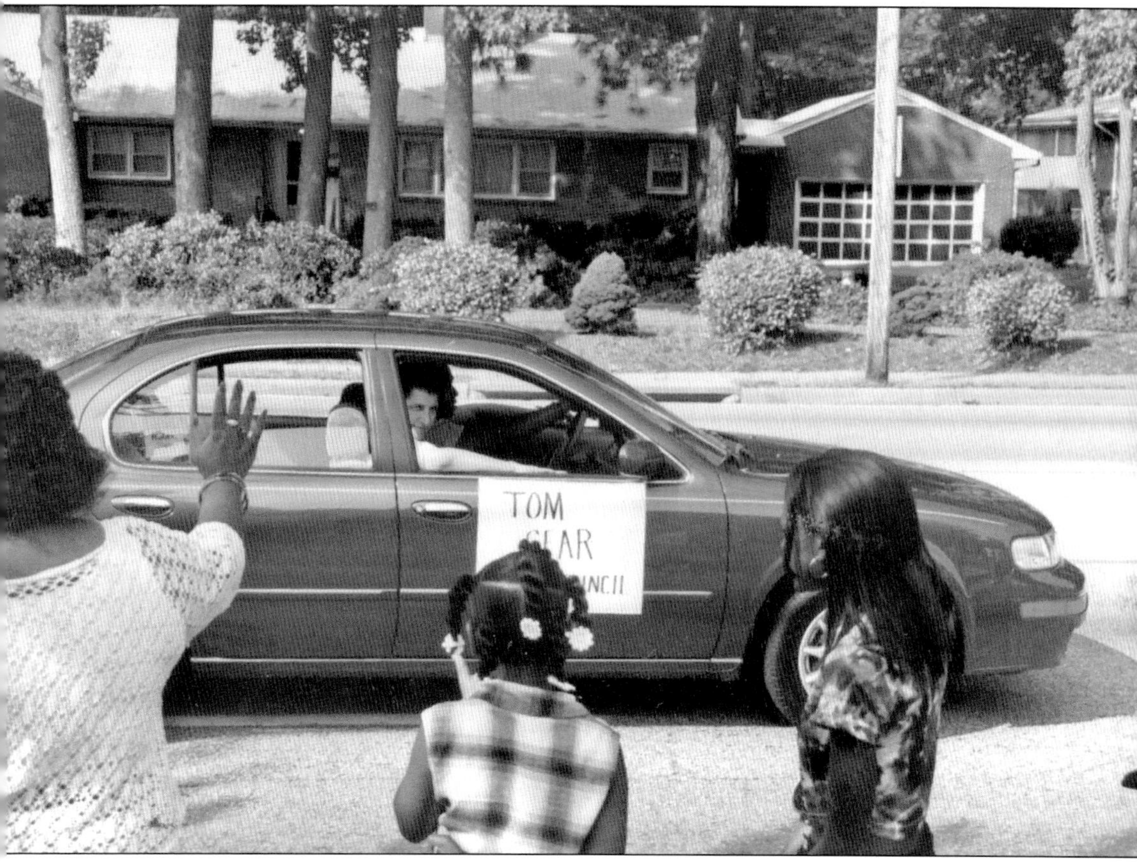

Granger Court, a west parcel of the 440 acres purchased in 1936, is diagonally across Aberdeen Road from Granger Court East. In 1958, the Hampton Institute established and organized a separate corporation, Granger Court, Inc., for the sole purpose of developing 25 acres of land to build single-family homes. In 1960, the lots were offered to Hampton Institute faculty, staff, alumni, and friends. Homes were custom-built according to owners' specifications. Brick and wood-veneer homes range from 1,500 square feet to 3,100-plus square feet of living space. The first to occupy the new homes were the families of Lloyd Alexander, Christopher Brown, and Alton Burns. Granger Court has a total of 45 homes located along Aberdeen Road, South Mary Peake Boulevard, and Lena Circle. Homes are featured in the background of the Deen's Day parade. Delegate Tom Gear is in the car. (Courtesy of Celestine Carter.)

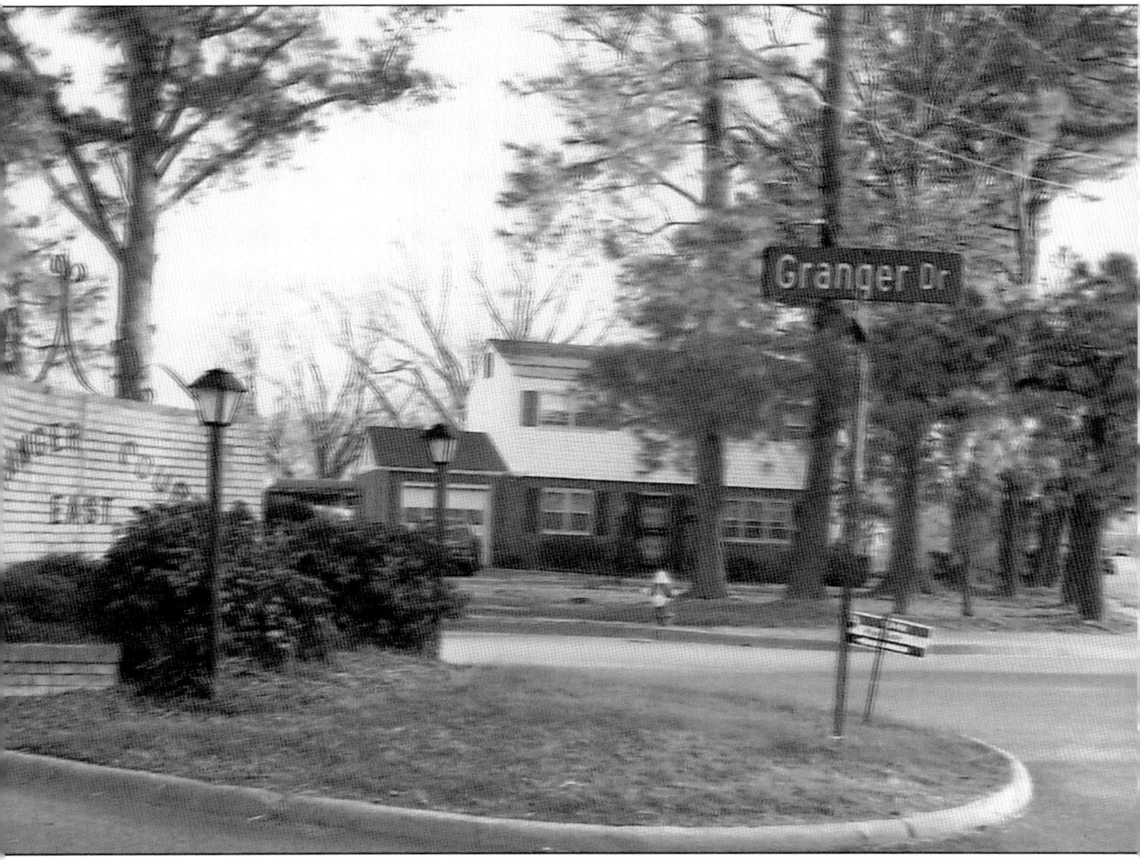

Granger Court East, an east parcel of the 440 acres purchased in 1936, was the land on which Hampton Institute's agricultural studies took place and which became known as Aberdeen Farms. In the mid-1960s, Granger Court East was constructed, consisting of 217 homes. This neighborhood is located behind the Aberdeen Gardens Historic District stretch of Langston Boulevard and parallel to East Russell Road, terminating at Aberdeen Road. With the exception of Granger Drive, which is a direct entry from Aberdeen Road, all other road accesses to this neighborhood involve going through the Aberdeen Gardens Historic District entry roads of East Davis and East Russell. These homes were also built to owner specification. Brick and wood-veneer home range from 1,000 square feet to 3,000 square feet of living space. The Newmarket Creek runs behind this neighborhood. The pictured front entry is at Granger Drive. Original residents and descendants of Aberdeen Gardens Historic District residents live in Granger Court East. (Courtesy of Catherine Howard.)

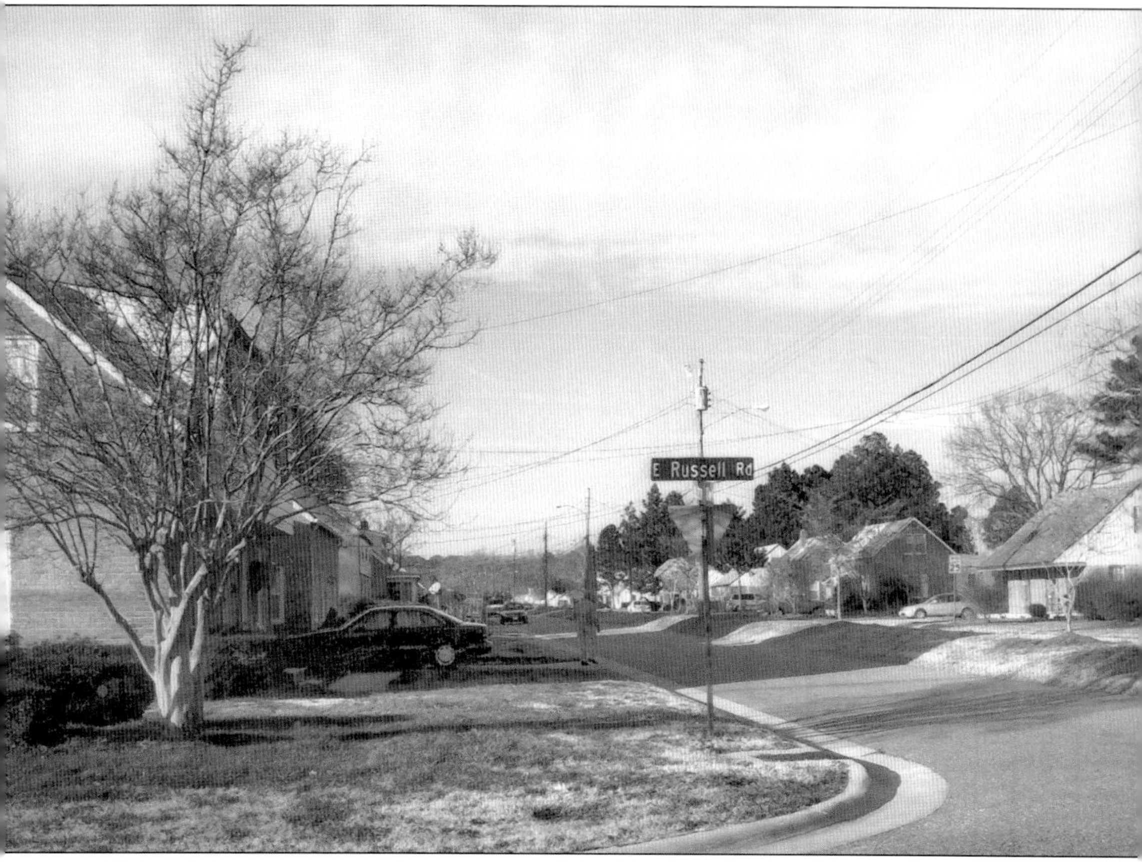

Eighty-six homes comprise the east sector of the Aberdeen Gardens Historic District. Langston Boulevard runs straight, and Aberdeen Elementary School separates Walker Road from the extension of Langston Boulevard; East Russell, East Davis, East Lewis, and East Weaver Roads connect with Langston Boulevard. The original wood and brick-veneer homes, completed in 1937, range from 830 square feet to 1,069 square feet. Most of the one-and-a-half-story homes have been remodeled but maintain the historic structure. The neighborhood east and south of Langston Boulevard is Granger Court East. This picture shows Langston Boulevard looking from East Russell Road. The curbing project of cemented entry walkways and driveways was completed in 2005. The blooming crepe myrtles and the neighborhood homes are intact after 70 years. (Courtesy of Aberdeen Gardens Historic and Civic Association, Inc.)

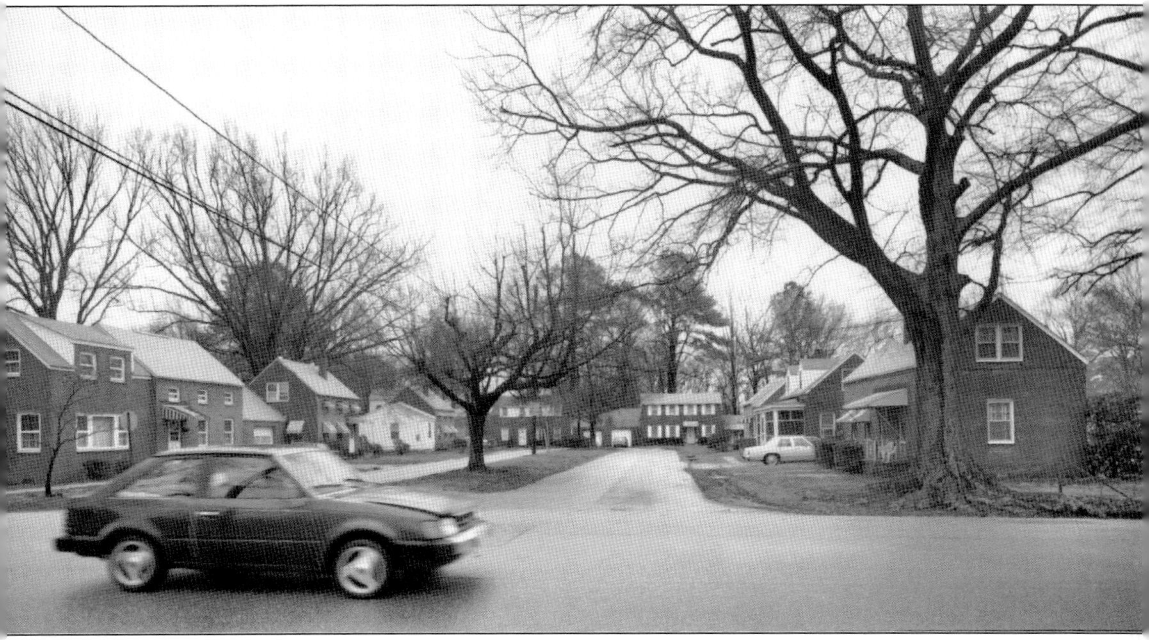

Seventy-two homes comprise the west sector of the Aberdeen Gardens Historic District. West Lewis, West Weaver, and West Walker Roads connect with Mary Peake Boulevard after crossing at Aberdeen Road. Mary Peake Boulevard is the home of the Historic Aberdeen Gardens Museum Complex. Directly west of Mary Peake Boulevard is the Big Bethel neighborhood and to the south is Granger Court. The Newmarket Creek is near the southern end of Mary Peake Boulevard. The Hampton City curbing project was completed after the east sector (Langston Boulevard) of the historic district was finished in 2005. (Courtesy of Catherine Howard.)

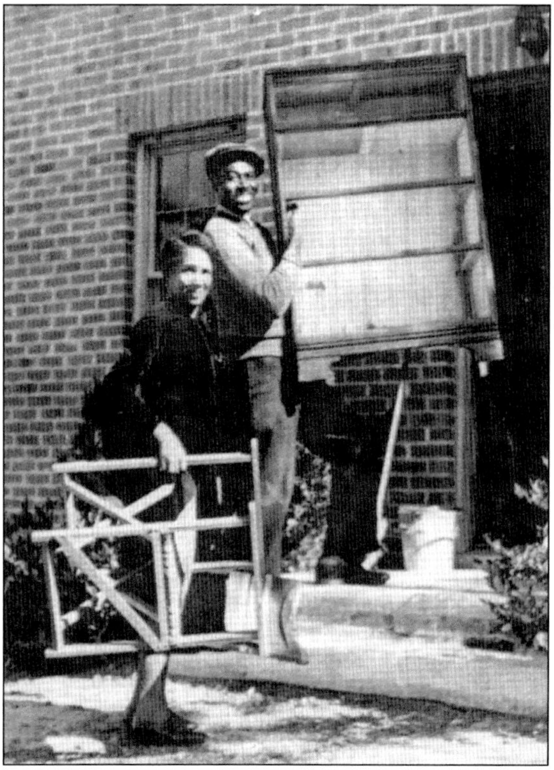

Moving-in day was happy among the residents. Many residents came from deplorable living conditions. The neighborhood is complete with landscaping, poles for electric wiring, and trees on the median. This 1937 FSA photograph of an unidentified couple was widely used to represent moving-in day in Aberdeen Gardens. (Courtesy of Rothstein.)

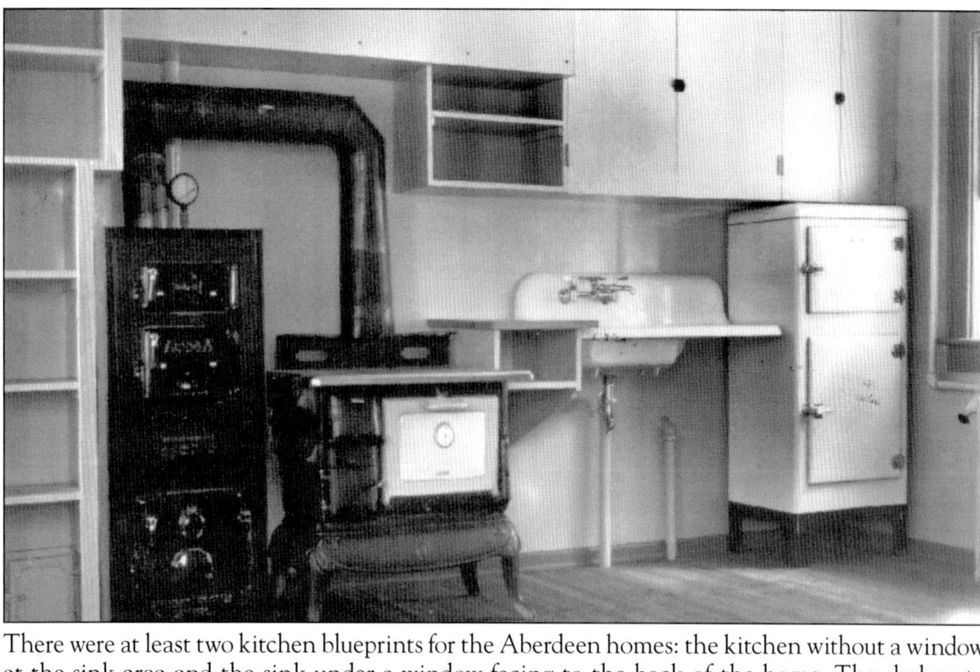

There were at least two kitchen blueprints for the Aberdeen homes: the kitchen without a window at the sink area and the sink under a window facing to the back of the home. The shelves to the left were use as a pantry for food or a cupboard for dishes. The Arcola heating system used coal for fuel. Note the small counter space. The open sink was usually covered with a decorative curtain to store items. (Courtesy of Heck Production Company.)

Two

Aberdeen Gardens 1966–1995

Hampton City's neighborhood office was created in 1993 to help the "people shape the look and feel of their neighborhood and meet needs they identify." Aberdeen Gardens was identifying the needs of the community and realizing that it had history to share. The Aberdeen Gardens Rattlers fast-pitch softball team members of 1946 rallied around the idea of being historic during their reunion in 1988. As written in the March 8, 1994, Proclamation in Recognition of the Preservation of Historic Aberdeen Gardens from the City of Hampton, signed by Mayor James L. Eason: "Whereas because of Aberdeen Garden's rich history, the Aberdeen Rattlers' Softball Club saw a need to preserve the rich history of their neighborhood and thus appointed the Aberdeen Gardens Historic Group which consisted of past and present residents including James C. Arrington, Evelyn Daniel Chandler, John H. Epps, Horace Goins, Walter P. Jackson, Lenrow Milo Jr., Claude Vann Jr., John P. H. Vann, Andre M. Vann, and Marsha Williams."

By 1994, the Aberdeen Gardens Historic and Civic Association, Inc., was formed, and Aberdeen Gardens was listed as a historic district on the Virginia State Register of Historic Landmarks, as well as on the National Register of Historic Places. The Aberdeen Gardens Historic and Civic Association's next challenges were to make everyone aware of these accomplishments and to be a role model to other neighborhoods. In 1998, the Foundation of Historic Aberdeen Gardens was formed; they set out to restore a 1936 Aberdeen Gardens house as a museum, collecting furniture and artifacts from around the neighborhood.

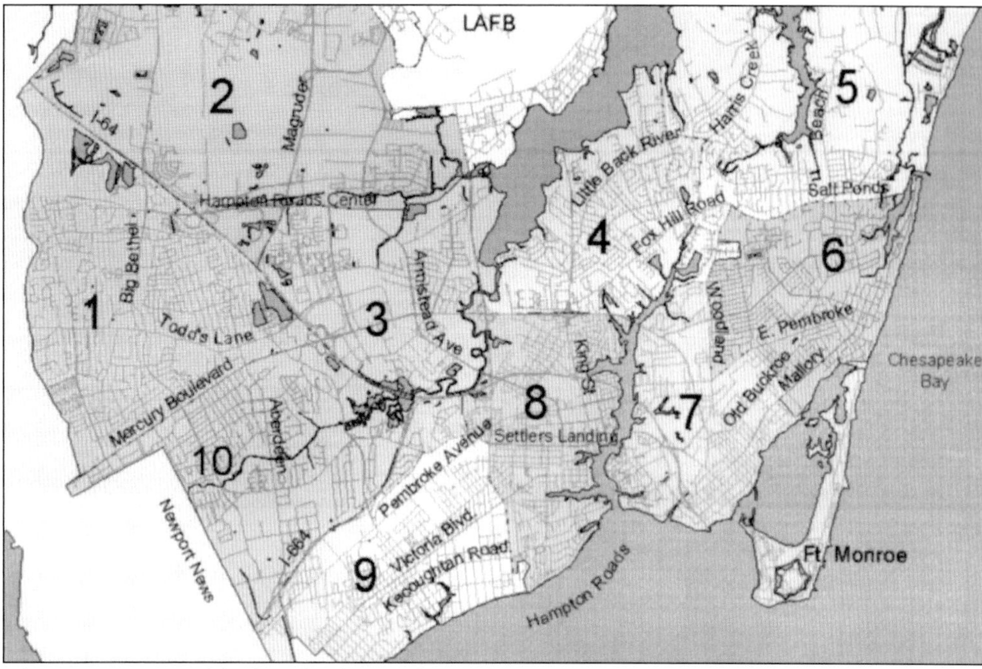

The Hampton Neighborhood Office is the guiding force in dividing the city into neighborhood districts and providing a neighborhood office contact facilitator to ensure that each neighborhood reaches its full potential and provides the people with the resources needed to meet their unique needs and goals. Each district has boundary lines and is represented by a neighborhood commissioner. The Aberdeen Gardens Historic District is in Hampton Neighborhood District 10. (Courtesy of Aberdeen Gardens Historic and Civic Association, Inc.)

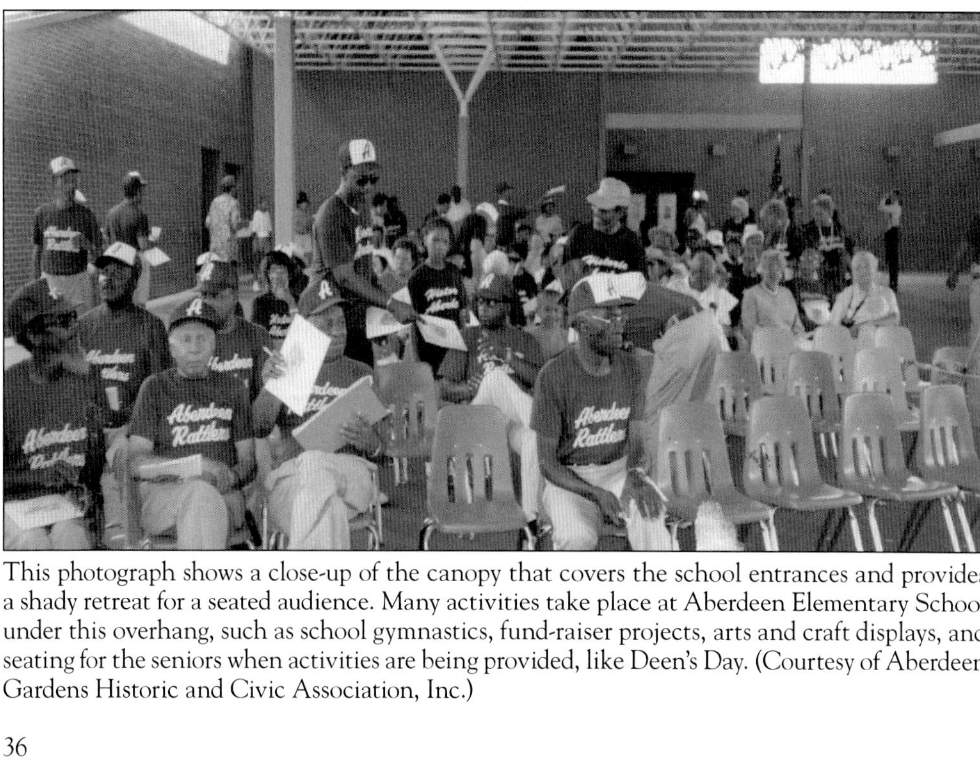

This photograph shows a close-up of the canopy that covers the school entrances and provides a shady retreat for a seated audience. Many activities take place at Aberdeen Elementary School under this overhang, such as school gymnastics, fund-raiser projects, arts and craft displays, and seating for the seniors when activities are being provided, like Deen's Day. (Courtesy of Aberdeen Gardens Historic and Civic Association, Inc.)

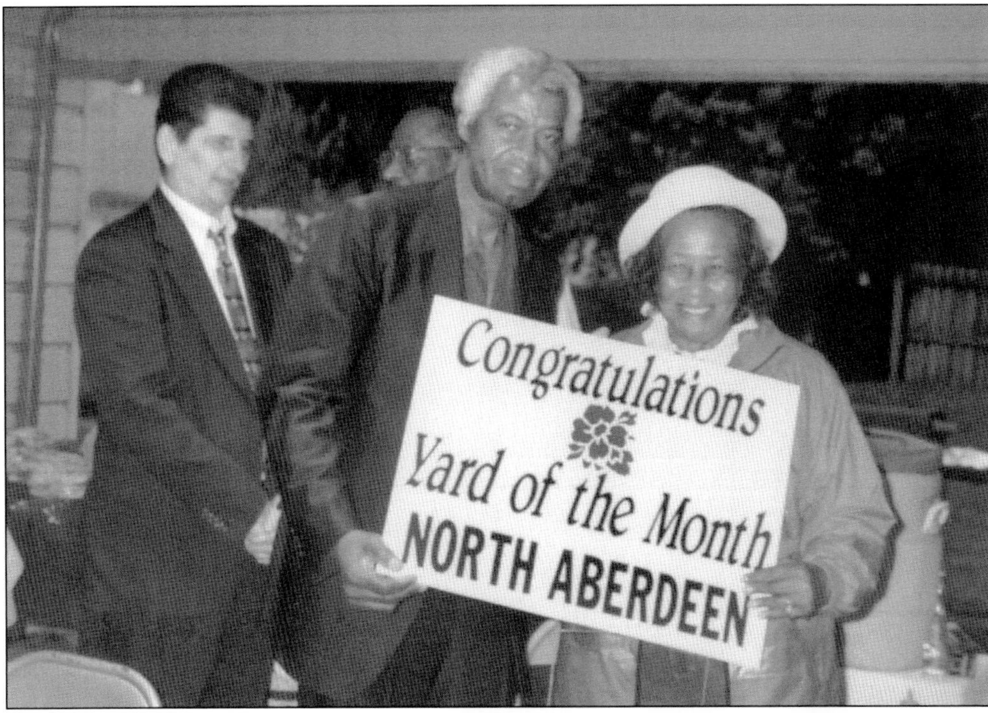

Lillian Gist had one of the first homes to receive the recognition of Yard of the Month. Pictured from left to right are Delegate Tom Gear of the 91st District; unidentified; Roosevelt Wilson, president of the Aberdeen Gardens Historic and Civic Association, Inc.; and Gist, who lives in North Aberdeen, north of the Aberdeen Gardens Historic District. (Courtesy of Aberdeen Gardens Historic and Civic Association, Inc.)

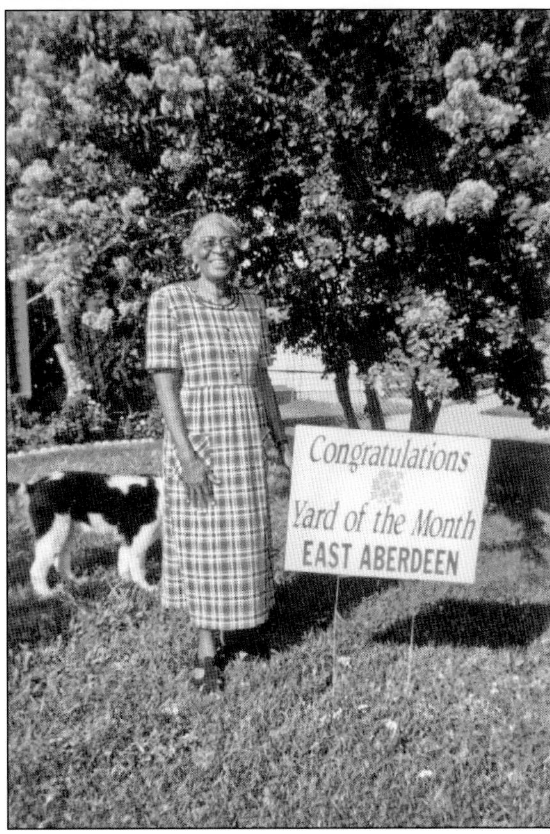

East Aberdeen's July Yard of the Month recognition was done by the beautification committee of the Aberdeen Gardens Historic and Civic Association, Inc. Myrtle Taylor, a retired music teacher and resident of Jordan Drive, had the award-winning yard. The lawn was well groomed with plants encased in orchestrated flowerbeds and a beautiful crepe myrtle in full blossom. (Courtesy of Myrtle Taylor.)

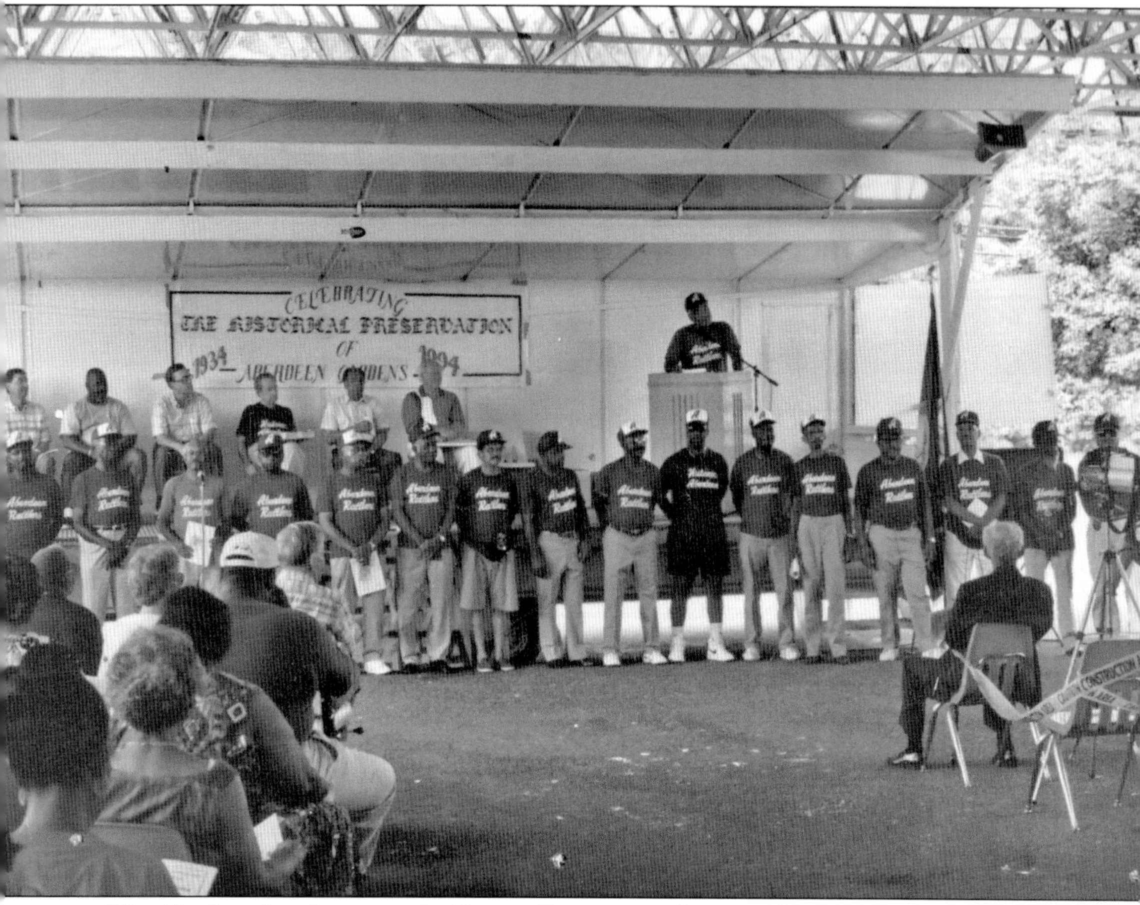

The Aberdeen Rattlers are at the Historic Preservation Program during Deen's Day at Aberdeen School. City officials, family, friends, and visitors are present. The Aberdeen Rattlers are well known in the Aberdeen Gardens Historic District. Upon reuniting in 1988, their offspring and new neighbors joined the Aberdeen Rattlers Softball Club. In honoring the Aberdeen Rattlers, the Aberdeen Gardens Historic and Civic Association titled its newsletter the *Rattler Chronicle*. (Courtesy of Jacqueline Arrington.)

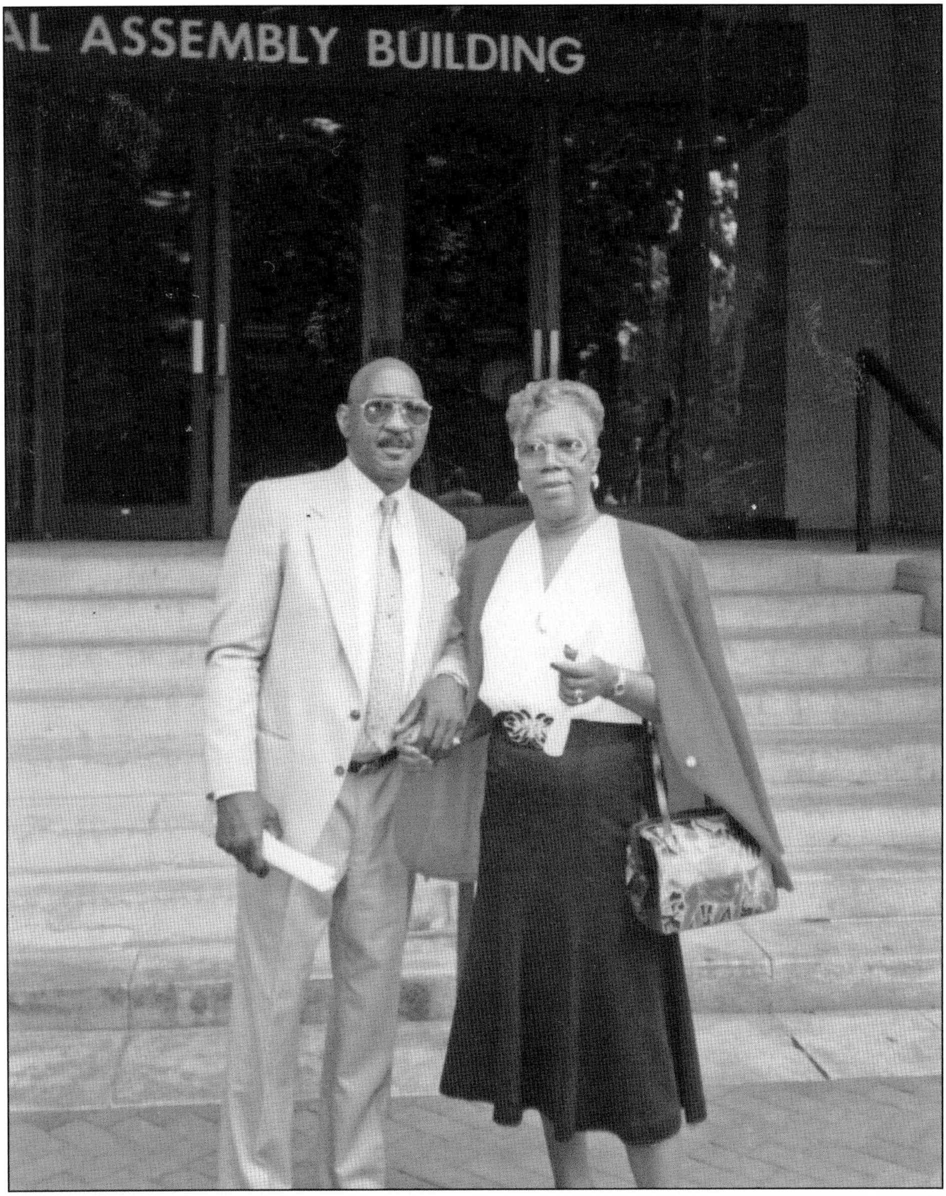

In 1937, like many of the first families, James W. and Vicy Arrington rented their 1936 Aberdeen Gardens home prior to buying it. James "Dusty" Arrington was nine years old. Jacqueline Arrington, James C. Arrington, and his wife, Shirley Arrington, reside in the family home on Langston Boulevard in the Aberdeen Gardens Historic District. James C. and Shirley Arrington have four sons—Arthur, Michael, Victor, and Marvin; all four later joined the Aberdeen Rattlers. James C., as chairman of the Aberdeen Gardens Historic Group, formed committees to meet the needs of the community, such as research, documents and applications for historic recognition, and fund-raising. In 1994, the Aberdeen Gardens Historic District became a historic landmark, and 158 homes and the Johnson Farm were listed on the National Register of Historic Places. James Arrington was the recipient of the Aberdeen Gardens Historic and Civic Association Historic Recognition Award in 1999, and Jacqueline Arrington was a recipient in 2005. (Courtesy of Aberdeen Gardens Historic and Civic Association, Inc.)

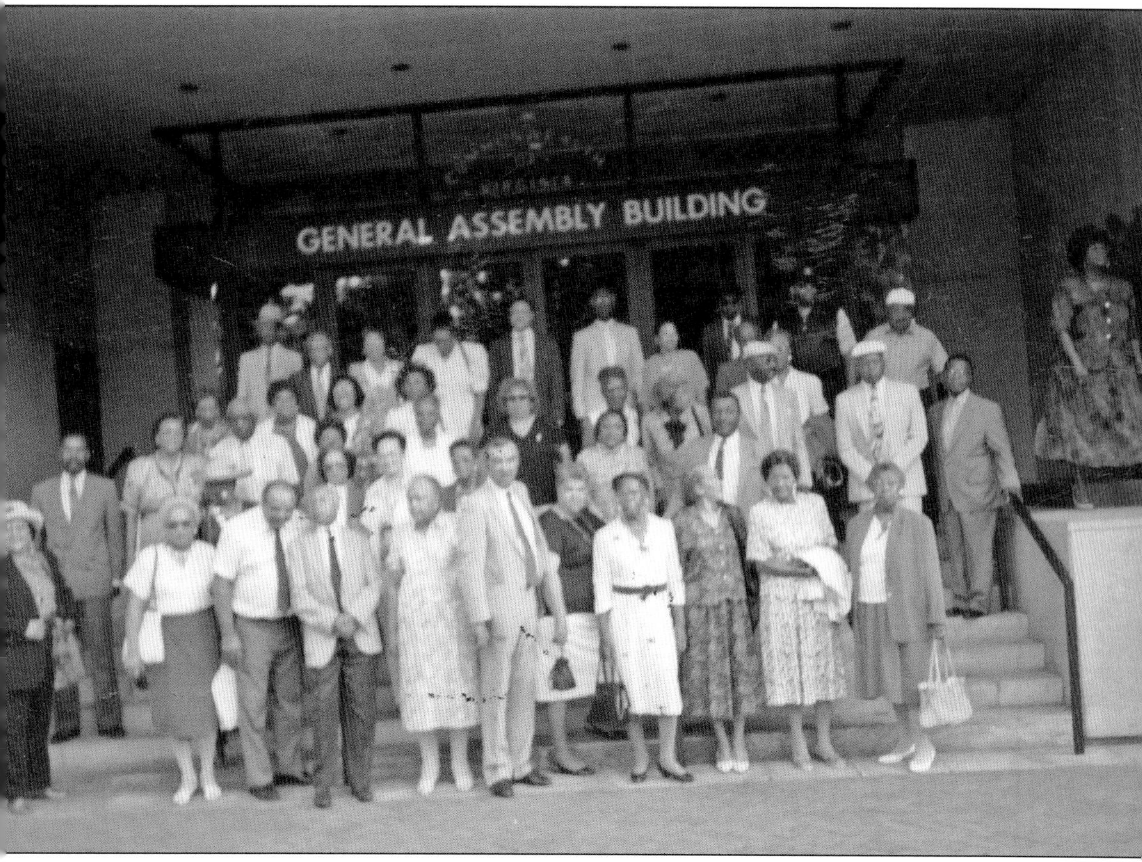

As research data was gathered, the association worked with the Virginia Department of Historic Resources to maintain continuity of documents to be returned in a timely fashion. Evelyn Daniels Chandler and Marsha Williams prepared and maintained documents accurately with the Aberdeen Gardens committee members' participation. The Aberdeen Gardens residents gathered in Richmond at the General Assembly Building in 1994 to hear the proclamation and witness the vote to accept Aberdeen Gardens' application to be placed on the historic register of Virginia. Two buses and many individual cars arrived in Richmond. The residents dined and signed the historic registry book in historic buildings. One such building is the Tredegar National Civil War Center Foundation Building. (Courtesy of Lenrow Milo.)

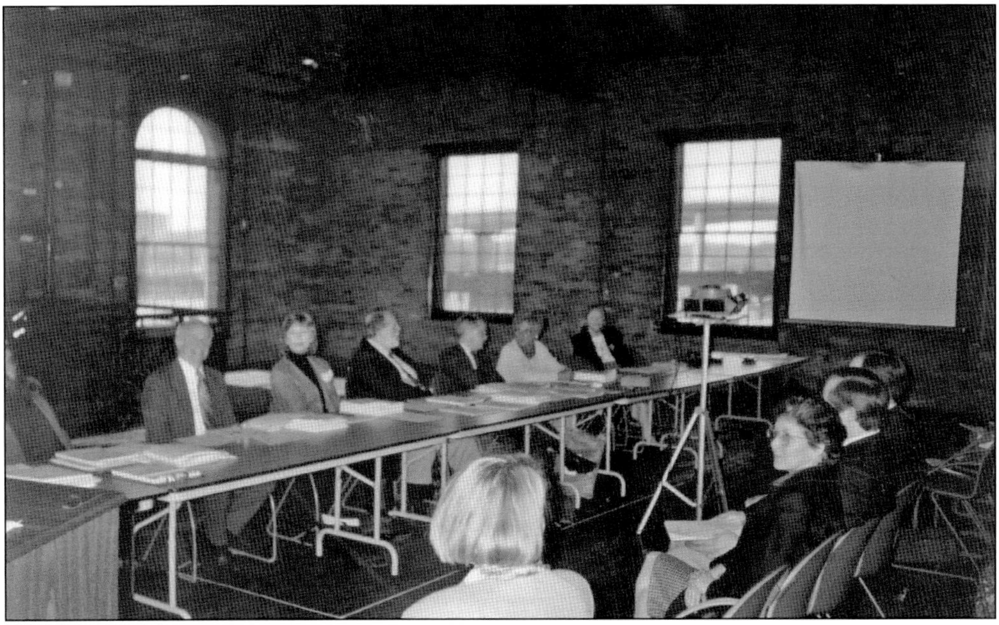

In 1994, Virginia Board of Historic Resources members and dignitaries prepare for Aberdeen Gardens Historic District resident signatures in the registry book in the Tredegar National Civil War Center Foundation Building in Richmond. Aberdeen Gardens, as well as many neighborhood members throughout Virginia, were present to hear their neighborhood presentation. (Courtesy of Lenrow Milo.)

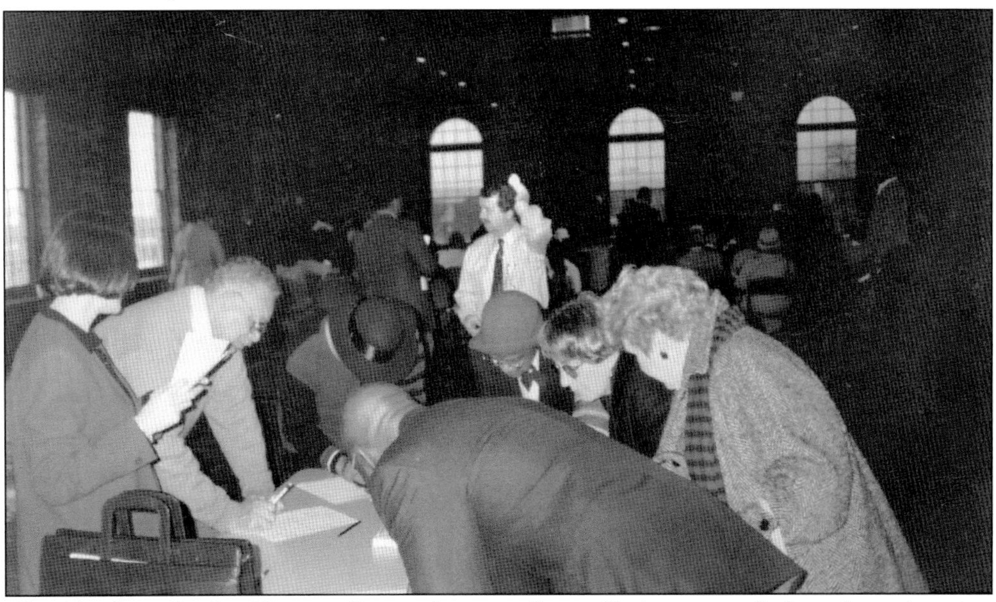

The Aberdeen Garden Historic Group chairman James C. Arrington, Robert Ayers (wearing glasses), and two other Aberdeeners (wearing hats) are assisted by the Virginia Board of Historic Resources clerks as they add their signatures to their registry book. Residents joyfully participated in naming the neighborhood a Virginia Historic Landmark in 1994 as Aberdeen Gardens Historic District, and the neighborhood was placed on the National Register of Historic Places by the U.S. Department of the Interior in May 1994. (Courtesy of Lenrow Milo.)

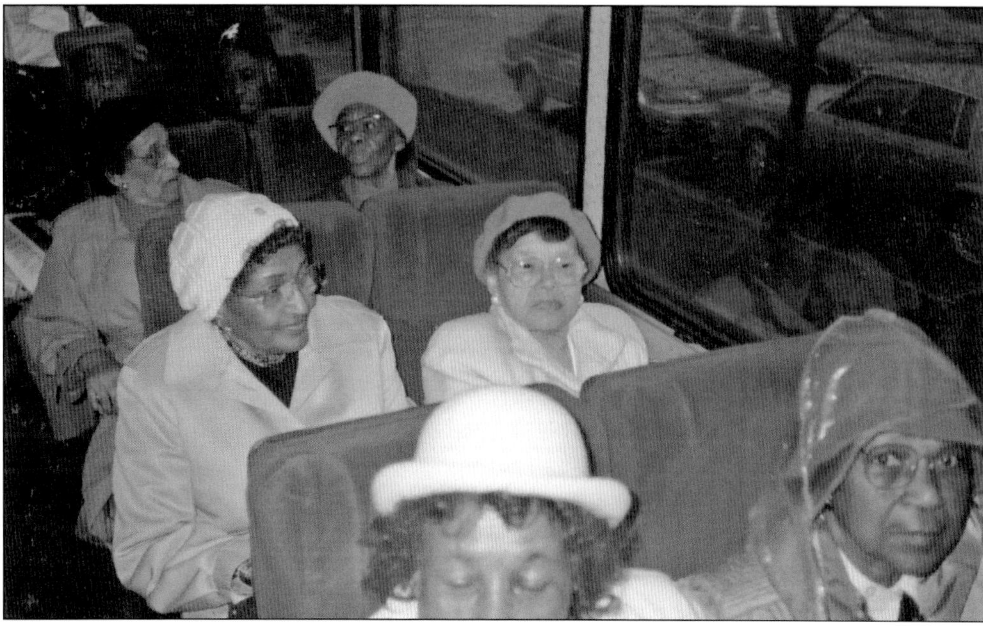

These are the faces of Aberdeeners coming home after a historic day in Richmond in 1994. Sixty years of neighborhood existence, socializing, quietly preserving home and land, and maintaining cultural, economic, religious, and social harmony have kept Aberdeen residents together with a desire for progress. (Courtesy of Lenrow Milo.)

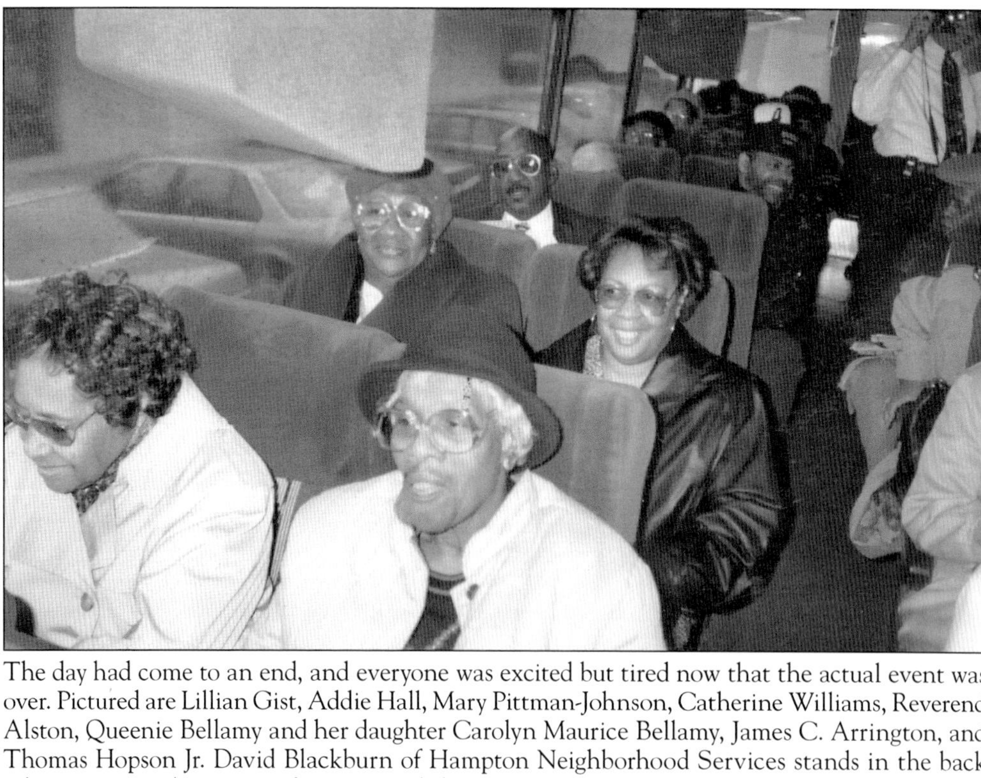

The day had come to an end, and everyone was excited but tired now that the actual event was over. Pictured are Lillian Gist, Addie Hall, Mary Pittman-Johnson, Catherine Williams, Reverend Alston, Queenie Bellamy and her daughter Carolyn Maurice Bellamy, James C. Arrington, and Thomas Hopson Jr. David Blackburn of Hampton Neighborhood Services stands in the back taking pictures. (Courtesy of Lenrow Milo.)

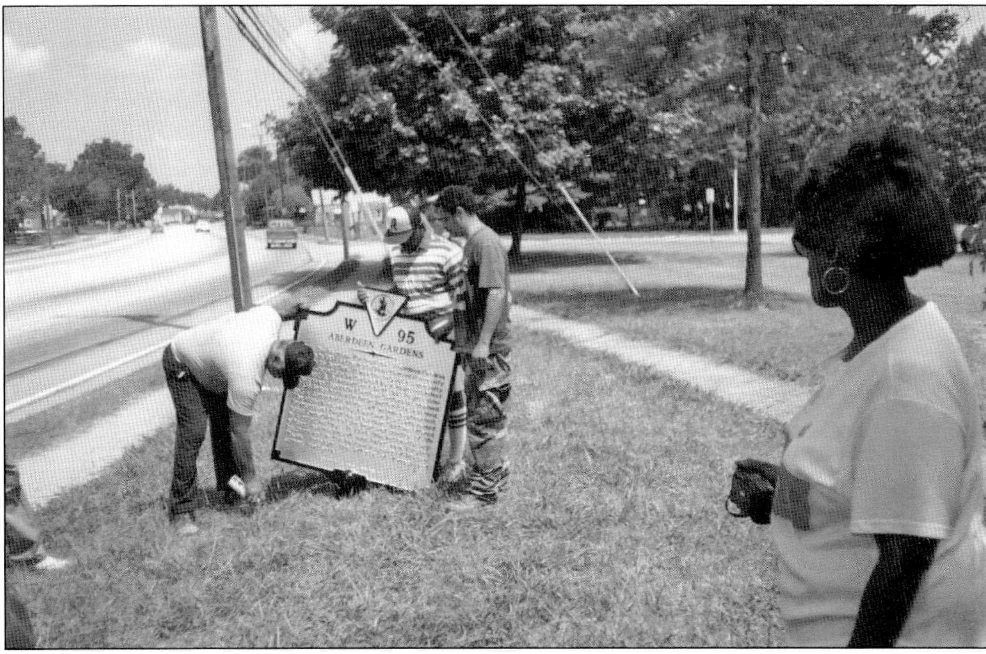

Virginia State Marker W95 is being erected in front of the Aberdeen Elementary School in Aberdeen Garden Historic District with assistance from residents and is being observed by Evelyn Daniels Chandler (right). As a result of a car accident, the original marker was damaged. The Virginia Department of Historic Resources was contacted, and the marker was replaced. (Courtesy of Lenrow Milo.)

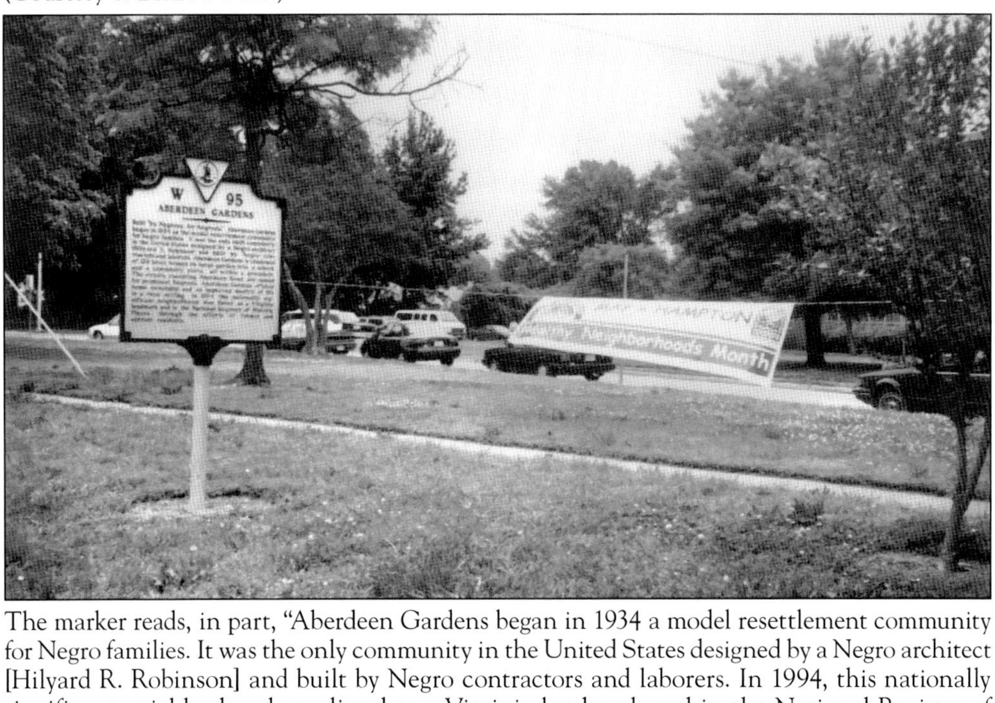

The marker reads, in part, "Aberdeen Gardens began in 1934 a model resettlement community for Negro families. It was the only community in the United States designed by a Negro architect [Hilyard R. Robinson] and built by Negro contractors and laborers. In 1994, this nationally significant neighborhood was listed as a Virginia landmark and in the National Register of Historic Places." (Courtesy of Lenrow Milo.)

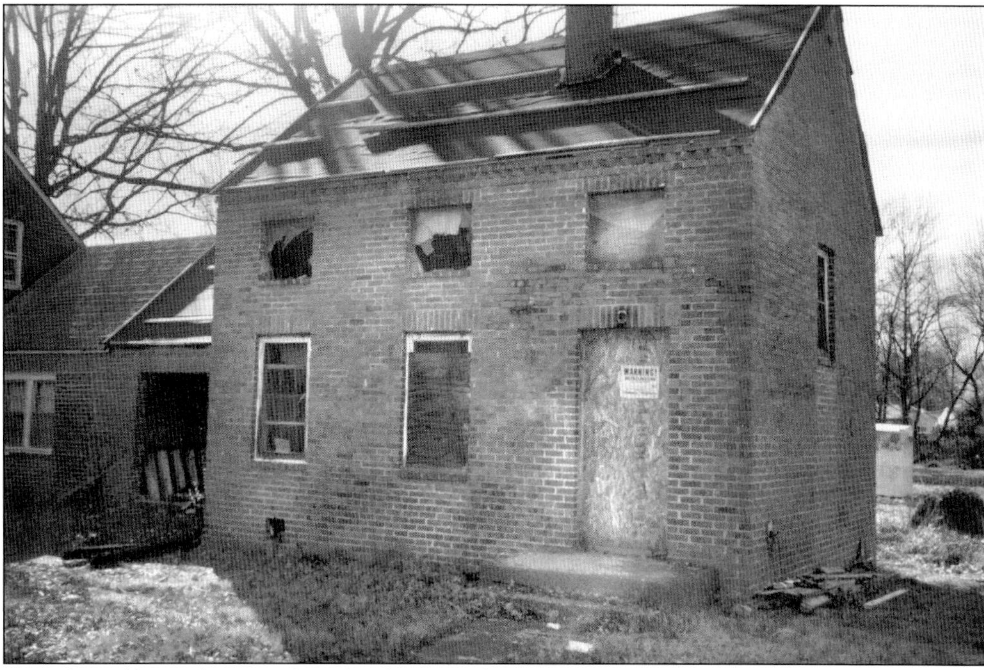

A neglected home became the Aberdeen Gardens Historic Museum on Mary Peake Boulevard. The suggestion came from Emma Taylor. Marsha Williams coordinated the procurement of the house for the museum; Hampton City's neighborhood office obtained the house; and Aberdeen Gardens Historic and Civic Association purchased the house for $1 in August 1995. The large tree inside and debris has been removed. (Courtesy of Aberdeen Gardens Historic and Civic Association, Inc.)

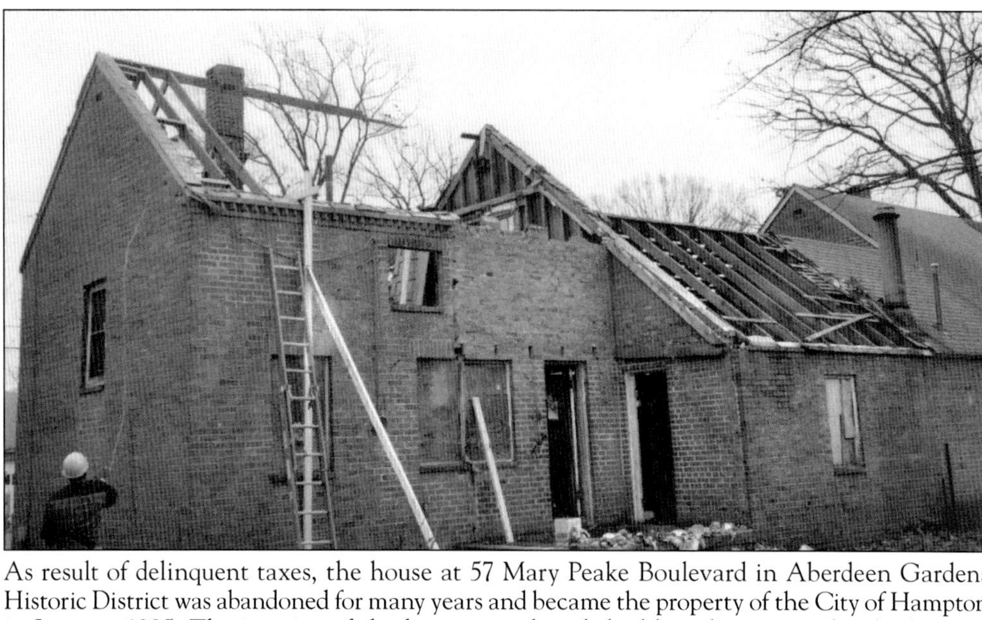

As result of delinquent taxes, the house at 57 Mary Peake Boulevard in Aberdeen Gardens Historic District was abandoned for many years and became the property of the City of Hampton in January 1995. The interior of the house was demolished by a large tree that had grown inside. The entire house had to be restored. (Courtesy of Aberdeen Gardens Historic and Civic Association, Inc.)

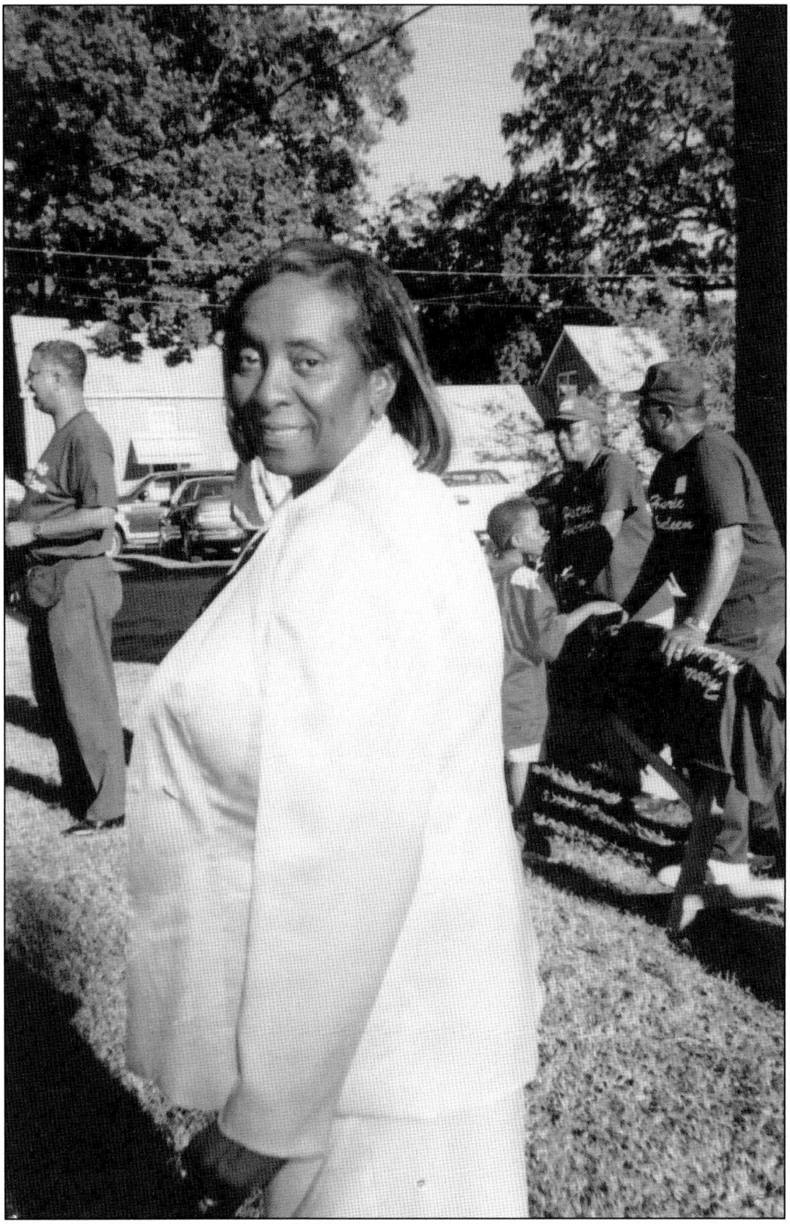

Burt S. and Marsha Williams are residents of Langston Boulevard in the Aberdeen Gardens Historic District. Marsha assisted with preparing the application for a $100,000 grant and presented it to the Virginia General Assembly in 1994 on behalf of the Aberdeen Gardens Historic and Civic Association. The grant was sponsored by Delegate Mary Taylor Christian. It was approved, and monies were received in increments of $50,000. Marsha has been a fervent worker for the Aberdeen Gardens Historic and Civic Association, Inc. She has worked on numerous committees, including the historian, hospitality, and program committees. As museum coordinator, she brought enlightening programs to the Aberdeen Gardens Historic Museum. She was the coordinator and mistress of ceremonies for the dedication of the Historic Aberdeen Gardens Museum on September 28, 2002. (Courtesy of Aberdeen Gardens Historic and Civic Association, Inc.)

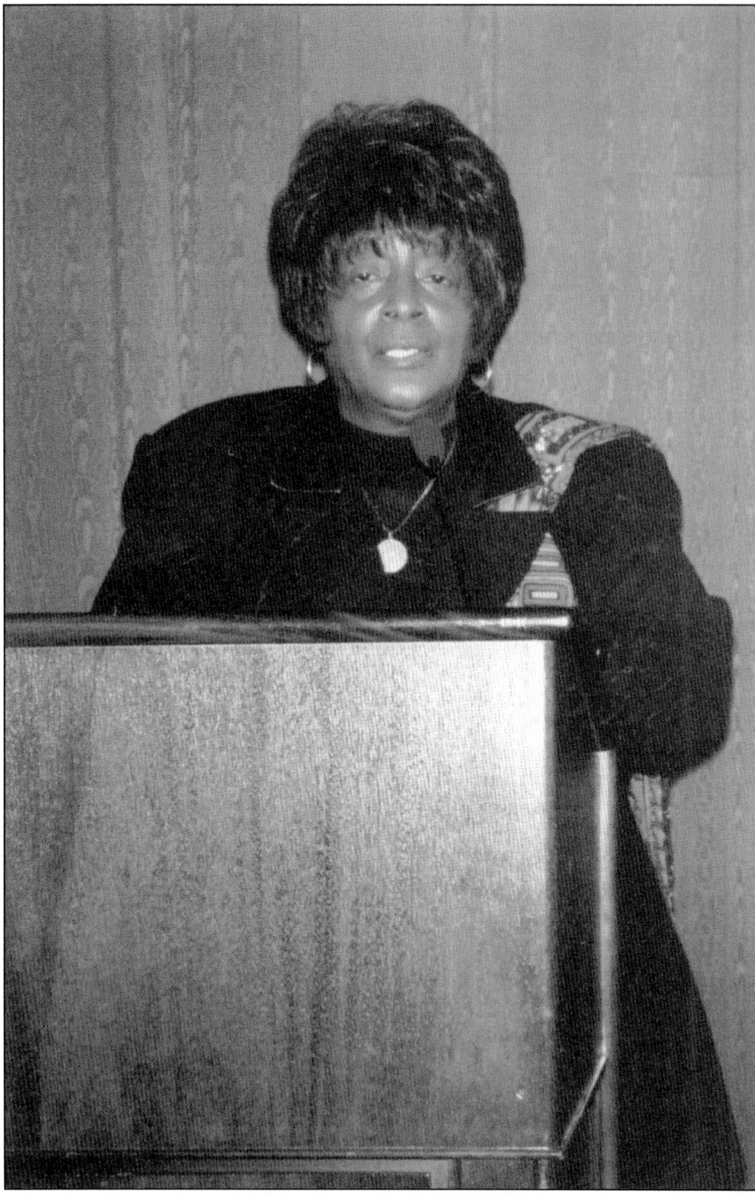

Evelyn Daniels Chandler is a descendant of Robert and Amaretha Daniels, who were original Aberdeen Gardens Historic District residents on Langston Boulevard. Chandler, as the Aberdeen Gardens Historic Group's program chair, brought awareness to the community and surrounding neighborhoods of the area's historic significance. Being an executive board member of the Preservation Alliance of Virginia, she bridged the gap between the Aberdeen Gardens Historic Group and collected data and the requirements needed for preservation. She and Marsha Williams worked collectively on the $100,000 preservation grant proposal. Chandler, as the black history program coordinator for the Aberdeen Gardens Historic and Civic Association, recognized three nurses, Agnes Stokes Chisman (an Aberdeen Gardens Historic District descendent), Patricia McKenzie, and Mildred Smith, with a plaque in recognition of their courage and achievement in the advancement of civil rights both in the community and the nation. (Courtesy of Aberdeen Gardens Historic and Civic Association, Inc.)

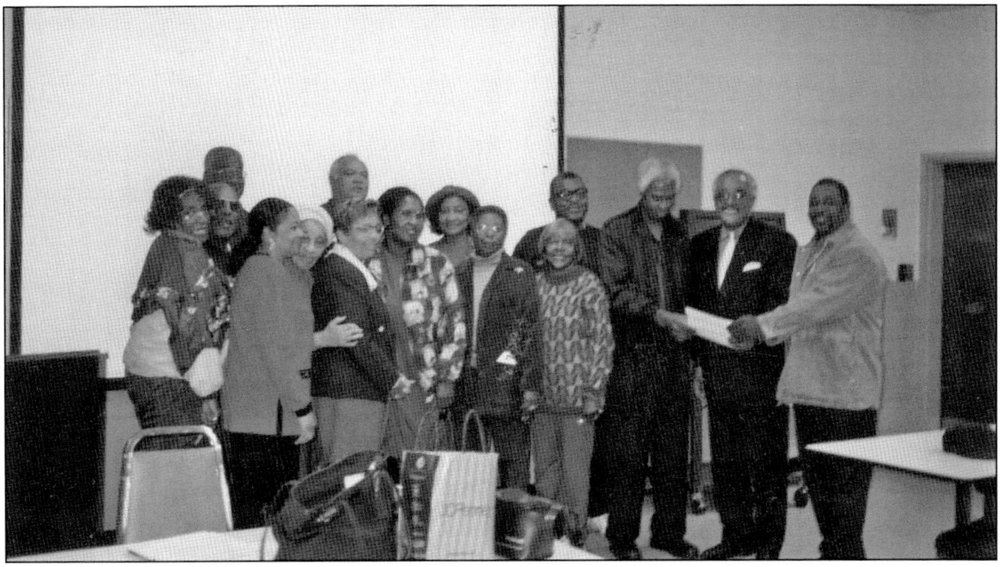

Three contractors applied to repair the Aberdeen Gardens Historic Museum. The 1999 meeting awarding the contract for this historic event took place at the Hampton Briarfield Fire Department conference room. Twelve Aberdeen Gardens Historic and Civic Association members witnessed the signing of the Aberdeen Gardens Historic Museum restoration contract awarded to Freeman Terry Contracting, Inc. Pictured holding the contract are (from left to right) association president Roosevelt Wilson, unidentified, and Hampton councilman Paige Washington. (Courtesy of Aberdeen Gardens Historic and Civic Association, Inc.)

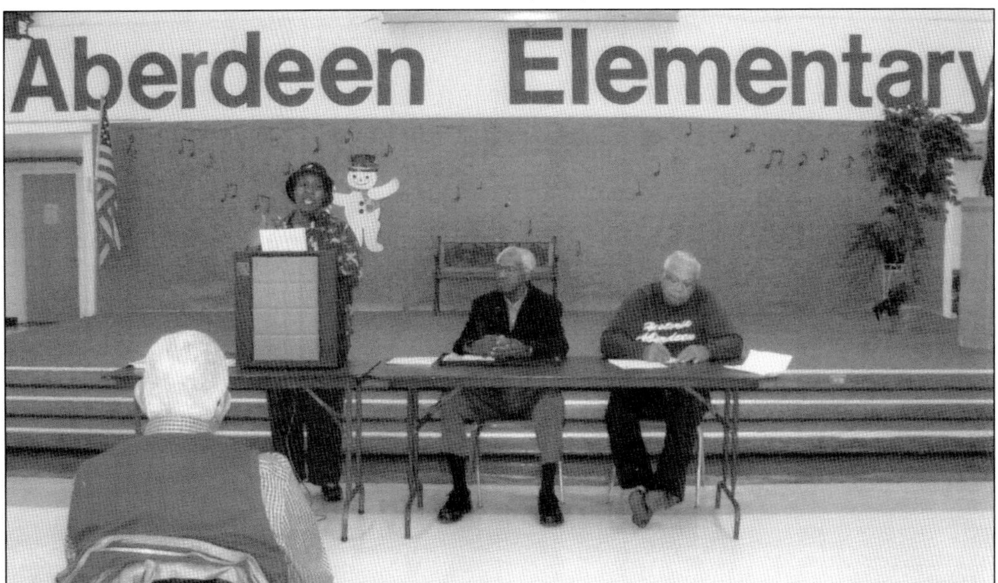

The neighborhood development plan of 1936 addressed Aberdeen Elementary School as a recreational and meeting place for the community. The Aberdeen Gardens Historic and Civic Association contacted the Hampton School Board to request that their meetings be held at the Aberdeen Elementary School. Meetings are held in the auditorium monthly. Shown are Jacqueline Arrington at the podium, Pres. Roosevelt Wilson (seated), and Claude Vann Jr. (writing). (Courtesy of Catherine Howard.)

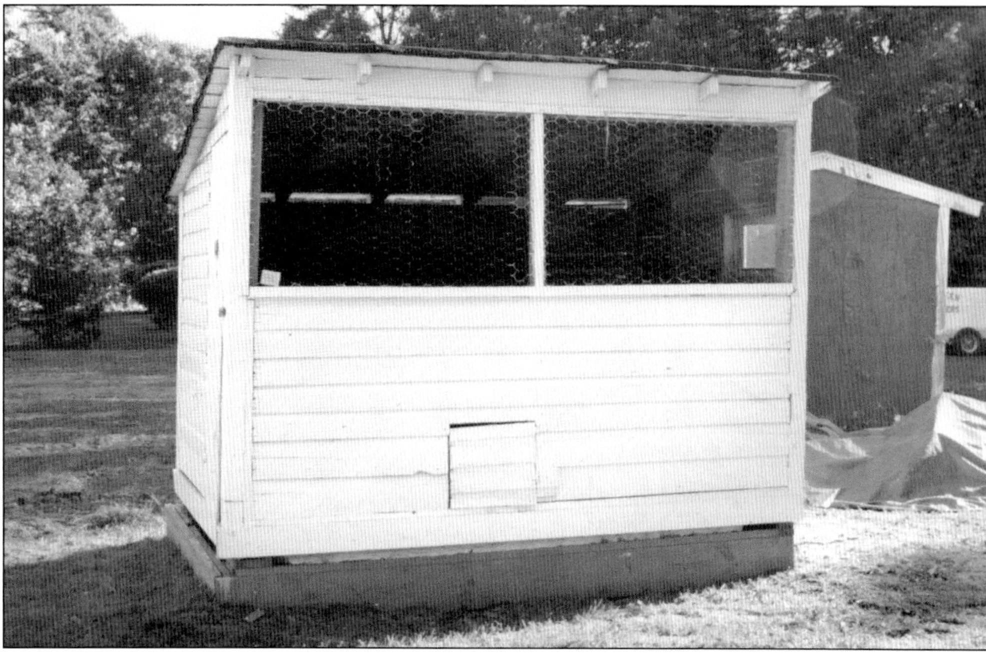

The only chicken coop left from 1936 was located in Sherman Roberts's backyard on East Russell Road in the Aberdeen Gardens Historic District. A close-up view of the coop reveals the side entrance and two large windows. A pre-measured area in the yard was for fencing the chickens. One resident was grandfathered in and allowed to maintain chickens until 2000. (Courtesy of Sherman Roberts.)

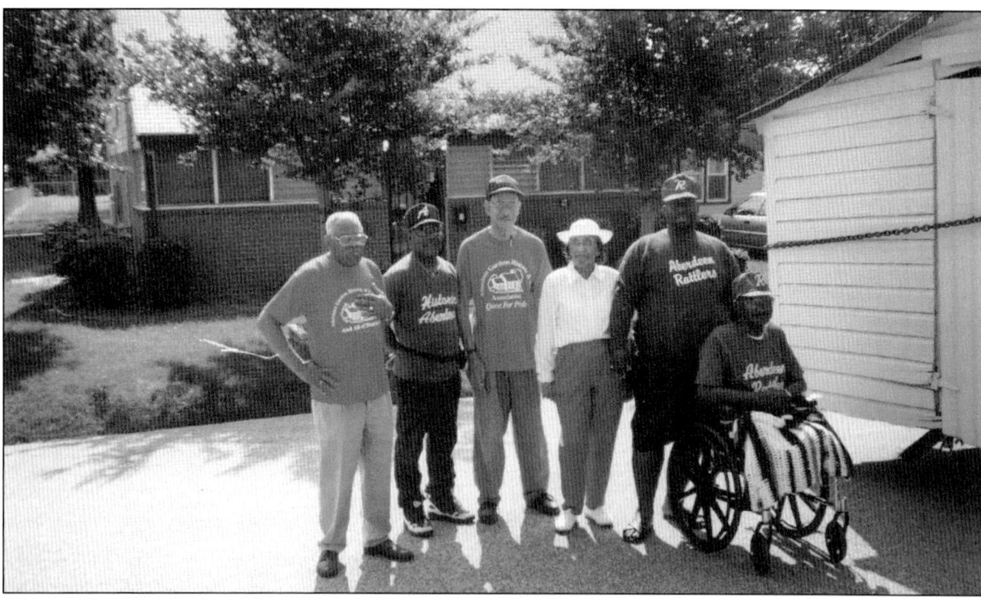

This well-preserved chicken coop from 1937, much like ones that once rested in each of the 158 backyards of the Aberdeen Gardens Historic District, is being moved to the Historic Aberdeen Gardens Museum. The move is being witnessed by the chairman of the Aberdeen Historic Group, James C. Arrington (seated), and, from left to right, Samuel Daniel, Howard Cary, Troy Smith Sr., Cora Johnson, and Arthur Arrington. (Courtesy of Jacqueline Arrington.)

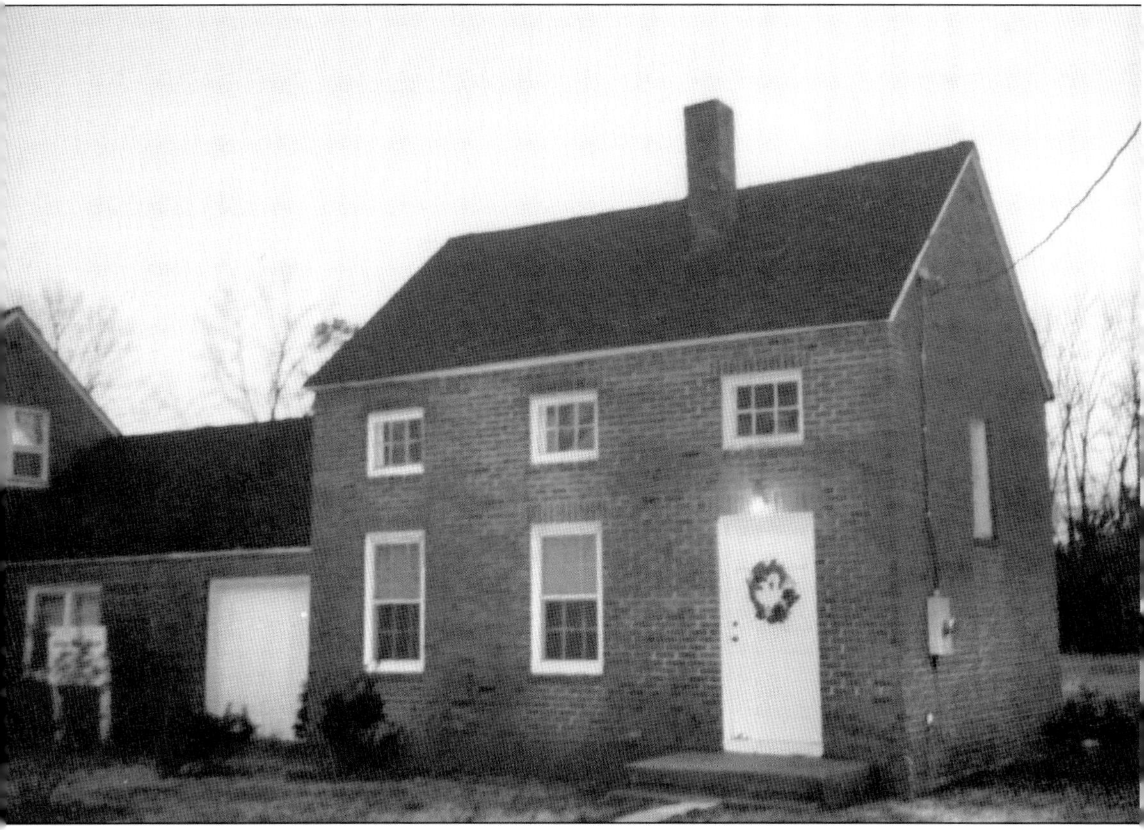

The Aberdeen Gardens Historic Museum restored the attached building, which was purchased for use as an administration building. The museum and administration building are referred to as the Museum Complex. Coordinator Marsha Williams worked diligently to solicit 1930–1950-era items from the neighborhood and artifacts of the 1930s from other localities. Contractors and subcontractors worked vigorously to meet deadline. Volunteer contractors within the Aberdeen Gardens Historic District who added their consultative outlook and expertise are Tennyson Garret Contracting, Smith Brothers Enterprise, the brick masonry of Walter Ford, and Claude Vann Jr. Hauling. There are still projects to be completed. (Courtesy of Aberdeen Gardens Historic and Civic Association, Inc.)

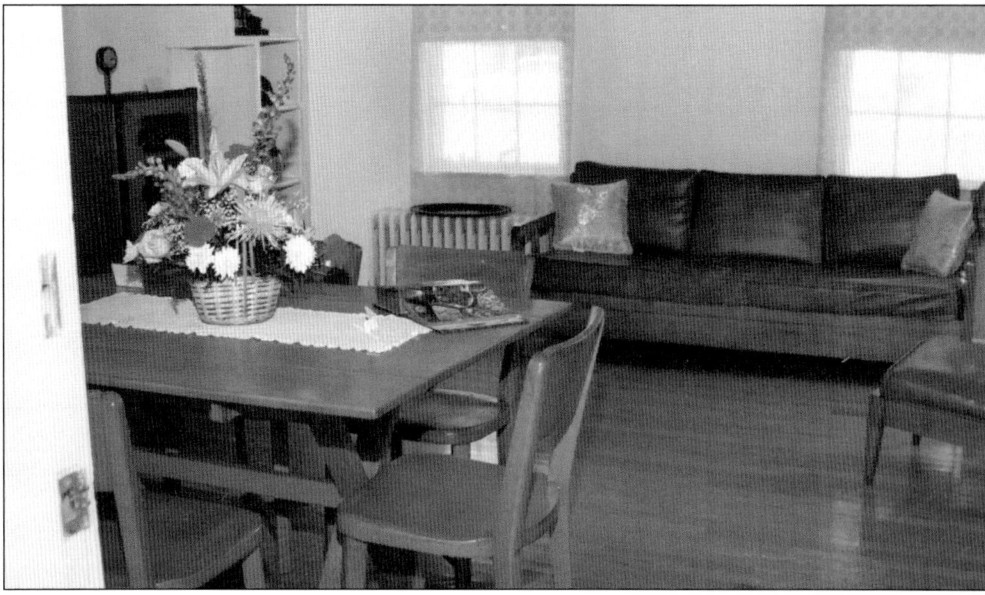

Restoring the Aberdeen Gardens Historic Museum took several years. While collecting, authenticating, and refurbishing furniture for the museum's interior, many artifacts were found in superb condition. The smaller first-floor plans show a dining/living room, kitchen, dining table, and six chairs. Wood floors are found throughout the home. There are two original versions of the dining table: one with A-style legs and one with four straight legs. (Courtesy of Aberdeen Gardens Historic and Civic Association, Inc.)

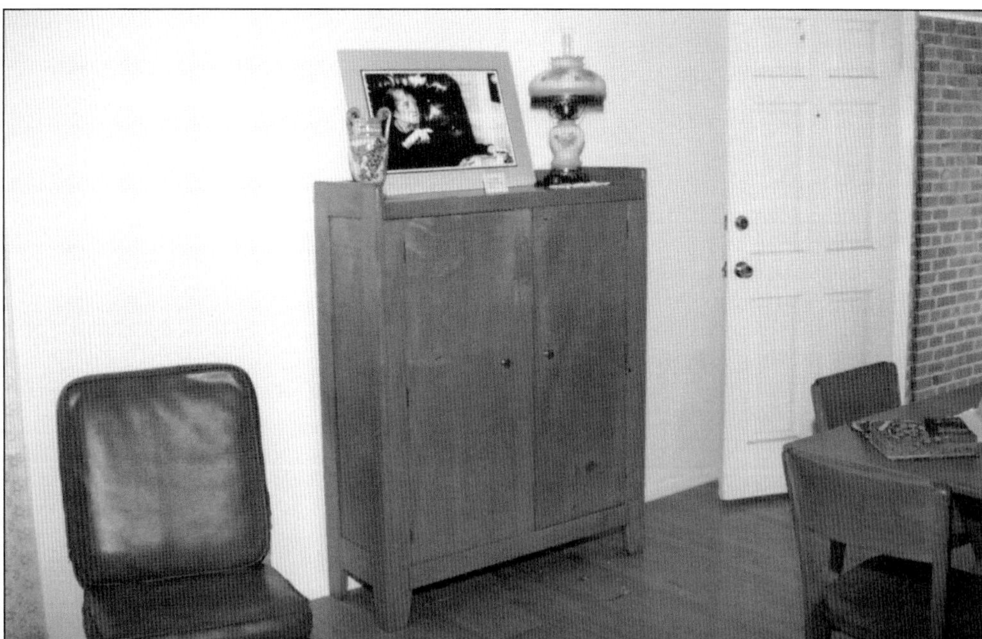

The wooden china cabinet is unique. It has three shelves, stump footing, and solid sides and back. The doors are solid with wooden knobs. It is heavy when empty. Several homeowners in the Aberdeen Gardens Historic District have kept and maintained similar pieces of furniture. (Courtesy of Aberdeen Gardens Historic and Civic Association, Inc.)

All Aberdeen homes were heated by a coal-fuel furnace-boiler radiator system called Arcola. The Arcola could be found in the kitchen of some homes and in a furnace room along the hallway in other homes. In the museum, a smaller floor plan, the Arcola furnace is by the cooking range. (Courtesy of Aberdeen Gardens Historic and Civic Association, Inc.)

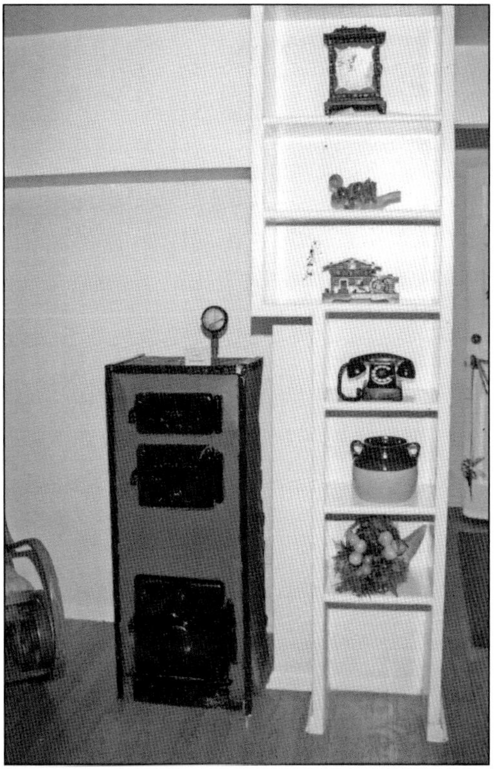

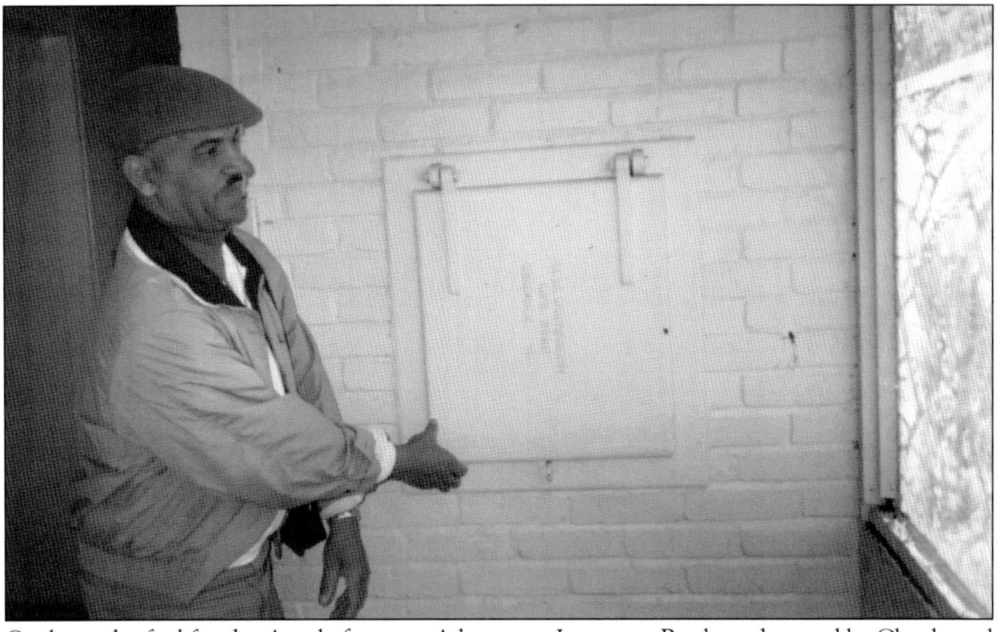

Coal was the fuel for the Arcola furnace. A home on Langston Boulevard owned by Claude and Rose Vann Jr. still has the brick wall, iron flip-up door, and coal bin room, which is located in the breezeway of the home (though coal is no longer in use). The coal storage room, furnace room, and breezeway porch had cement slab flooring. Pictured next to the flip-up door is Lenrow Milo. (Courtesy of Walter Jackson.)

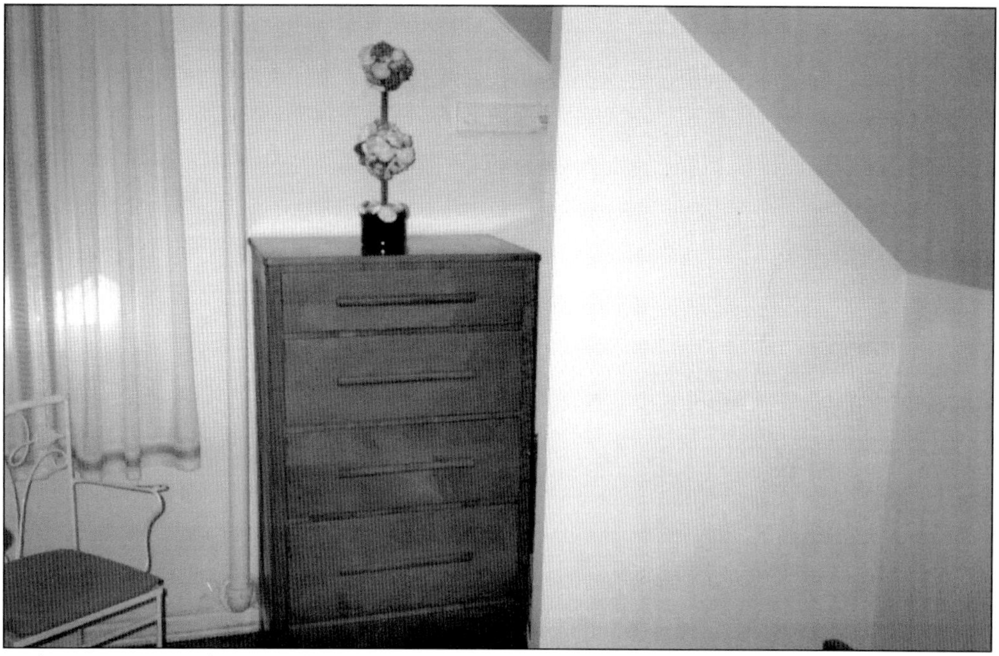

Bedrooms were on the second floor of each home. A bedroom dresser and chest of drawers set is utilized every day in the Langston Boulevard home of Lillie Jones. Many residents held on to their 1936 furniture as antique pieces to pass down through the generations. (Courtesy of Aberdeen Gardens Historic and Civic Association, Inc.)

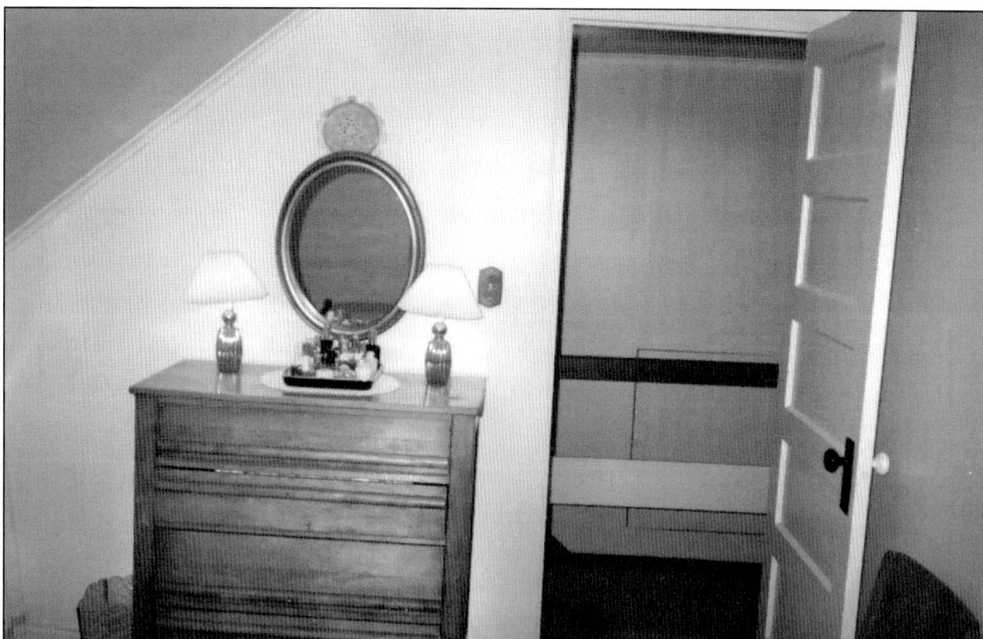

Chests of drawers, like dresser drawers, are all solid frames. There was more than one style. Each drawer could be a closed compartment, and anything falling out of the drawer would be held within the drawer compartment. It could also be open, and anything falling out of the drawer fell to the bottom of the chest. (Courtesy of Aberdeen Gardens Historic and Civic Association, Inc.)

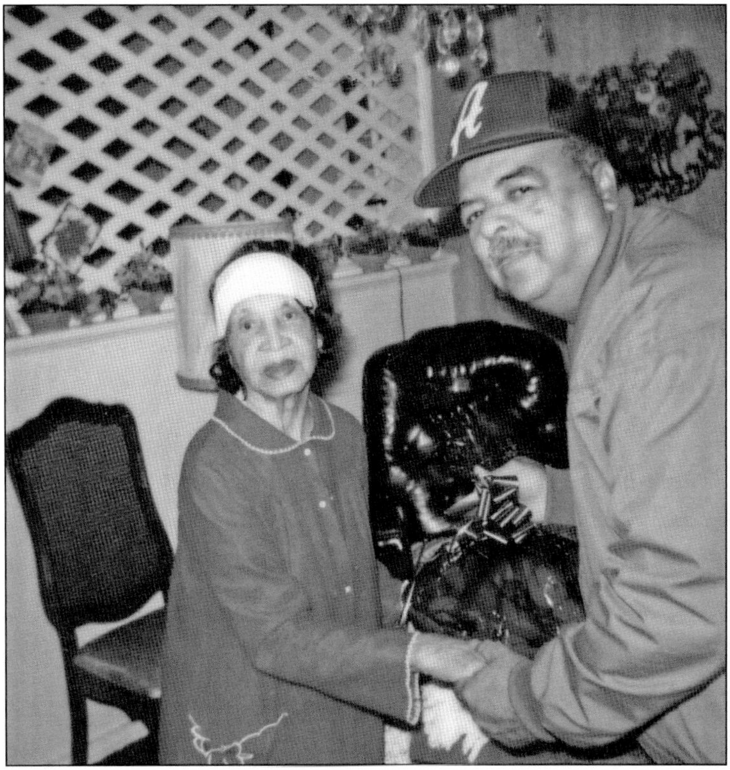

Aberdeen Rattlers always remember Rattler widows and family members with a basket of fruit or candies during the holidays. Andre' "Monk" Vann presents a smiling Maggie Jones, at 90-plus years old, with a basket of fruit in her home. (Courtesy of Lenrow Milo.)

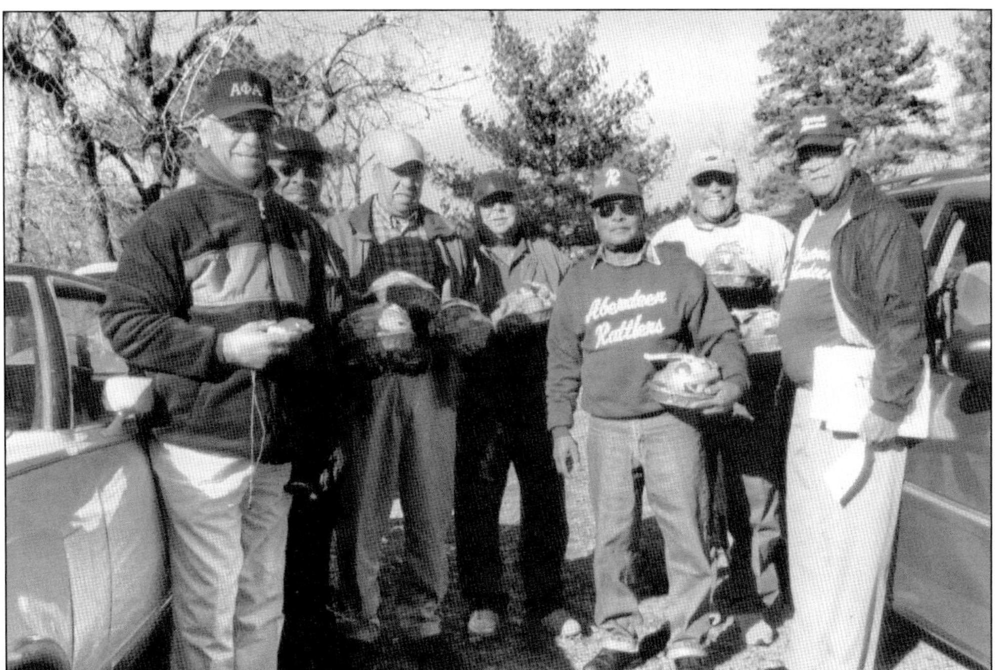

On a sunny day in December, the Aberdeen Rattlers met with checklist handy, prepared to deliver their last baskets. The Aberdeen neighborhood residents can call on the Aberdeen Rattlers for just about anything, and they will aid anyway they can. (Courtesy of Lenrow Milo.)

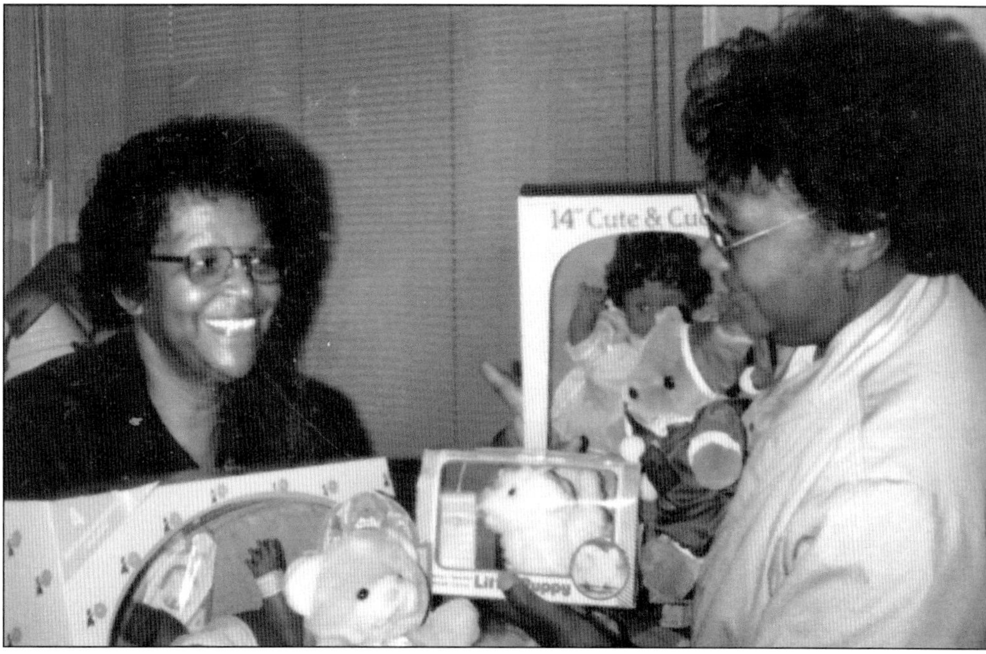

Giving back to the neighborhood is what Mamie Batchelor enjoys doing. She annually gives toys to needy children during the holidays. She is the owner of the Aberdeen Fashion Flair Hair Styling, Manicure, and Pedicure shop in the remodeled mini-mall across from Aberdeen Elementary School in the Aberdeen Gardens Historic District. (Courtesy of Mamie Batchelor.)

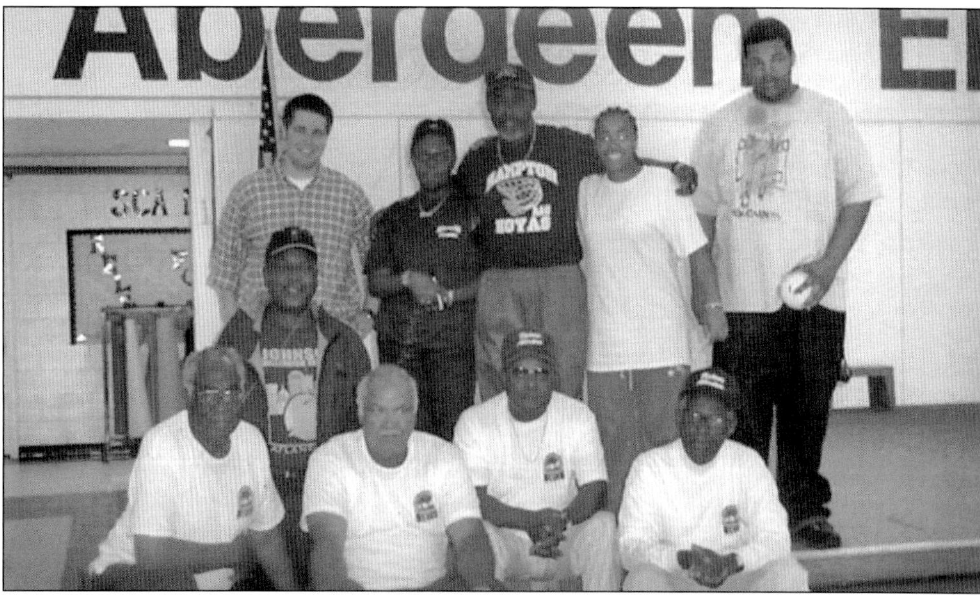

Aberdeen Deen's Day has been hosted annually since 1994 by the Aberdeen Athletic Association and the Aberdeen Gardens Historic and Civic Association. Linwood "Butch" Harper, the athletic association's president, is at center in the Hampton Hoyas shirt; five members of the civic association are seated. Standing with Butch are athletic association members and Youth Alternative members. This photograph was taken in Aberdeen Elementary School's auditorium. (Courtesy of Aberdeen Gardens Historic and Civic Association, Inc.)

Three

Aberdeen Gardens 1996–2007

As a result of empowerment, the Aberdeen Gardens Historic and Civic Association, Inc., is a registered neighborhood in the city of Hampton. The district became Neighborhood of the Year nationally and inspired Hampton Neighborhood District 10 and the City of Hampton to build the West Hampton Community Center. The district also gained representation on Hampton's city council (the former president of the civic association is on the city council) and has been on the Home and Gardens television (HGTV) network twice.

The Historic Foundation of Aberdeen Gardens, Inc., hosts activities that enhance the full usage of the Aberdeen Gardens Historic Museum. Their Gala Celebration recognized Aberdeen Gardens Historic District residents with Pioneer and Legacy awards. The museum is open three days a week: Monday, Wednesday, and Friday, from 10:00 a.m. to 2:00 p.m.

The association's next challenges will be to strengthen and maintain the neighborhood's cohesiveness. The neighborhood residents, along with the Aberdeen Gardens Historic and Civic Association, Inc., and the Historic Foundation of Aberdeen Gardens, Inc., will continue to work in collaboration to establish a nature park and hopefully build a small recreation center in the Aberdeen Garden Historic District, as mentioned in the 1936 original plans but never built.

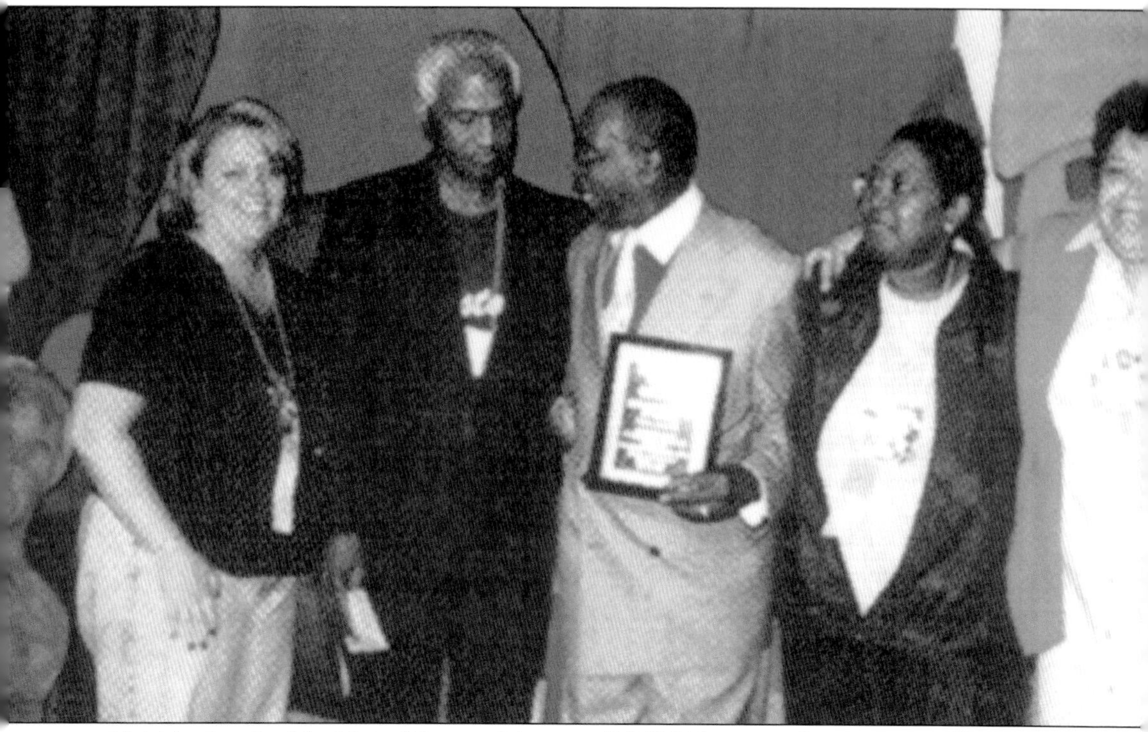

Neighborhoods of the United States of America (NUSA) hosts conferences annually throughout the United States. According to Who is NUSA?, the organization is "a national non-profit organization committed to building and strengthening neighborhood organizations." The City of Hampton supported the Aberdeen Gardens Historic and Civic Association president Roosevelt Wilson, secretary Jacqueline Arrington, historian Claude Vann Jr., District 10 facilitator Shellae Blackwell, and neighborhood marketing specialist Tammy Flynn in a trip to the NUSA conference held from May 23–25, 2002, in Houston, Texas. There the Aberdeen Gardens Historic and Civic Association presented a project to restore an Aberdeen Gardens Historic District house into the Aberdeen Gardens Historic Museum. The presenting four-member team had eight minutes to speak about the 65-year-old neighborhood. The presenters' topics were the origin of Aberdeen, grassroots, partnerships, and challenges. The Aberdeen Gardens Historic and Civic Association won first place for Multi Partnerships and the overall prize: Neighborhood of the Year 2002. (Courtesy of Hampton Neighborhood Office.)

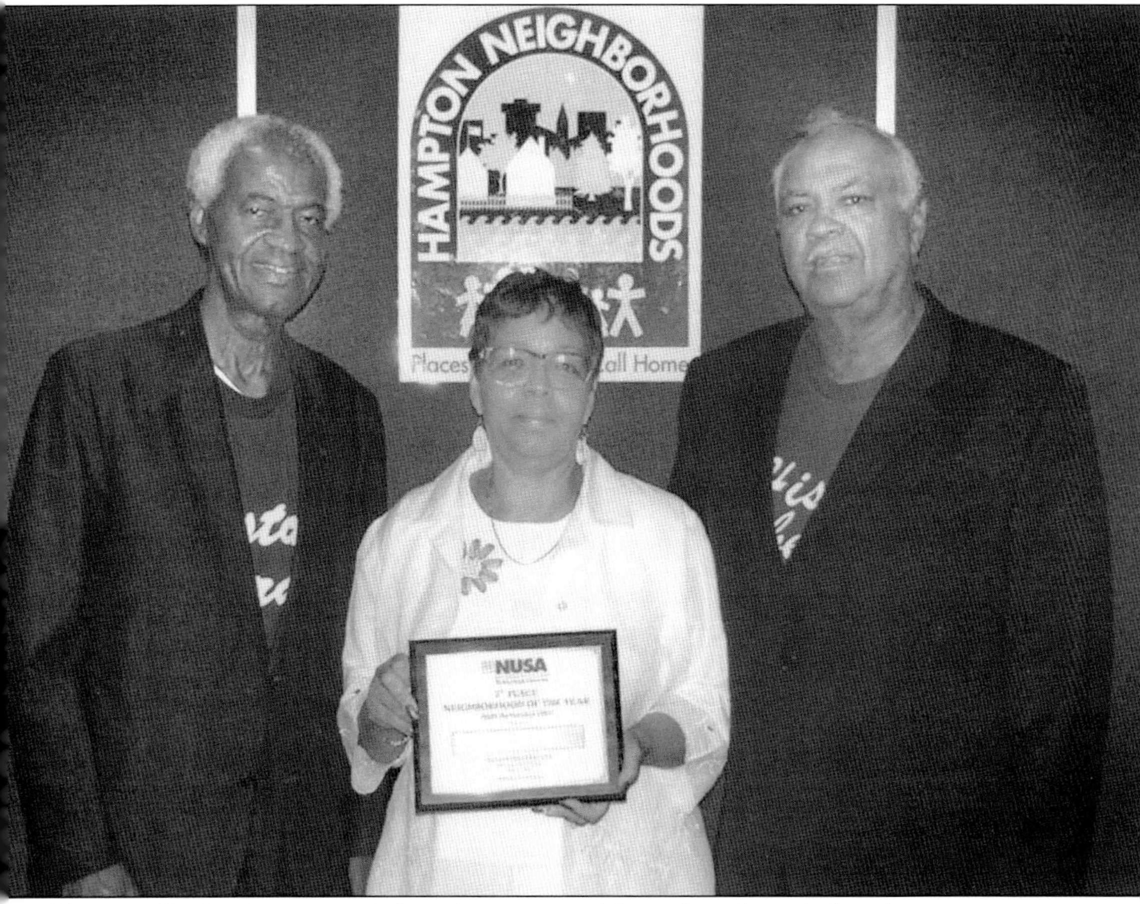

Aberdeen Gardens Historic and Civic Association adults and youth worked to obtain input on a community recreation center–needs survey. The West Hampton Community Center, a $3-million structure, was built in 2004 and credited to the Aberdeen Gardens Historic and Civic Association, who presented this entry at the NUSA competition. The Aberdeen Gardens Historic and Civic Association was awarded first place in the category of Neighborhood Improvement in 2005. The City of Hampton supported association president Roosevelt Wilson, secretary Eunice Peele, historian Claude Vann Jr., and parks and recreation superintendent Art Thatcher at the conference. The West Hampton Community Center has over 24,000 square feet, including a gymnasium, fitness room, indoor climbing wall, lounge, multipurpose room, and community room. Other partners instrumental in the development of the West Hampton Community Center are the Neighborhood Development Committee, the City of Hampton Parks and Recreation Department, the Hampton Neighborhood Office, and the Coalition for Youth Alternatives. (Courtesy of Hampton Neighborhood Office.)

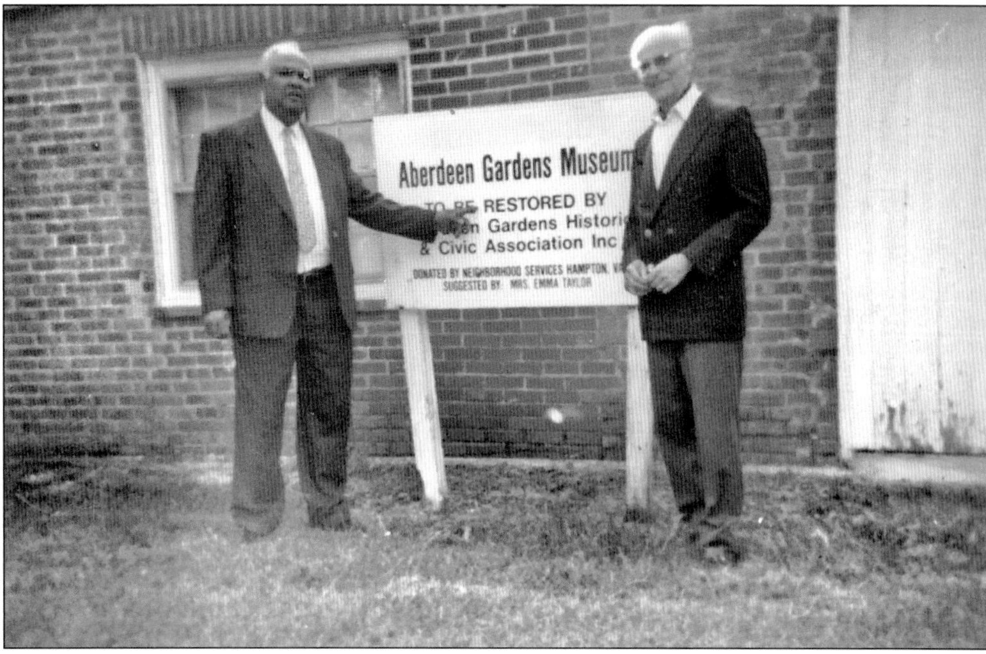

Claude Vann Jr. (left) and William R. Walker Jr. (right), the 1936 manager of Aberdeen Gardens Homes, are pictured at the Aberdeen Gardens Historic Museum's dedication on September 28, 2002. Many dignitaries from the state and local levels arrived for this occasion. (Courtesy of Aberdeen Gardens Historic and Civic Association, Inc.)

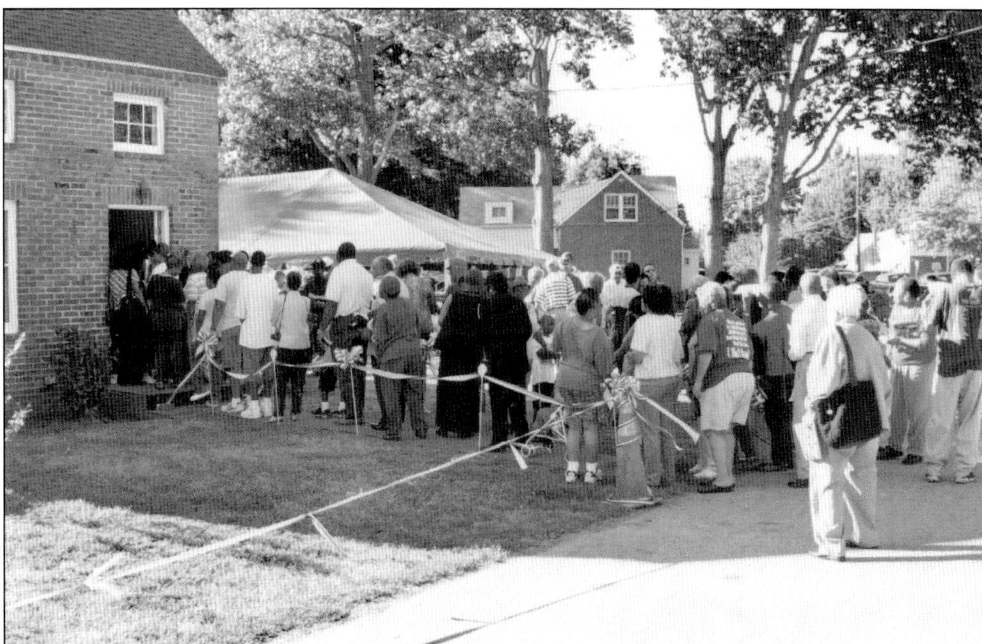

Residents from far and near participated in or witnessed the historic ribbon-cutting event. On dedication day of the Aberdeen Gardens Historic Museum, many people stood in this long line to tour the museum. (Courtesy of Aberdeen Gardens Historic and Civic Association, Inc.)

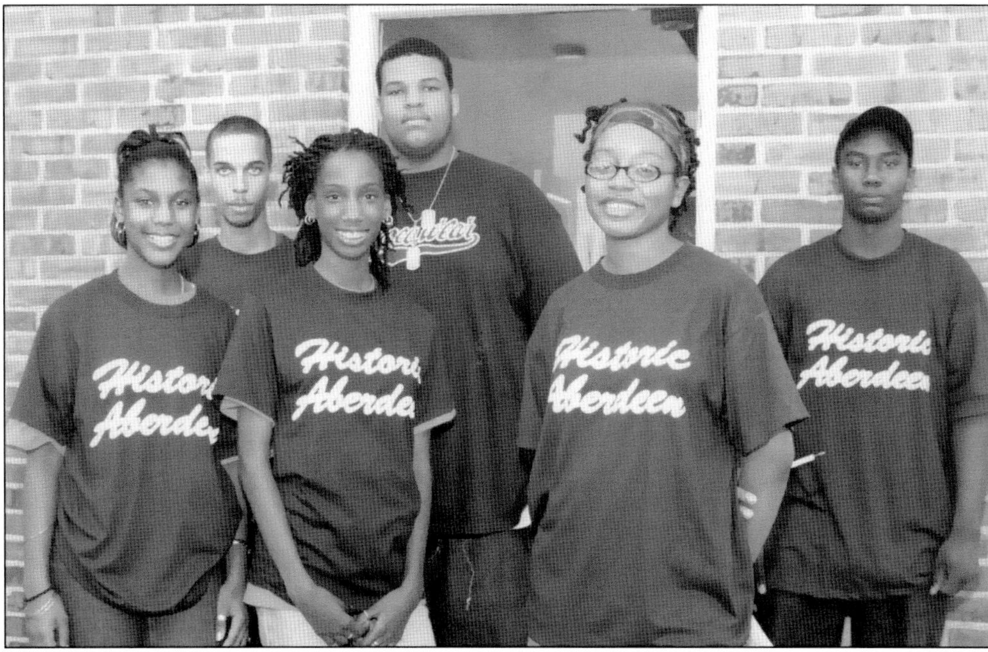

During the dedication of the Aberdeen Gardens Historic Museum, many historic district and partnering neighborhood youths were on hand to assist as docents and escorts. Marsha Williams was significant in suggesting that the youth be trained for this honor. (Courtesy of Aberdeen Gardens Historic and Civic Association, Inc.)

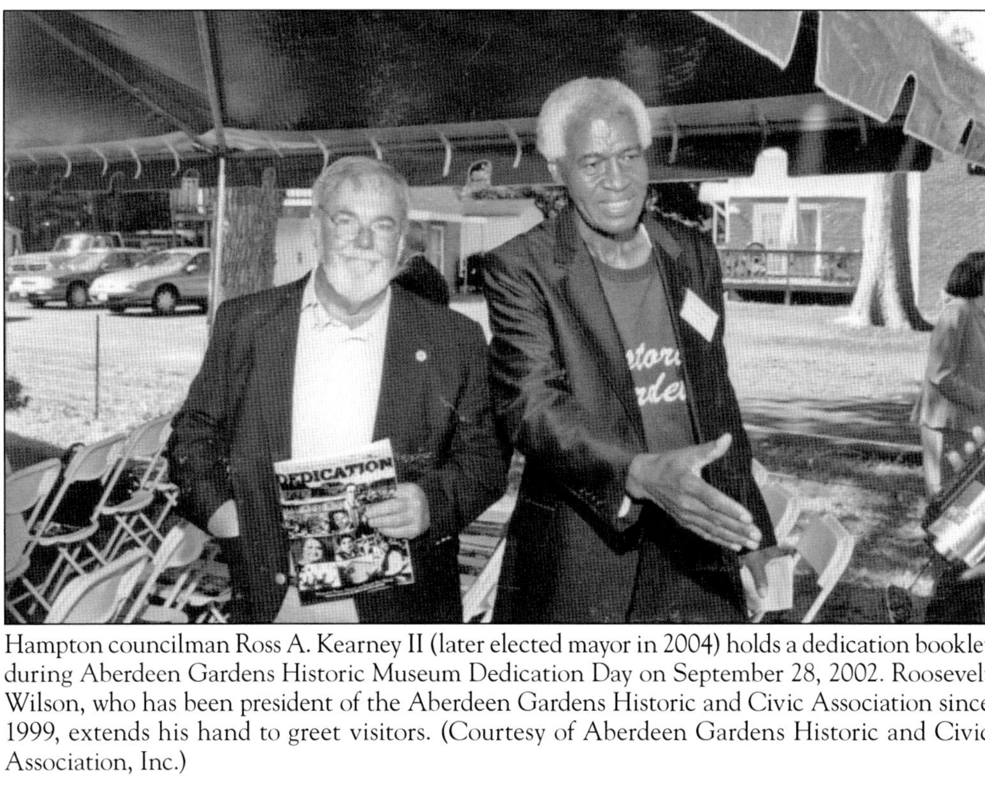

Hampton councilman Ross A. Kearney II (later elected mayor in 2004) holds a dedication booklet during Aberdeen Gardens Historic Museum Dedication Day on September 28, 2002. Roosevelt Wilson, who has been president of the Aberdeen Gardens Historic and Civic Association since 1999, extends his hand to greet visitors. (Courtesy of Aberdeen Gardens Historic and Civic Association, Inc.)

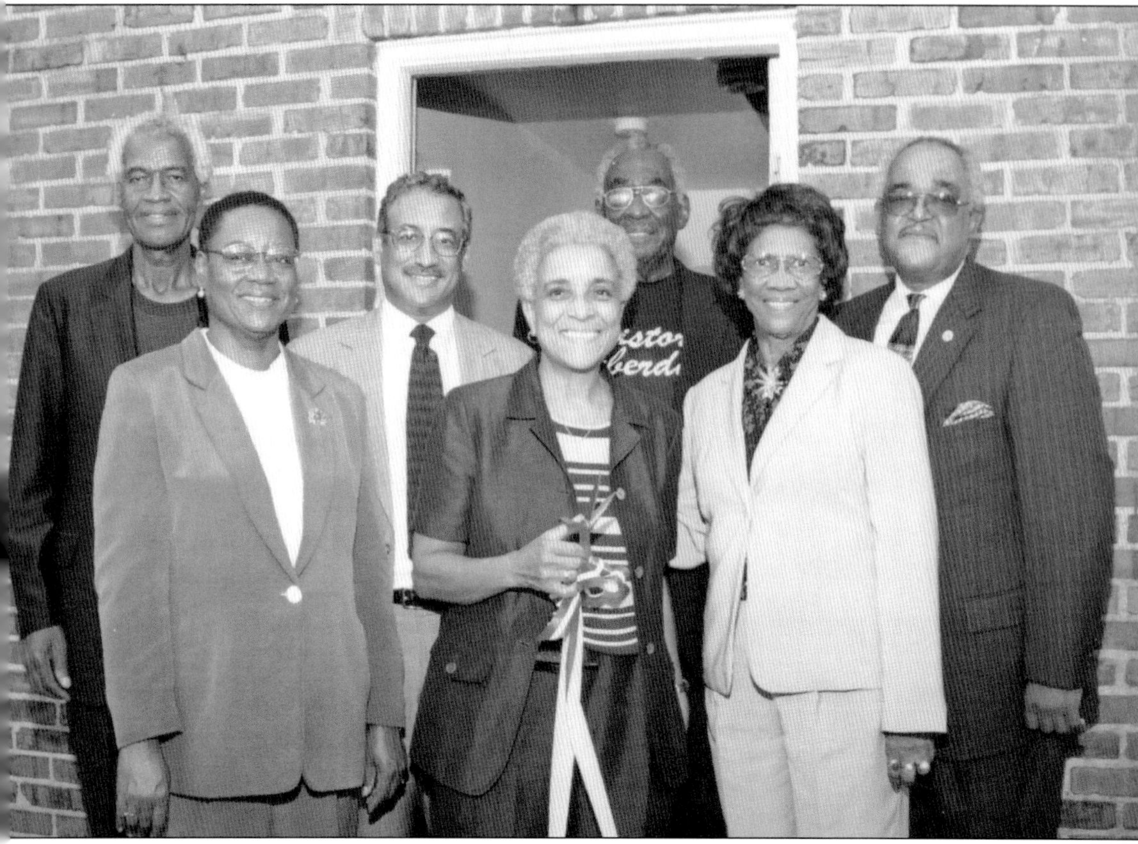

Pictured at the Aberdeen Gardens Historic Museum Dedication Day ceremony are the following: (first row) Hampton mayor Dr. Mamie E. Lock; Amy T. Billingsley, and Virginia delegate Dr. Mary T. Christian, honored guest; (second row) Roosevelt Wilson, Aberdeen Gardens Historic and Civic Association president; Congressman Robert C. "Bobby" Scott; Harmon Stokes, Aberdeen Gardens Historic and Civic Association safety officer; and Paige Washington, Hampton vice mayor. These distinguished guests gladly responded to an invite to this occasion. Delegate Christian is the first African American to represent the City of Hampton in the Virginia House of Delegates, and she sponsored the $100,000 preservation grant for the restoration of this museum in the General Assembly. Congressman Scott represents the 3rd Virginia Congressional District. He has truly been a people's advocate. Mayor Locke was guest speaker. Amy Billingsley is a descendant of Charles Duke, the civil engineer of Aberdeen Gardens' construction in 1936. Vice mayor Washington was the president of the Aberdeen Gardens Historic and Civic Association when he decided to run for Hampton's city council. (Courtesy of Aberdeen Gardens Historic and Civic Association, Inc.)

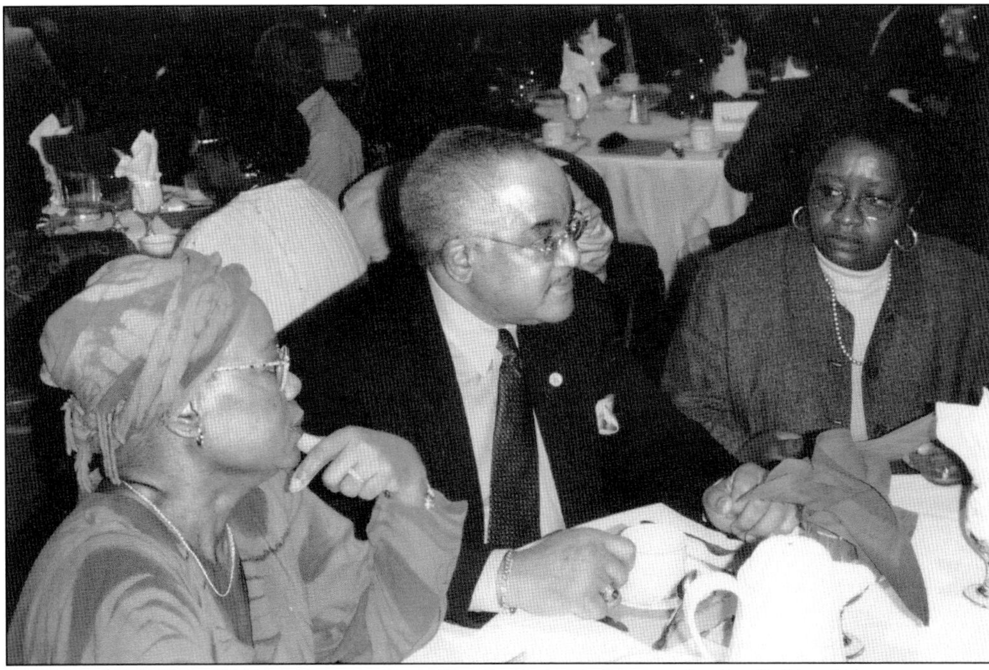

Paige and Carolyn Washington are seated with Senator Mamie Locke (left) of Virginia at the Black History Program. Paige is an Aberdeen Gardens Historic District resident, former vice mayor, the Aberdeen Gardens Historic and Civic Association president, and as of 2007, a Hampton City councilman. Councilman Washington received the Historic Recognition Award in 1999. (Courtesy of Aberdeen Gardens Historic and Civic Association, Inc.)

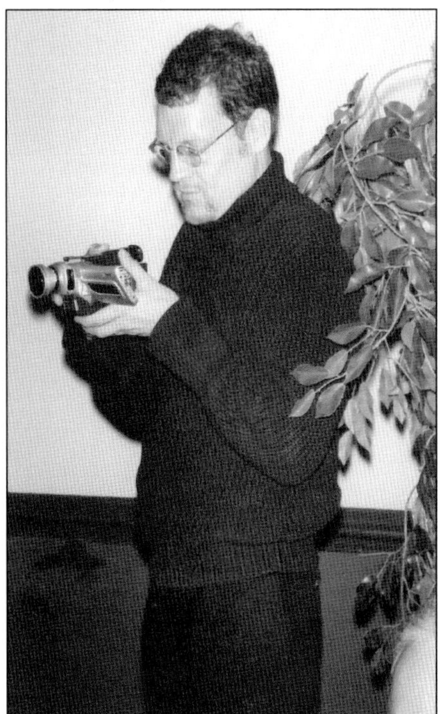

Stuart Patterson selected two of Pres. Franklin D. Roosevelt's New Deal neighborhoods—Arthurdale Heritage in West Virginia and Aberdeen Gardens Historic District in Virginia—as his doctorate dissertation while enrolled at Emory University. He joined the Aberdeen Gardens Historic and Civic Association and was enthusiastic about the cohesive bond of the residents. (Courtesy of Aberdeen Gardens Historic and Civic Association, Inc.)

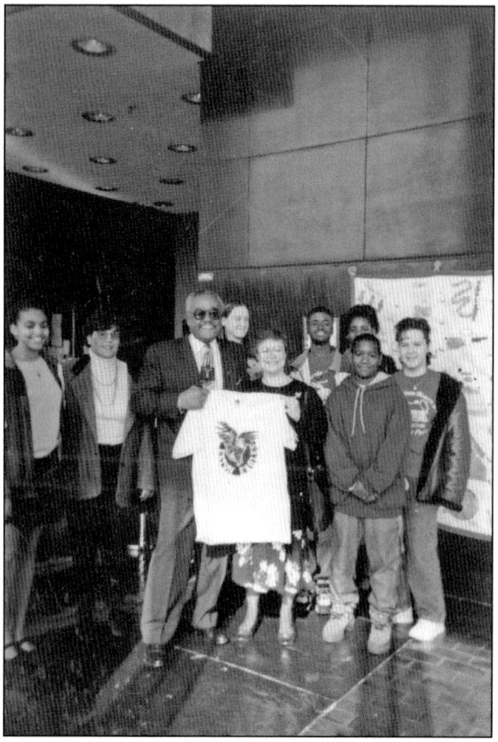

Students and teacher pose in front of the Thomas Eaton Fundamental School with a display of a beautiful handmade quilt in appreciation for the Aberdeen Gardens Historic and Civic Association's inclusiveness and tutoring of the youth of the school and the surrounding neighborhoods. (Courtesy of Aberdeen Gardens Historic and Civic Association, Inc.)

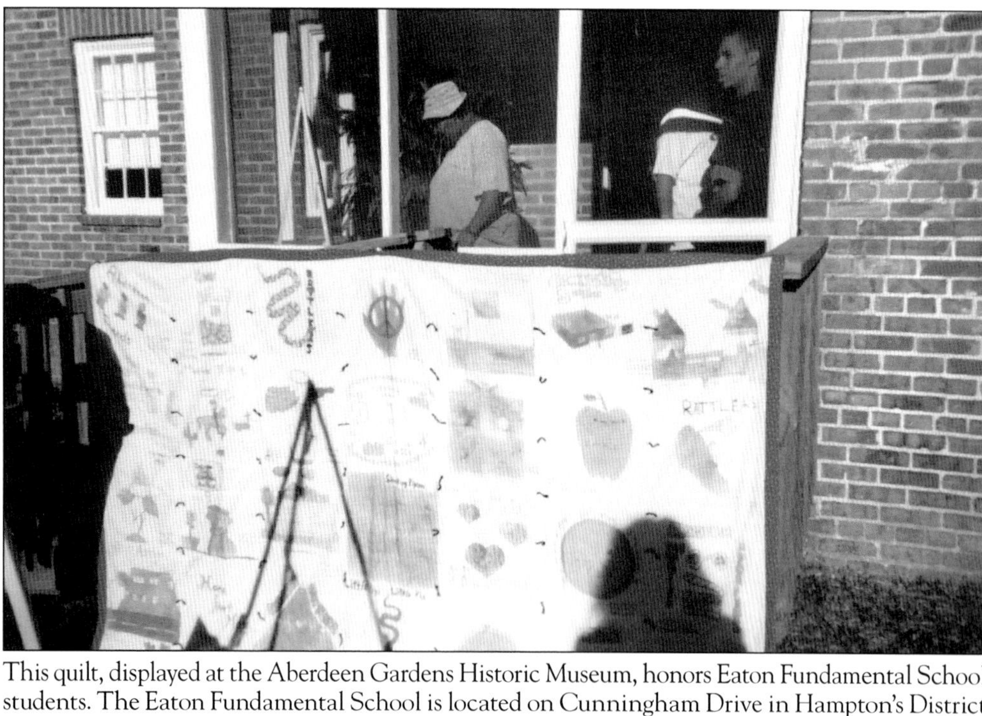

This quilt, displayed at the Aberdeen Gardens Historic Museum, honors Eaton Fundamental School students. The Eaton Fundamental School is located on Cunningham Drive in Hampton's District Three neighborhood. The quilt relays a message of the early years of Aberdeen Gardens. Images of Aberdeen Gardens are presented, such as rattlesnakes, people, and the Eaton Fundamental School children's signatures. (Courtesy of Catherine Howard.)

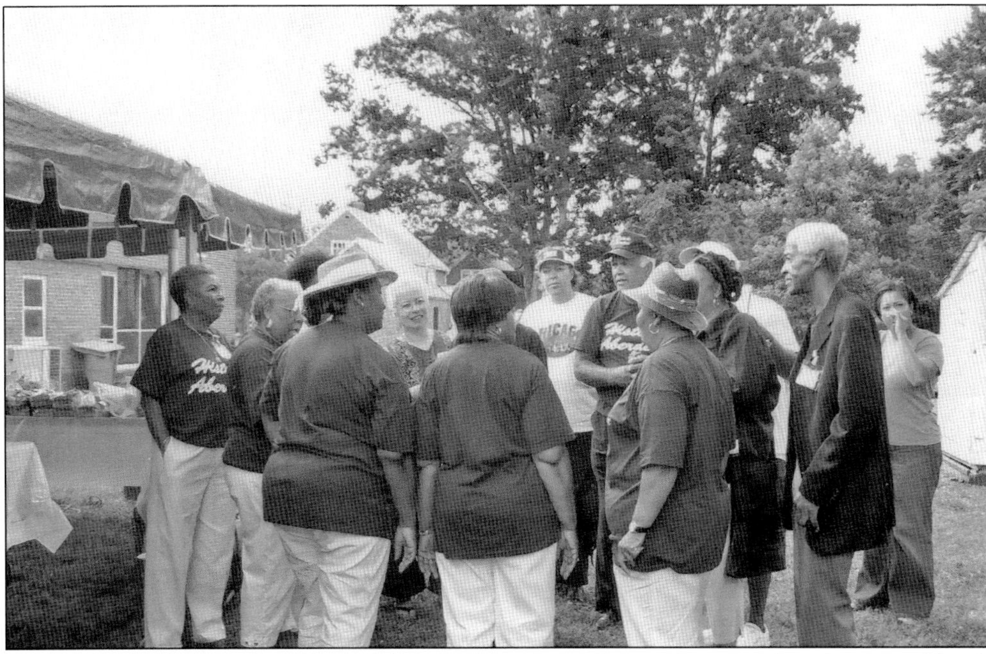

A group of visiting Chicago journalists and Heritage Committee members listen as Claude Vann Jr., the Aberdeen Gardens Historic District's historian, narrates the history of Aberdeen Gardens along with many comical anecdotes during a Heritage Day Celebration on the lawn of the Aberdeen Gardens Historic Museum in June 2006. (Courtesy of Catherine Howard.)

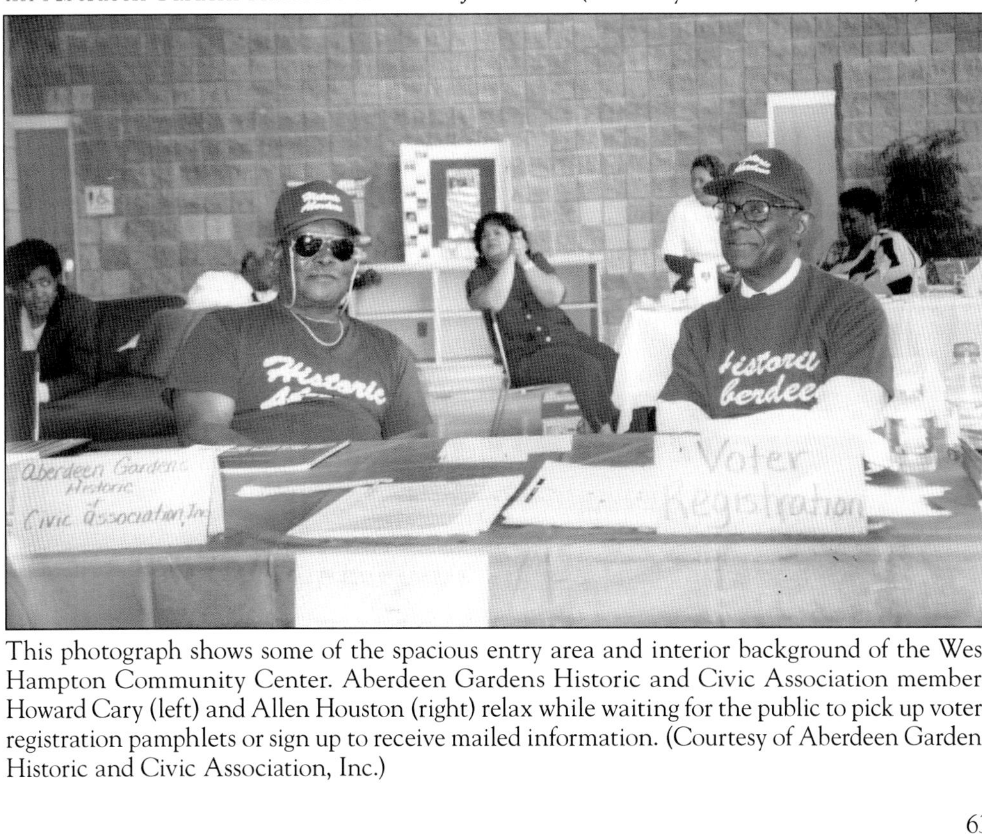

This photograph shows some of the spacious entry area and interior background of the West Hampton Community Center. Aberdeen Gardens Historic and Civic Association members Howard Cary (left) and Allen Houston (right) relax while waiting for the public to pick up voters registration pamphlets or sign up to receive mailed information. (Courtesy of Aberdeen Gardens Historic and Civic Association, Inc.)

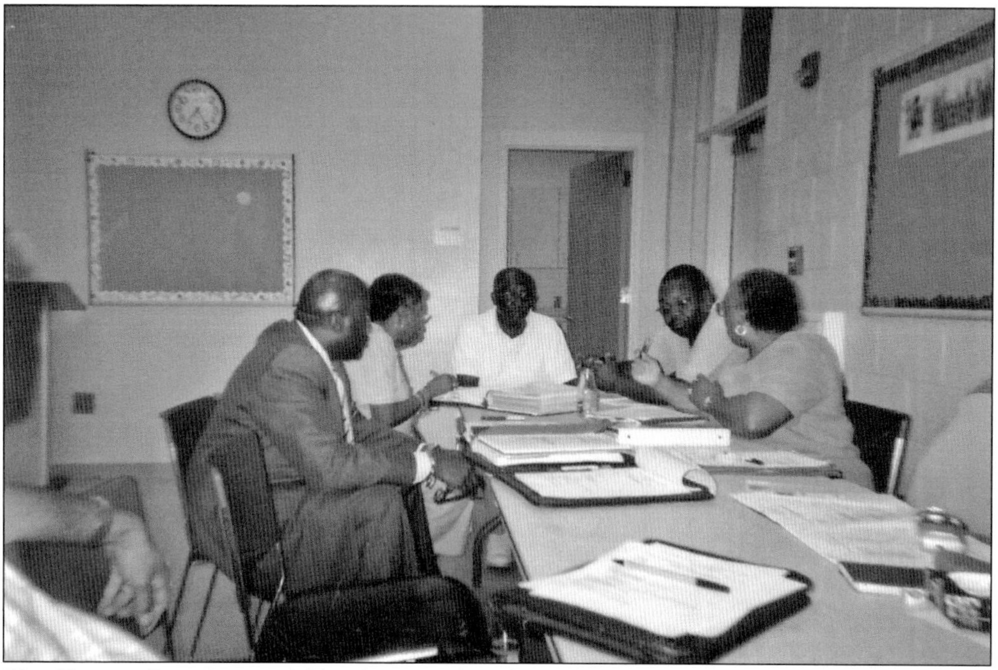

The Historic Foundation of Aberdeen Gardens hosted golf tournaments in 2005 and 2006 at the Woodland Golf Course in Hampton. Tournament chairman Derwin W. Brewster (below, seated), a resident of Granger Court East, constantly worked to obtain sponsors and coordinate final activities for the tournaments. Trophies and gifts included a car for a hole in one and first-, second-, and third-place team and individual recognitions. All of the trophies were on display. Pictured (above) from left to right are Rev. Hallie Richardson, Geneva Cooper, Joseph Holland, Brewster, and Margaret Wilson. Jacqueline Arrington (below, standing) tallied the final team scores. No one received the Pomoco car for the hole in one. (Both courtesy of Catherine Howard.)

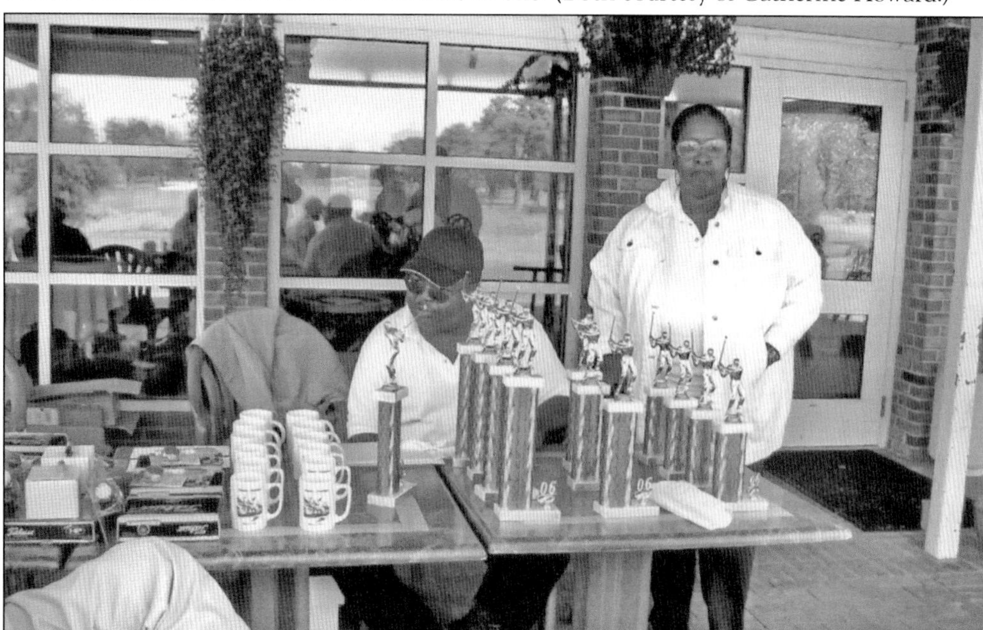

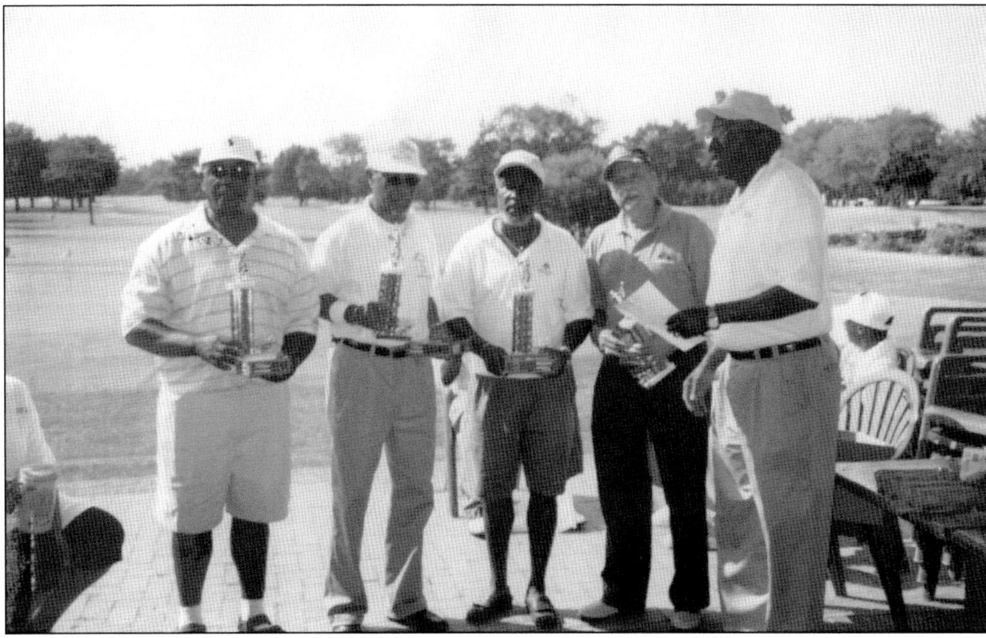

The 2005 Historic Foundation of Aberdeen Gardens Golf Challenge took place on June 10. First-place winners were James Flythe, Walter Washington, Rick Duvall, and Glenn Hughes. Second-place winners and New Town Junior Golf Club members Sherman Keyes, Nathan Mack Jr., Darren James, and Marcus Hofler get congratulations from their coach, Glenn Hughes (below, third from left). They were also congratulated by Joseph Holland, president of the Historic Foundation of Aberdeen Gardens, at the Woodlands Golf Course. (Both courtesy of Catherine Howard.)

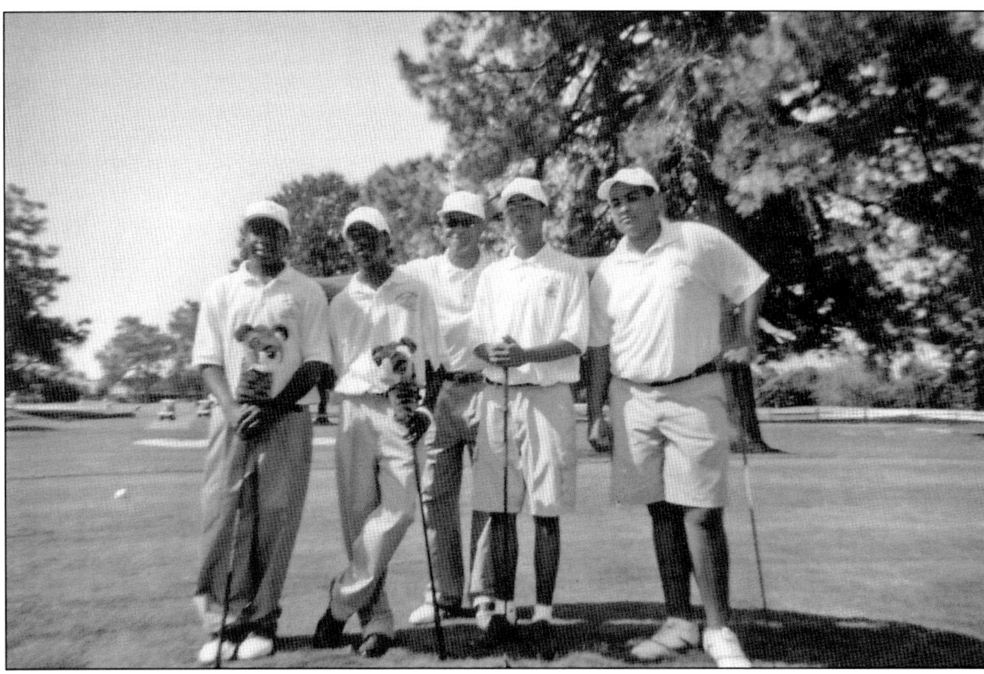

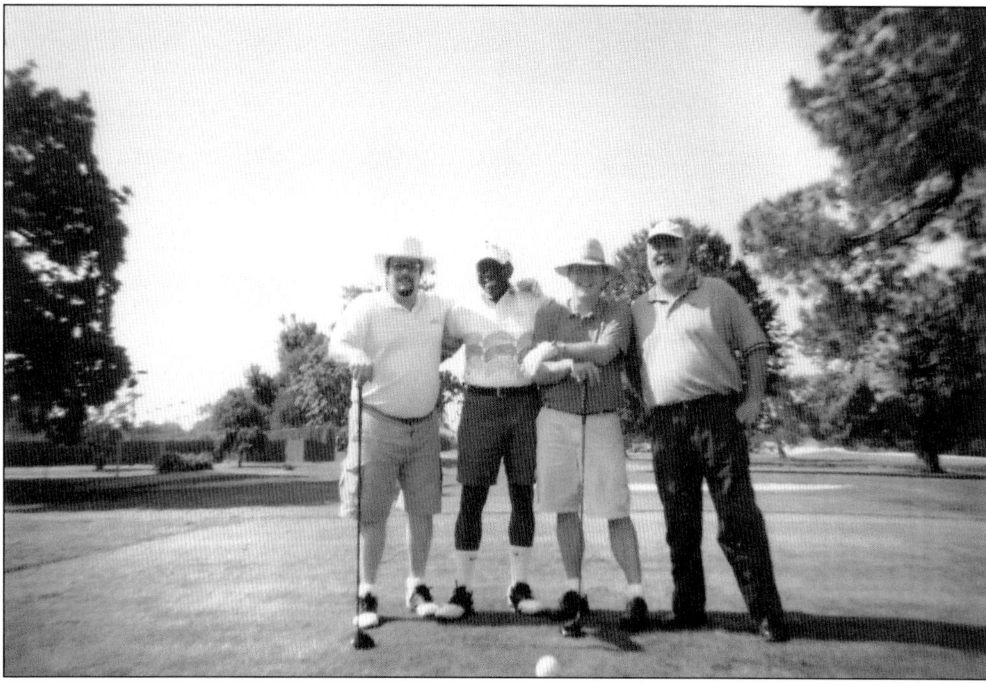

Third-place winners in 2005 are Joe Riche, James Butler, Shawn Smith, and Mike Hayes. The Second Annual Historic Foundation of Aberdeen Gardens Golf Challenge was held September 30, 2006. The hole-in-one prize was sponsored by Pomoco, and the group sponsors vice president was Stephen C. Adams, CPA (not pictured). Derwin Brewster (below) holds a sign promoting Chrysler Plymouth of Hampton. (Both courtesy of Catherine Howard.)

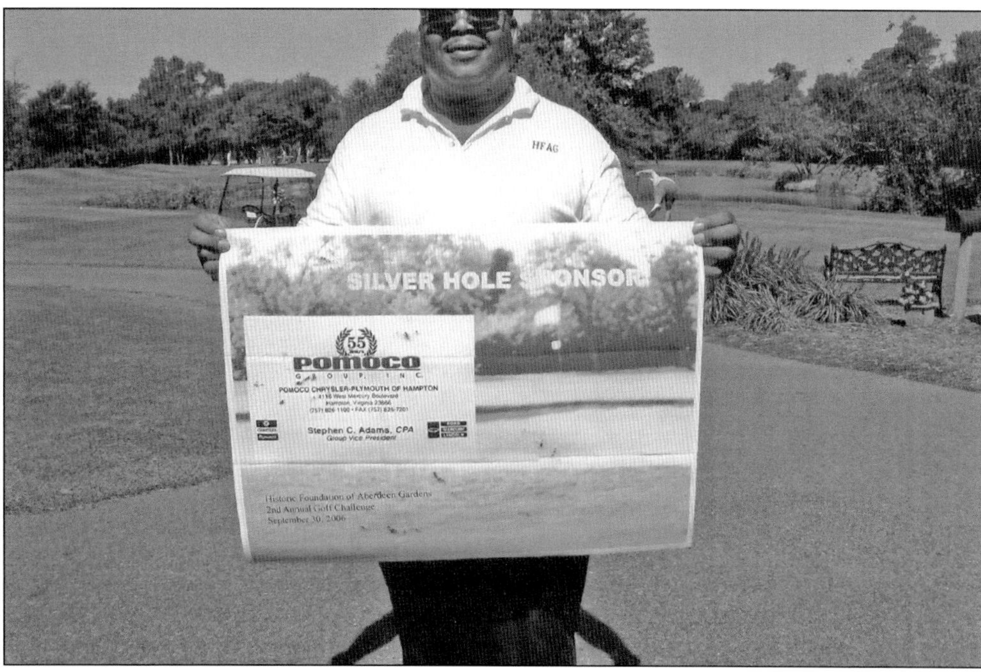

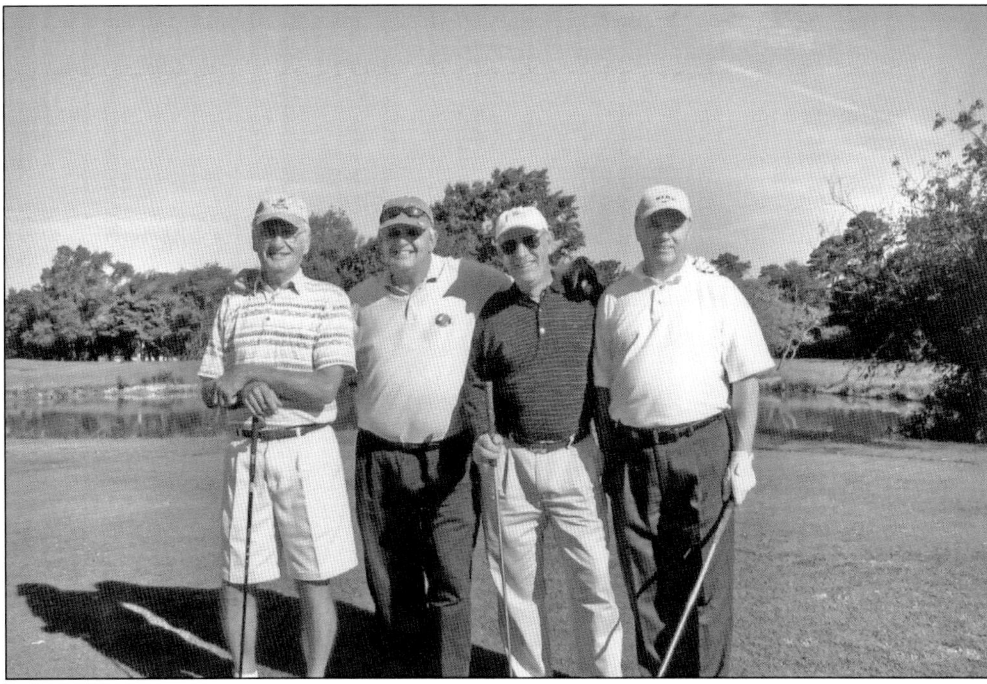

Shown above, the first-place winners in 2006 are (from left to right) Larry Parker, Billy Blackmond, Richard Scott, and Charley Johnson. Below, the third-place winners, (from left to right) Glenn Hughes, Walter Washington, Earnest Marshall, and Felix L. Hilton, are congratulated by Historic Foundation of Aberdeen Gardens president Joseph Holland (far right) on September 30, 2006, at the Woodlands Golf Course. (Both courtesy of Catherine Howard.)

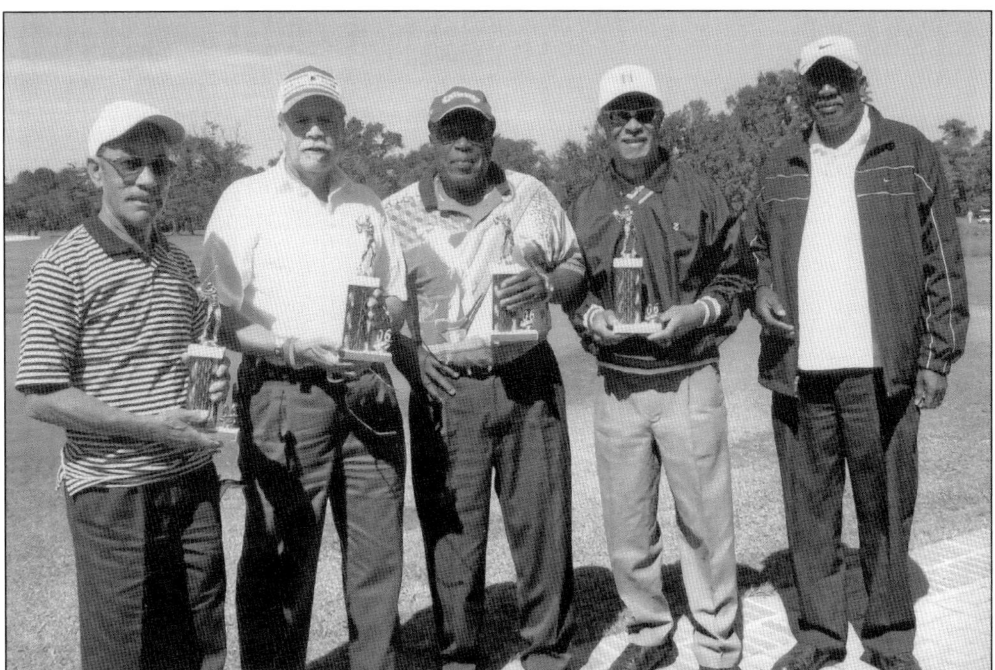

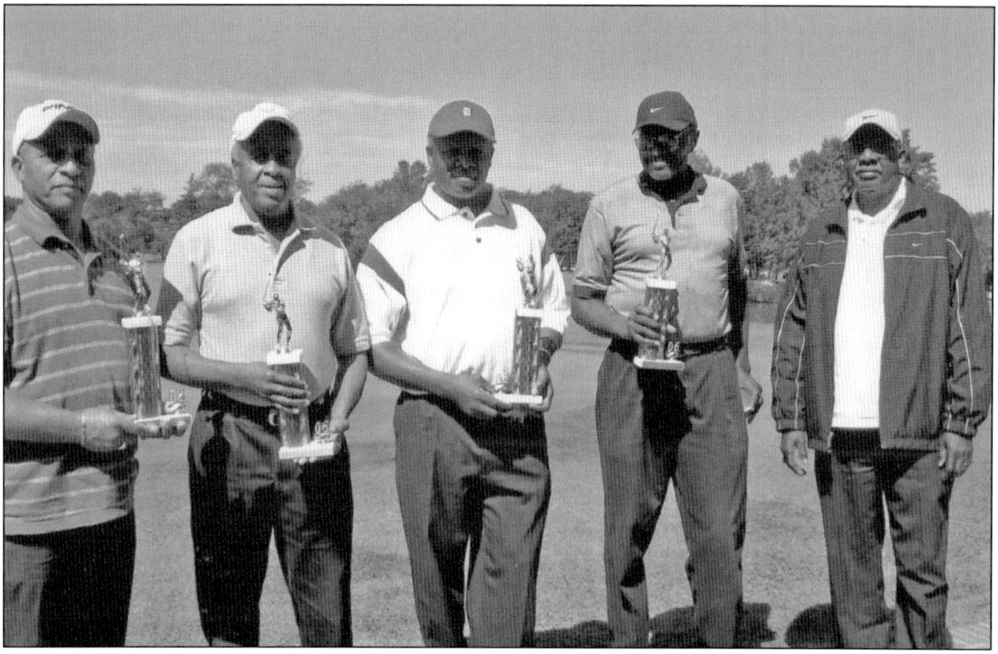

Second-place winners (from left to right) Wayne White, Aaron White, John Arson Woodard, and Casey Aursby receive congratulations from Historic Foundation of Aberdeen Gardens president Joseph Holland. Holland presented trophies to all the teams. Lunch was provided for all players and volunteers in 2005 and 2006. (Courtesy of Catherine Howard.)

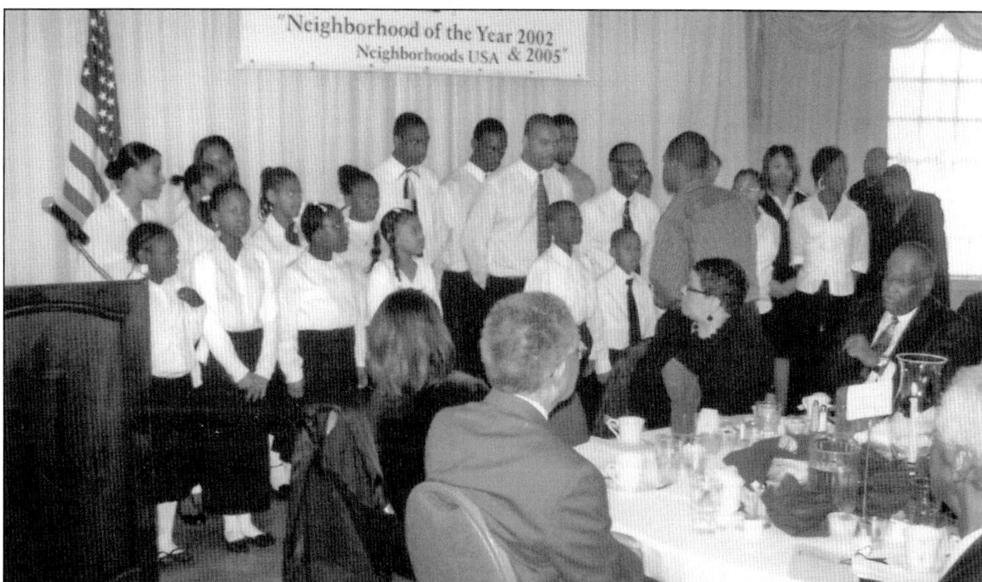

The Annual Black History Program, hosted by the Aberdeen Gardens Historic and Civic Association, brings together many remaining first- and second-generation Aberdeen families, as well as partnering neighborhood members, businesses, and visitors. Little Zion Baptist Church is one of the historic churches available to Aberdeeners from 1937 to the present, and their youth choir performs at the 2006 Black History Program. (Courtesy of Catherine Howard.)

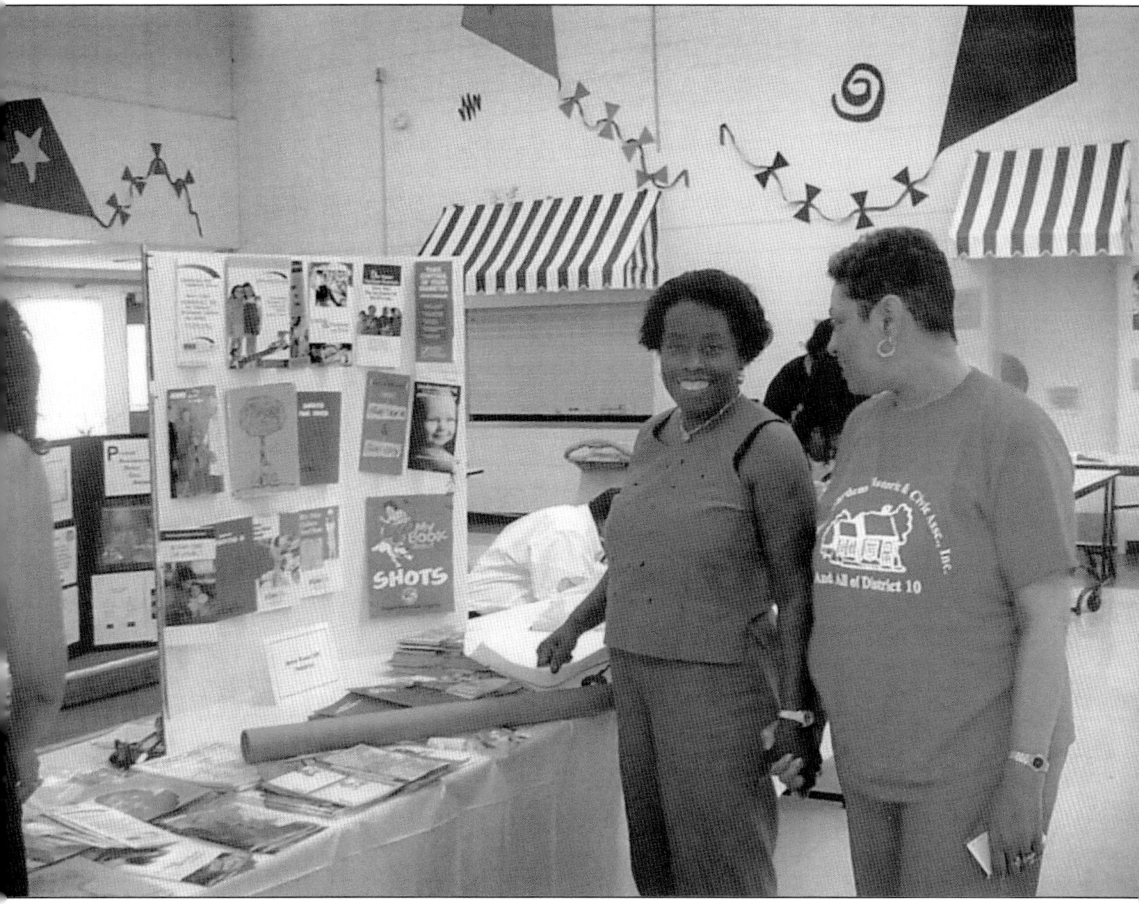

Patricia Mainor (right) is a business entrepreneur. She is the owner and chief executive officer of Tender Care Health Services, Inc. Her business provides health care to clients on a daily basis, sometimes around the clock. Mainor has been the chair of the Health Fair since 2001. She has hosted the health fair at the Aberdeen Elementary School and the West Hampton Community Center. Here she looks over some of the displays used for the health fair. The two-day fair started with one day of general vendor displays covering a variety of health issues. The second day was usually for children and their special needs. On many occasions, the health fair would be taken to the four schools—Tarrant Elementary, Aberdeen Elementary, Robert E. Lee Elementary, and Francis Mallory Elementary—in Hampton's Neighborhood District 10. (Courtesy of Aberdeen Gardens Historic and Civic Association, Inc.)

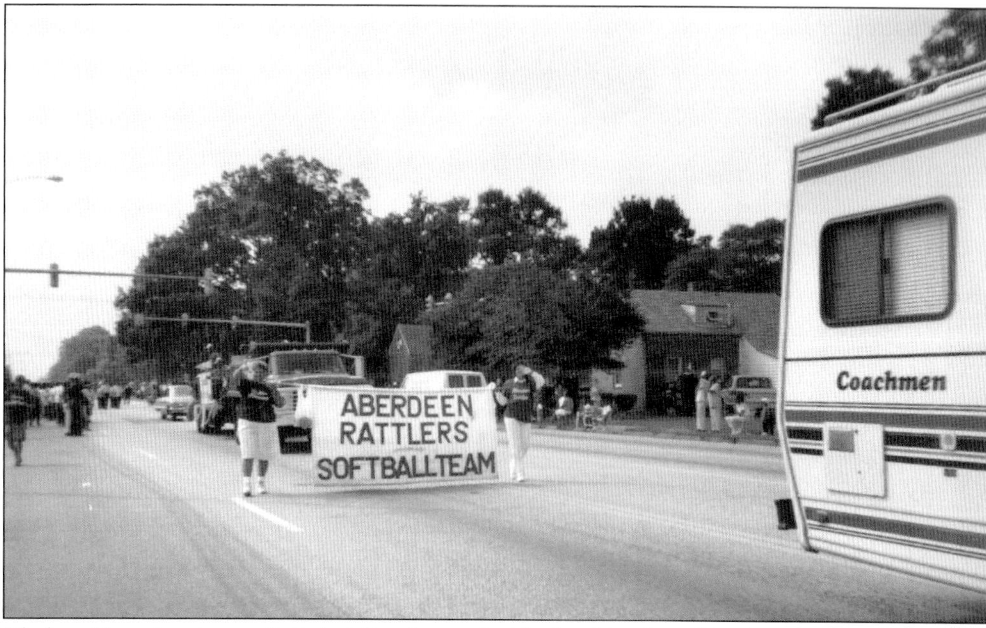

Thelma Vann Lattimore (left, holding banner) aids the Aberdeen Rattlers in their annual fish fry held in the neighborhood. She volunteered to assist with carrying the banner in the Deen's Day parade. Lattimore lives on Langston Boulevard in the Aberdeen Garden Historic District. She was one of the first majorettes for George P. Phenix High School, located on the campus of Hampton University. (Courtesy of Aberdeen Gardens Historic and Civic Association, Inc.)

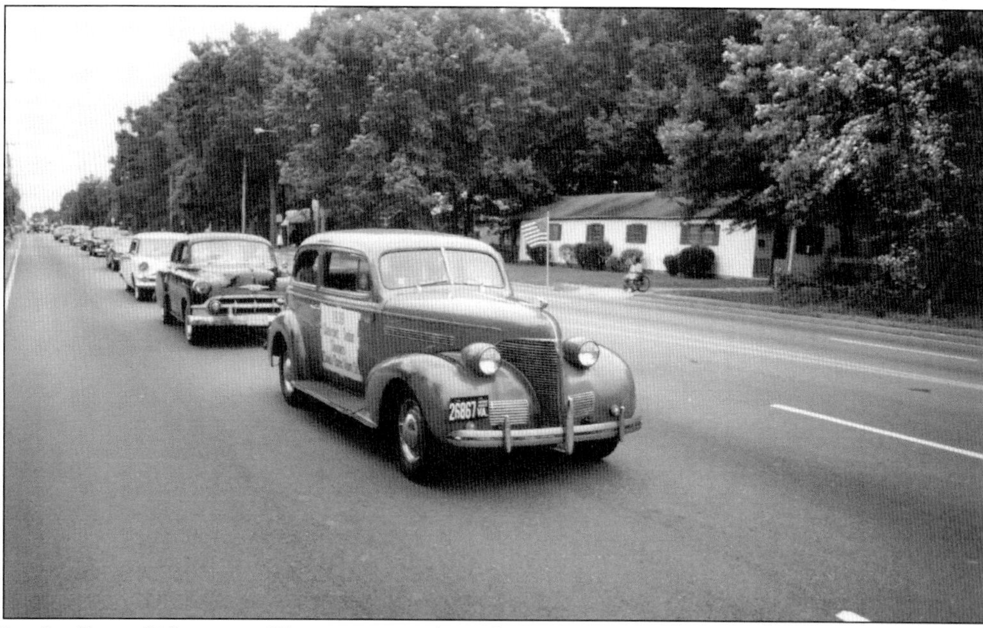

In the City of Hampton Christmas parade each year, several residents of Aberdeen Gardens, along with friends from neighboring cities, drive their antique cars. Pictured is a 1939 Chevy leading the 10 to 15 cars featured in the parade. The drivers are joined by their families to greet the many residents who stand along the parade route. (Courtesy of Aberdeen Gardens Historic and Civic Association, Inc.)

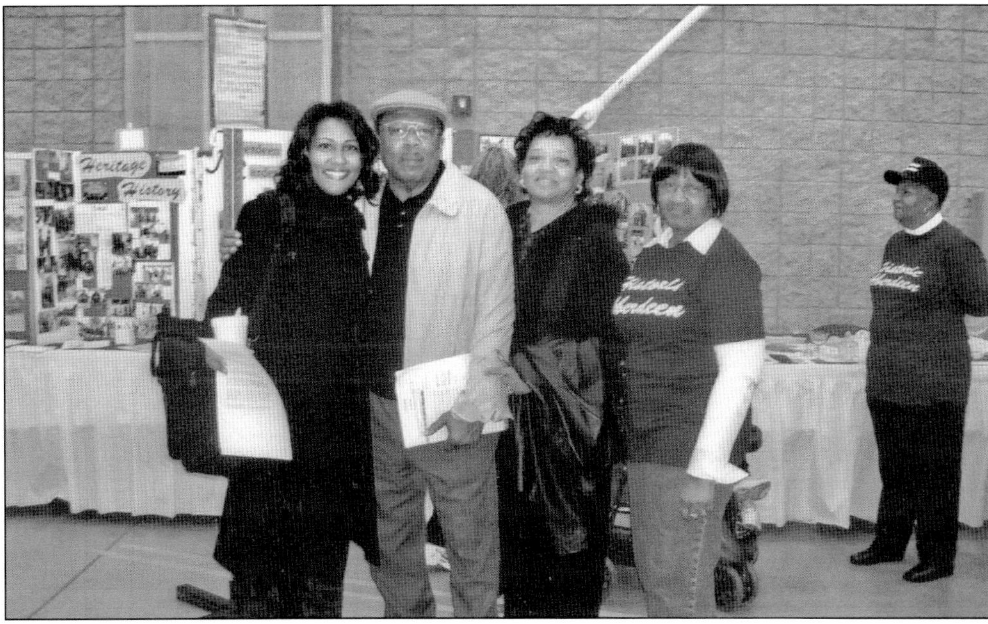

The Aberdeen Gardens Historic and Civic Association had three very large board displays for the Hunt for Hampton's History event. Catherine Howard is the association's historian and photographer; thus, pictures were available for this display. Many pictures came from residents, friends, and family members. It was truly a pictorial display of the Aberdeen Gardens Historic District and partnering neighborhoods. (Courtesy of Aberdeen Gardens Historic and Civic Association, Inc.)

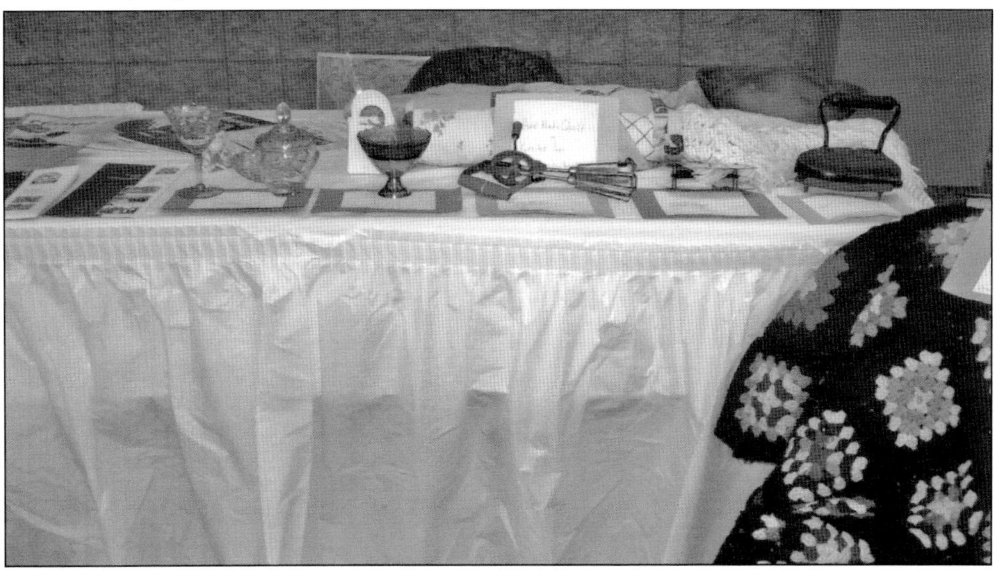

The Hunt for Hampton's History event brought together neighborhoods to display and talk about their community history. The Aberdeen Gardens Historic and Civic Association had program folders and magazines that highlighted Aberdeen; household items from 1930 to 1955 displayed on a table; Thomas Eaton Fundamental School's beautiful quilt given to the Aberdeen Gardens Historic and Civic Association; and a hand-crocheted quilt of the 1950s. (Courtesy of Aberdeen Gardens Historic and Civic Association, Inc.)

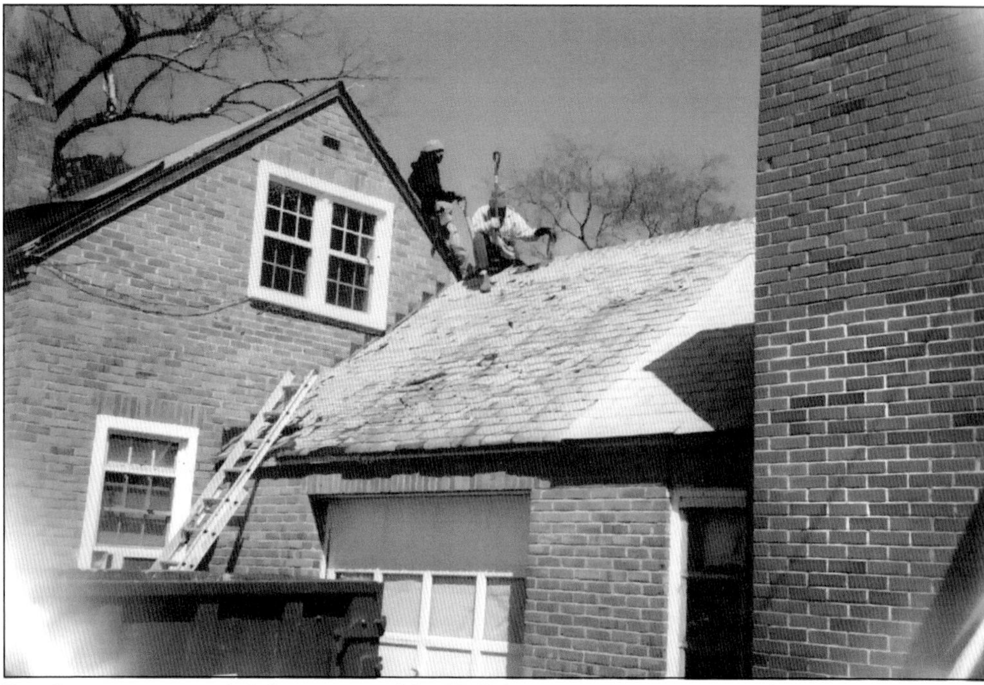

Parade magazine awarded the winner of the "Tell America's Story" contest, the Aberdeen Gardens Historic District, monies for historical restoration of windows and for roof repairs. The original 1936 Aberdeen home of William Taylor Sr.'s family in the Aberdeen Gardens Historic District was selected for this project and was highlighted in *Parade* magazine in 2006. William Taylor Jr. resides in the family home. He and his sisters, Lois and Geneva, and brother Rudolph were extremely happy that their family home was chosen. The roofing project is in progress. The workers are seen finishing over the garage. (Both courtesy of Catherine Howard.)

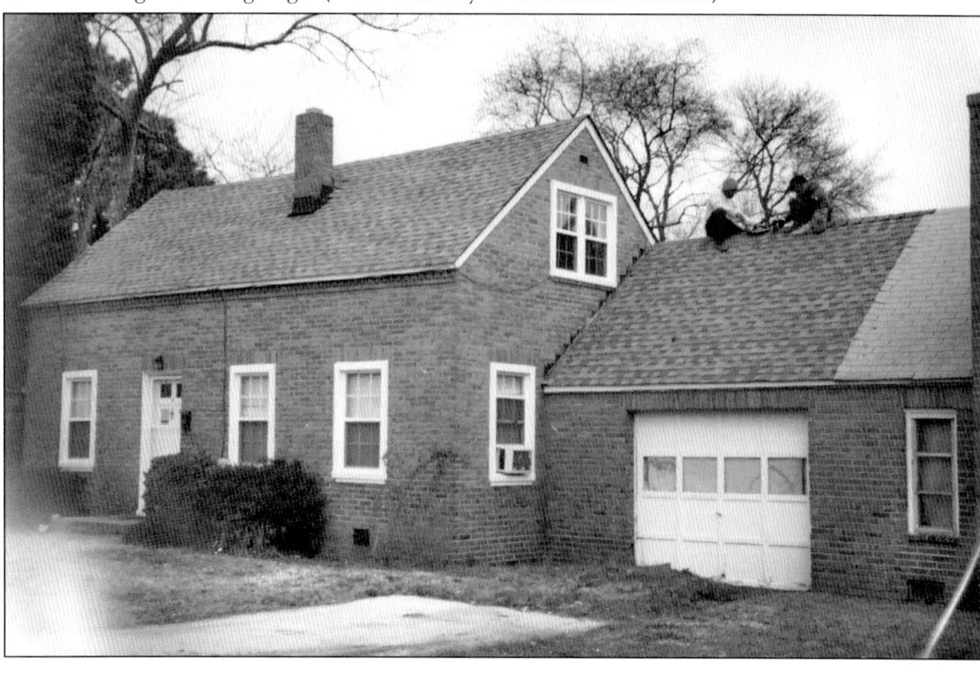

Four

COUNCIL OF ELDERS 2000–2007

The Council of Elders of Aberdeen Gardens Historic and Civic Association, Inc., are inductees who have lived 30 or more years in their locality. Elders pass on traditions in all neighborhoods.

The Council of Elders provides a resource of mature men and women to demonstrate the dedication, commitment, and compassion needed to educate the children, retain the history of the community, and demonstrate to youth the values of love, togetherness, and life in general. They are here to help maintain a healthy atmosphere in which to live and to share their history in the community. In return, the community promotes a sense of dignity, security, and well-being to all elders. The elders who received their medallions for whom pictures are not available are Beatrice Edwards Jennings, Annie Mae Davis Williams, Bertha O. Graham, and Leon H. Kerry.

The Aberdeen Gardens elders were truly essential in the early years. All the neighbors knew one another and their children. If a wrong was seen, it was addressed by the neighbor and reported to the parents. People's relationship to their heritage is the same as the relationship of a child to its mother. As the African proverb states, "When as elder dies, a library is burnt."

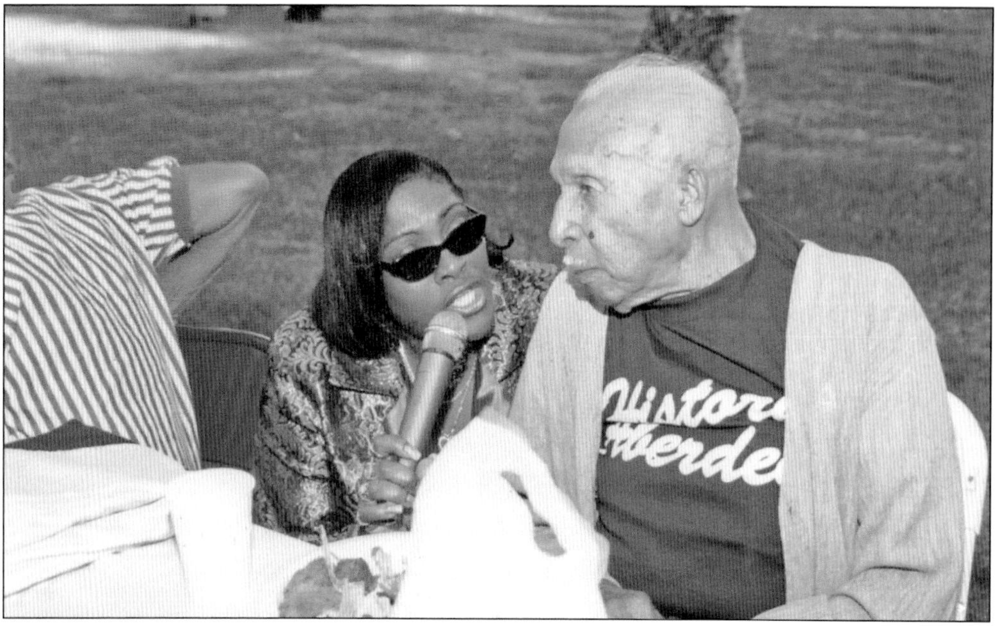

In February 2001, the first Council of Elder award was given, recognizing the most senior individual in the Aberdeen neighborhood. Burum Walker Jr. was a Buffalo Soldier. He received his Elder Medallion in 2002. At 94 years of age, he is shown here being interviewed by Robin Williams. Both were Langston Boulevard residents in the Aberdeen Gardens Historic District. (Courtesy of Aberdeen Gardens Historic and Civic Association, Inc.)

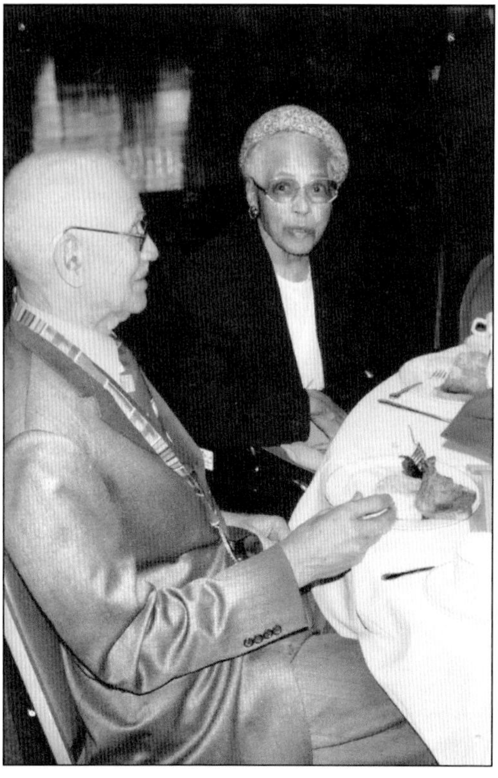

In 2001, Troy Smith Sr., at 83 years of age, was inducted into the Aberdeen Gardens Historic and Civic Association Council of Elders, thus receiving an engraved medallion. He and his wife, Olivia, live on West Walker Road in the Aberdeen Gardens Historic District. Troy Smith Sr. has three children: Edna, Linda, and Troy Smith Jr. He is also a business entrepreneur, running Smith Enterprises, Inc. (Courtesy of Aberdeen Gardens Historic and Civic Association, Inc.)

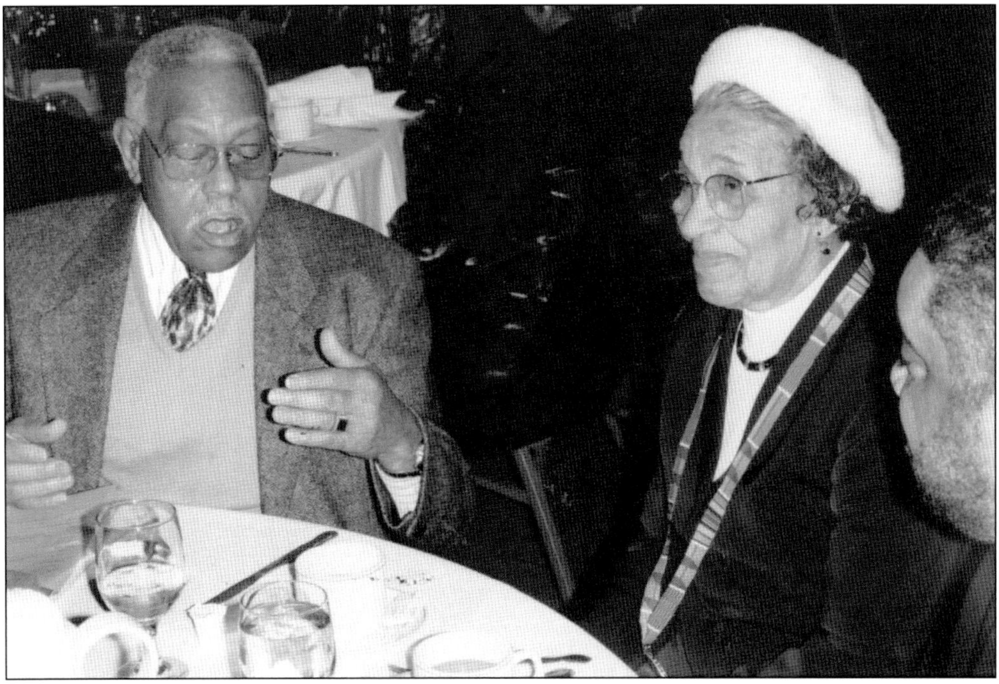

In 2005, Cora Pierce Johnson was inducted into the Aberdeen Gardens Historic and Civic Association Council of Elders and received an engraved medallion. She lives on Mary Peake Boulevard in the Aberdeen Gardens Historic District. She served as financial secretary for the association and was instrumental in helping set up the interior decor of the Aberdeen Gardens Historic Museum. (Courtesy of Jacqueline Arrington.)

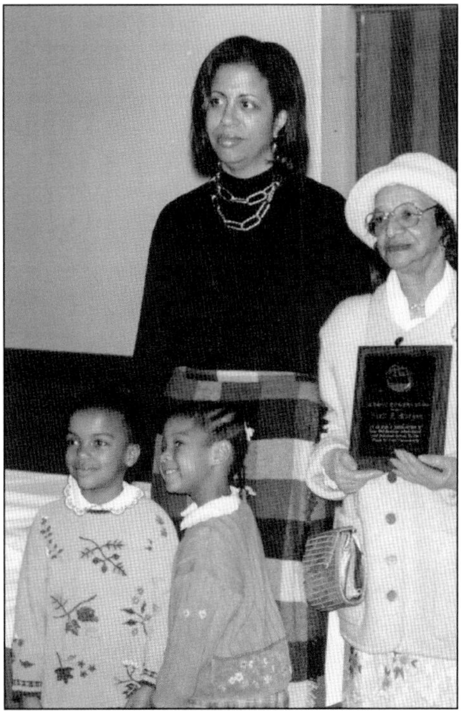

Adell F. Morgan was inducted into the Aberdeen Gardens Historic and Civic Association Council of Elders and received her engraved medallion in 2004. She stands with her daughter and grandchildren. She lives on Mary Peake Boulevard in the Aberdeen Gardens Historic District. (Courtesy of Jacqueline Arrington.)

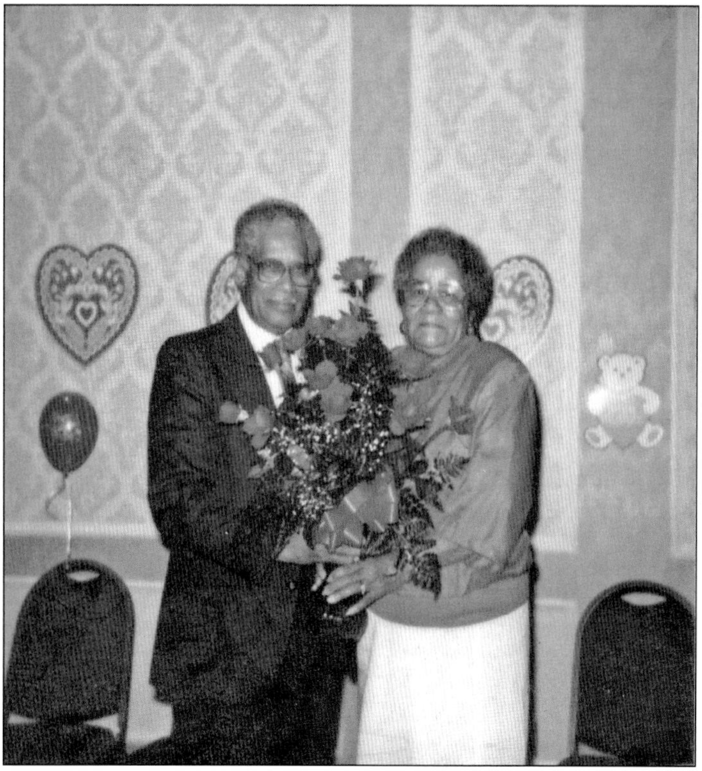

Celebrating their 50th wedding anniversary, John W. and Emily Pierce are original residents of the Aberdeen Gardens Historic District, dating from 1936. Having raised two sons, they were the oldest living, married couple residing in Aberdeen Gardens as of 2006. In 2004, John was inducted into the Aberdeen Gardens Historic and Civic Association Council of Elders. (Courtesy of John W. Pierce.)

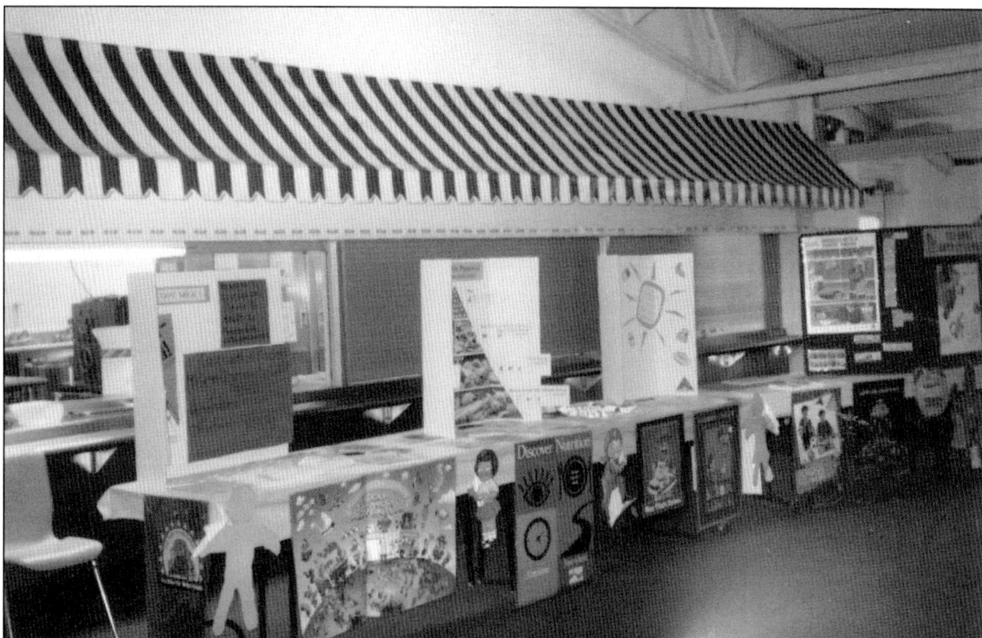

During the health fair, many vendors specify food choices for healthy bodies in contrast to much medication and bad food habits. The elderly are targeted to eat more fruits and vegetables. Patricia Mainor is the chair of the Aberdeen Gardens Historic and Civic Association Health Fair. (Courtesy of Aberdeen Gardens Historic and Civic Association, Inc.)

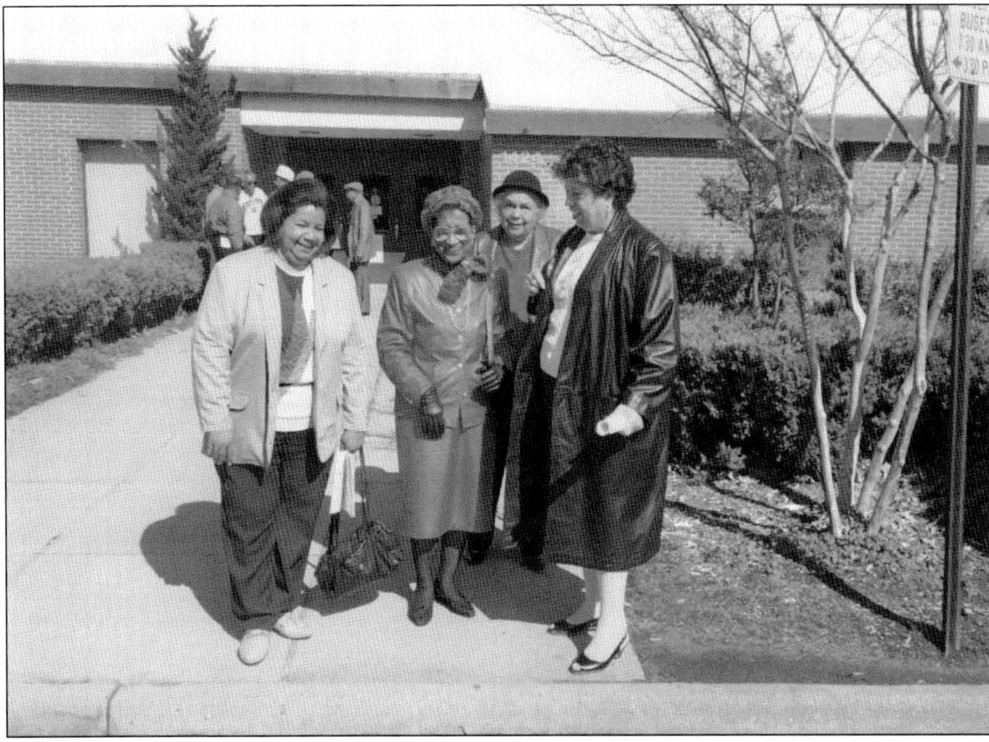

After the opening of the Aberdeen School, many residents visited to see the renovations. Pictured from left to right are an unidentified Aberdeen Elementary teacher, Lillie M. Jones (featured on the cover and a staff member of the Aberdeen Gardens Rental Office, 1942–1947), Gladys Walker, and Ann Thornton. With the exception of the teacher, all of these ladies are Aberdeen Gardens Historic District residents. (Courtesy of Aberdeen Gardens Historic and Civic Association, Inc.)

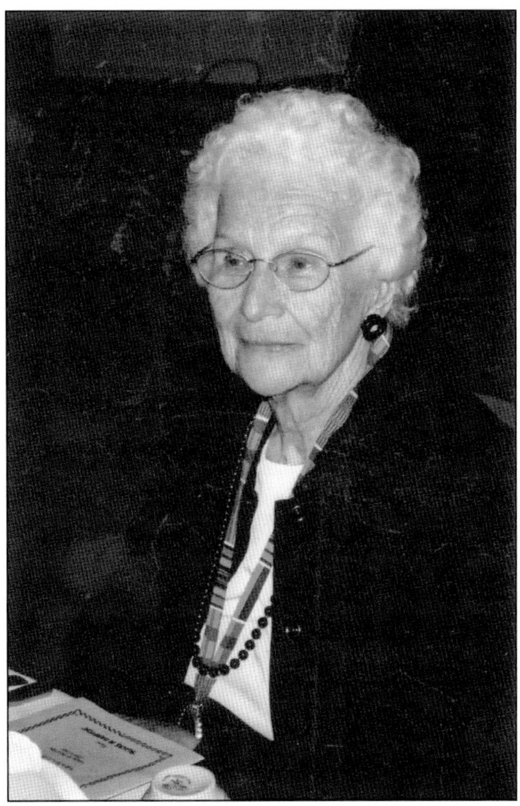

In 2006, Beulah Hunter was inducted into the Aberdeen Gardens Historic and Civic Association Council of Elders and received an engraved medallion. She lives on East Lewis Road in the Aberdeen Gardens Historic District. She was married to the late Bradshaw Hunter and has two daughters, Carolyn and Romaine. (Courtesy of Aberdeen Gardens Historic and Civic Association, Inc.)

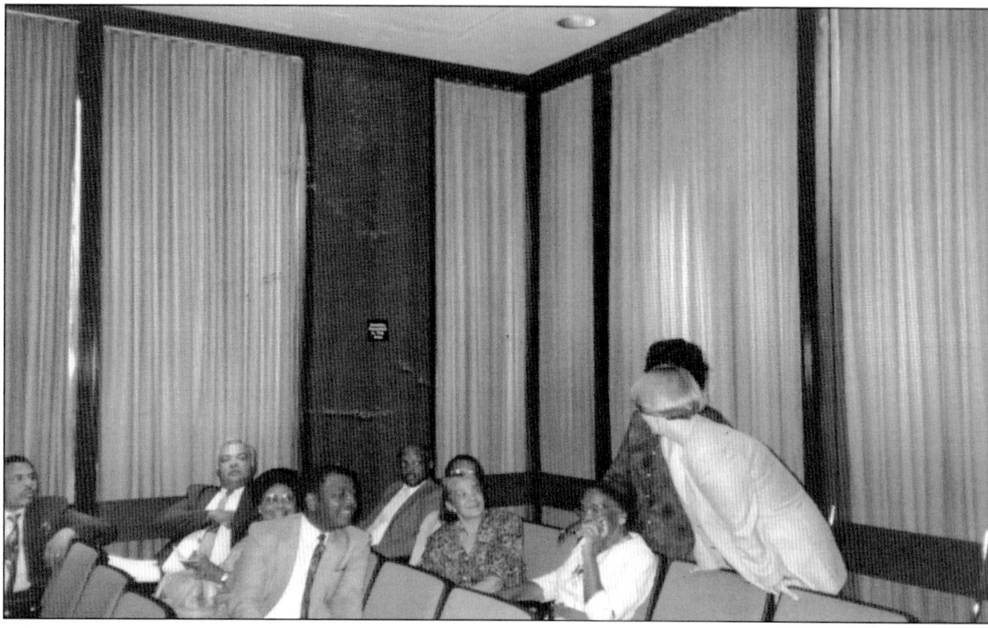

Alva Ruth Foster Jackson was inducted into the Aberdeen Gardens Historic and Civic Association Council of Elders in 2006 and received her engraved medallion. She was 12 years old when she arrived on Mary Peake Boulevard in the Aberdeen Gardens Historic District. For 70 years, she has remained in the family home on Mary Peake Boulevard. Post 69 of the American Legion is named after her brother, Harry S. Foster. (Courtesy of Aberdeen Gardens Historic and Civic Association, Inc.)

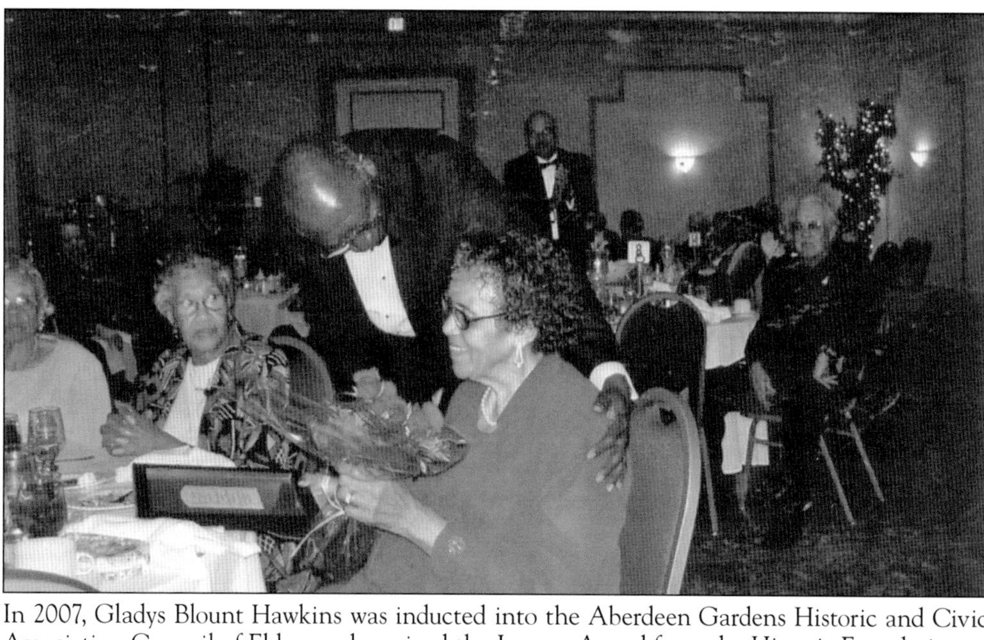

In 2007, Gladys Blount Hawkins was inducted into the Aberdeen Gardens Historic and Civic Association Council of Elders and received the Legacy Award from the Historic Foundation of Aberdeen Gardens. She was 83 years of age at the time and lives on East Russell Road in the Aberdeen Gardens Historic District. She receives roses from President Holland as Alma Landis looks on. (Courtesy of Aberdeen Gardens Historic and Civic Association, Inc.)

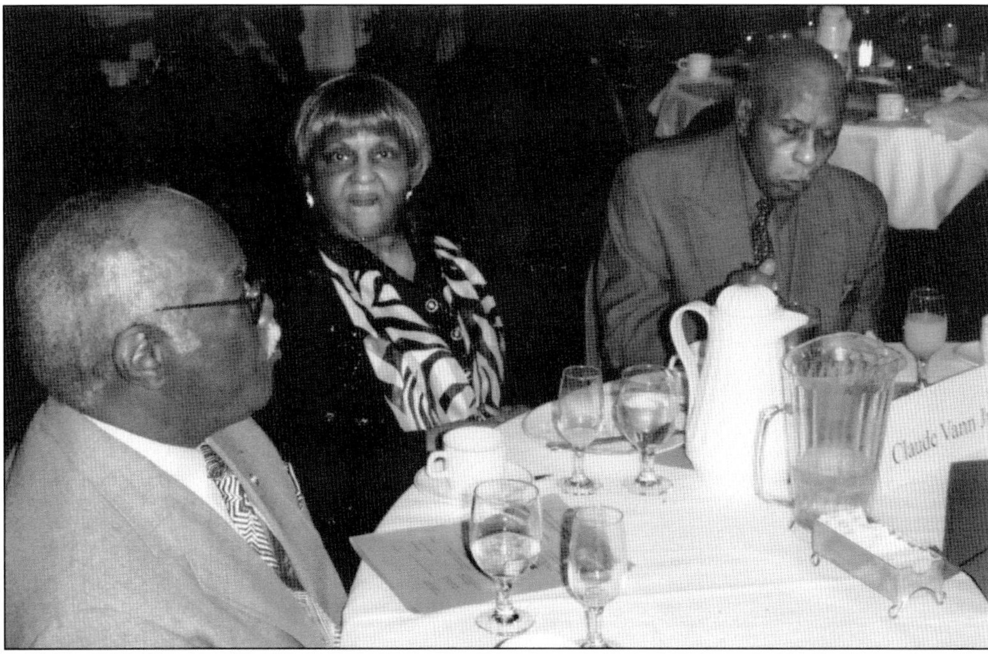

In 2007, Mildred Lee Hopson was inducted into the Aberdeen Gardens Historic and Civic Association Council of Elders. She lives on East Walker Road in the Aberdeen Gardens Historic District. She was married to the late Theodore Hopson (shown to her left in 2002) and has three children: Theodore, Gwendolyn, and Gayle. (Courtesy of Aberdeen Gardens Historic and Civic Association, Inc.)

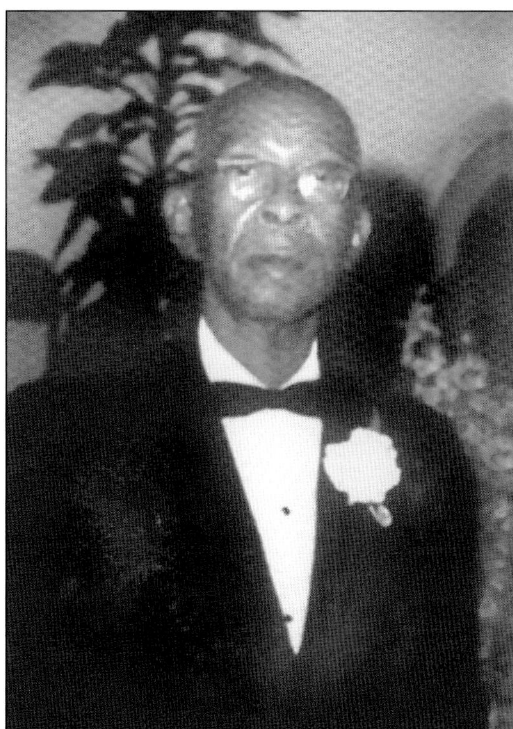

Harrison Brown, the son of John T. and Laura Brown, was born and reared in Hampton, Virginia. Like his father and three brothers, Harrison Brown was a businessman. He worked as a butcher in several markets in Hampton before starting his own business. He owned and operated Brown's Grocery in the Aberdeen Association mini-mall for more than five years. When a major grocery chain caused rivalry, he closed his store because he could not compete. He worked at other local businesses until his retirement. He died in 1983. (Courtesy of Margaret Wilson.)

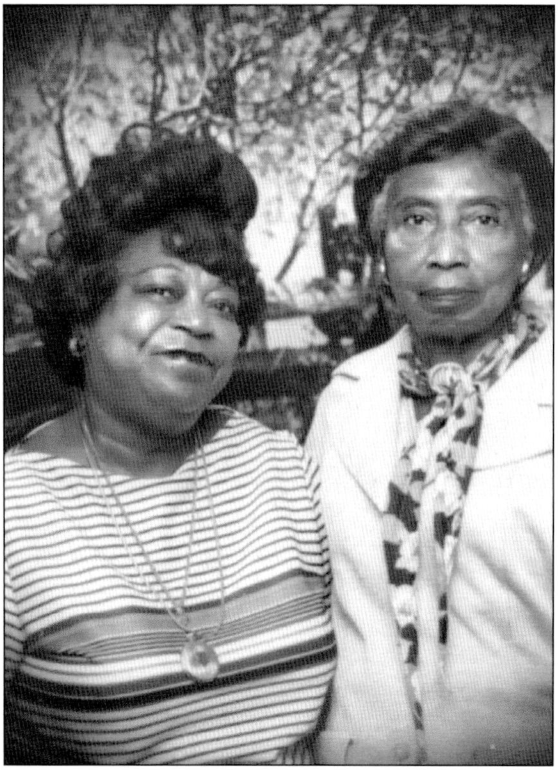

Ethel (left) and her mother, Ellen Grannison (right), lived on Langston Boulevard in the Aberdeen Gardens Historic District. Everyone liked them, and they were friendly, sharing, and caring. Memories of the Grannisons waving from the porch at everyone going by will last. Ellen Grannison's snowball bushes (Roseum viburnum opulus) were beautiful. (Courtesy of Aberdeen Gardens Historic and Civic Association, Inc.)

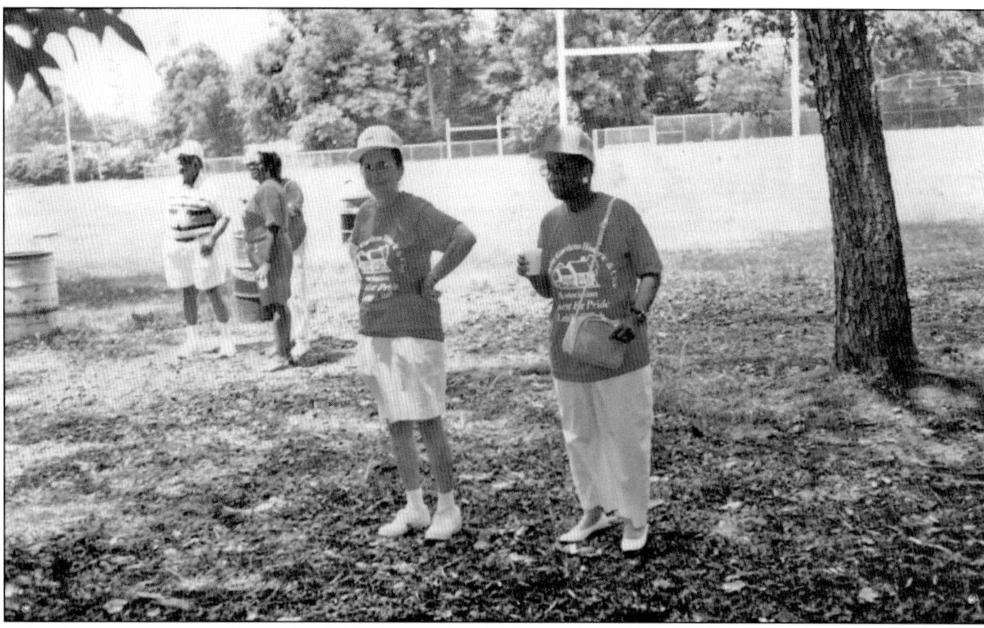

After the Aberdeen Gardens Deen's Day parade, Lillie M. Jones (right) socializes with Alice Walker. Both are residents of the Aberdeen Gardens Historic District. Jones was inducted into the Aberdeen Gardens Historic and Civic Association Council of Elders in 2005 and received an engraved medallion. She resides on Langston Boulevard and was married to Edward Jones. (Courtesy of Aberdeen Gardens Historic and Civic Association, Inc.)

Five

Aberdeen's Who's Who 1937–2007

The Aberdeen Gardens Historic District has its fame to claim. The Aberdeen Gardens neighborhood, finished in 1936, drew people from all walks of life, including Christians and secular groups who realized that this community spelled opportunity. Opening a neighborhood for blacks by blacks was different and exciting. It was an attraction to everyone. How many houses available for blacks in the 1930s were brick and had electricity and indoor plumbing, not to mention a radiator heat fueled by an Arcola coal-burning boiler furnace? The neighborhood welcomed not only the railroad and shipbuilding and dry dock workers, but also doctors, teachers, lawyers, business entrepreneurs, and military families. They were thrown together in an opportunity-of-a-lifetime environment that has lasted for 70 years, from 1937 to 2007.

The attraction remains the same as in the past. The Aberdeen Gardens Historic District has its own who's who, as well as an invited who's who that have influenced, advised, supported, and participated in Aberdeen Gardens neighborhood activities over the years.

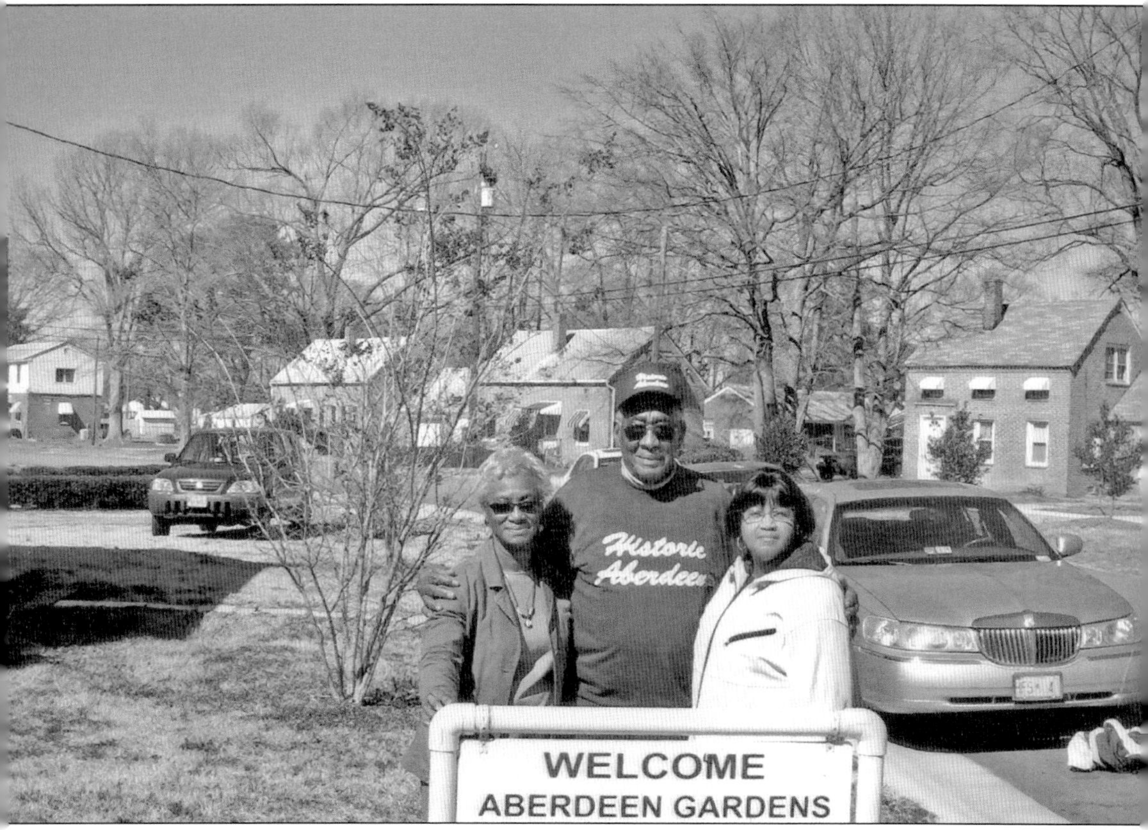

Catherine Howard, Harmon Stokes, and Jacqueline Roundtree stand behind the sign welcoming everyone to visit Aberdeen Gardens. The three represent the Aberdeen Gardens Historic and Civic Association and the Historic Foundation of Aberdeen Gardens. The Aberdeen Gardens Historic District is a friendly and mostly quiet neighborhood. Driving through the neighborhood, one will see remodeled houses and landscaped yards. The flowers are prevalent throughout, though only a few residents still have snowball bushes. Traffic patterns are definitely different from yesteryear, and they are constantly changing today. Years ago, residents cut the medians and trimmed the trees; the City of Hampton does that now. After 5:00 p.m. in the 1950s, the only sounds heard in Aberdeen Gardens were crickets, frogs, and an occasional rattlesnake. Lightning bugs could be seen throughout the neighborhood. Today businesses, eateries, and malls are within minutes of the Aberdeen Gardens Historic District. (Courtesy of Historic Foundation of Aberdeen Gardens, Inc.)

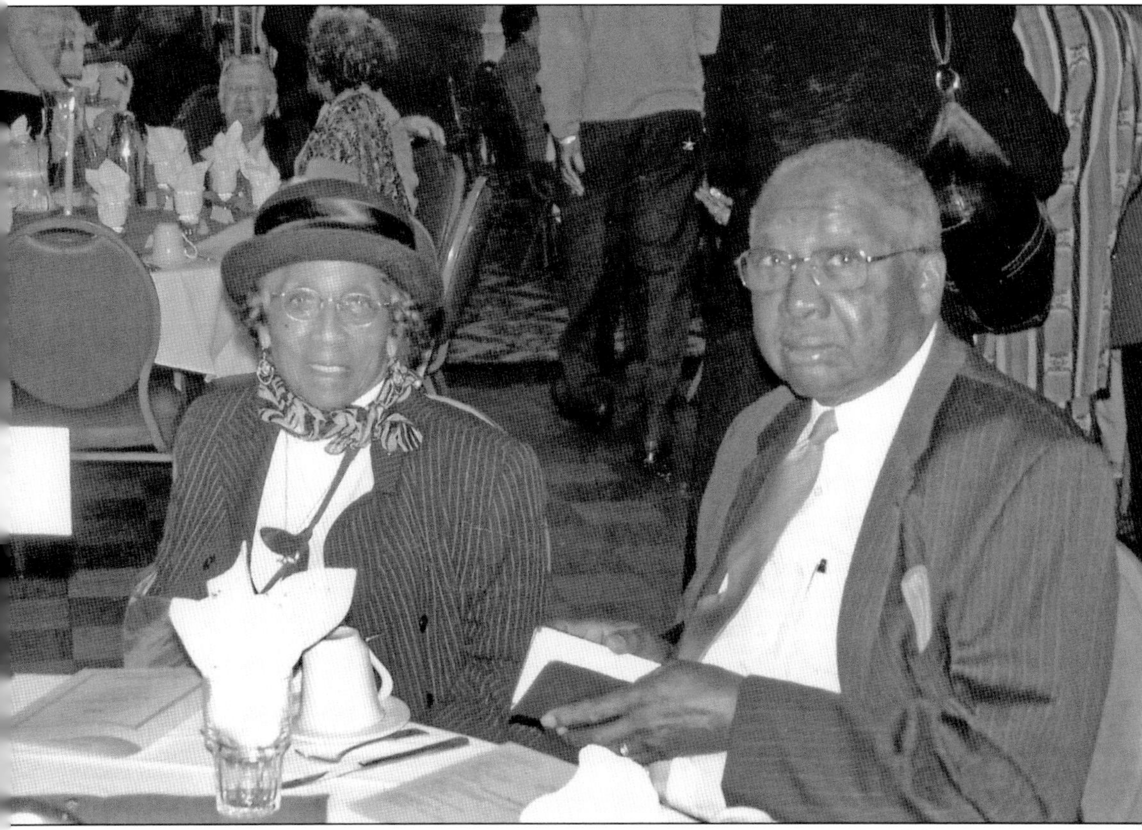

Gladys and Joseph Holland are seated at the head table at the Harvest Fest gala of the Historic Foundation of Aberdeen Gardens, Inc. The gala is a newly annual fund-raising event hosted by the foundation. President Holland was the former Hampton City District 10 commissioner. He performed his duties along with the 20 members of the commission to expand the level of involvement in Healthy Neighborhoods; assist neighborhoods with projects; and be a resource person to the neighborhoods. He and his wife reside on Randall Court in Granger Court, south of the Aberdeen Gardens Historic District corridor. President Holland oversees the maintenance and management activities at the Aberdeen Gardens Historic Museum. (Courtesy of Catherine Howard.)

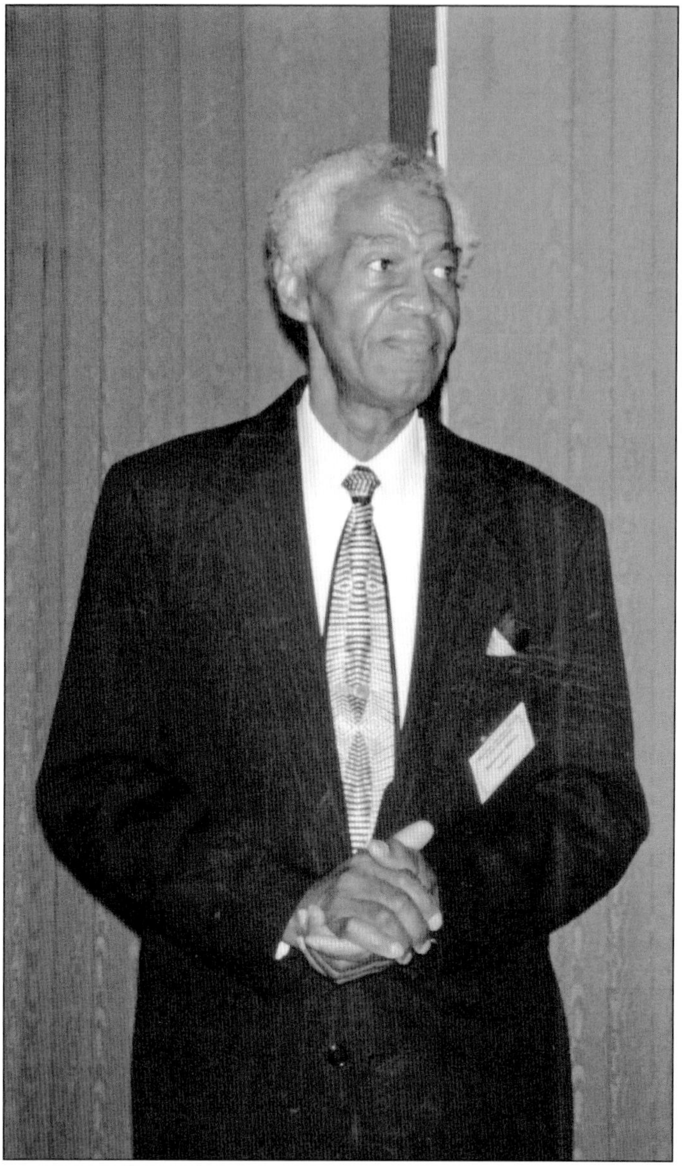

Roosevelt Wilson is a resident of Micott Drive in Granger Court East, which is east of the Aberdeen Gardens Historic District. He was president of the Aberdeen Gardens Historic and Civic Association from 1999 to 2007. The association members and community have gained recognition through award-winning successes during his leadership. Wilson keeps abreast of issues influencing the neighborhood. To empower the neighborhoods, representatives of the association and the community are urged to attend Hampton's Neighborhood College, Hampton's Citizens Code Academy, and Hampton's Citizens Police Academy, to name a few institutions. He makes sure that the association and community members are present at council meetings. He invites guest speakers involved in issues that impact the community. The annual health fair and Heritage Day were initiated during Wilson's presidency. He constantly tries to unite all neighborhoods that have membership in the Aberdeen Gardens Historic and Civic Association. Wilson received the Aberdeen Gardens Historic and Civic Association Historical Recognition Award at the association's 2001 Black History Program. (Courtesy of Catherine Howard.)

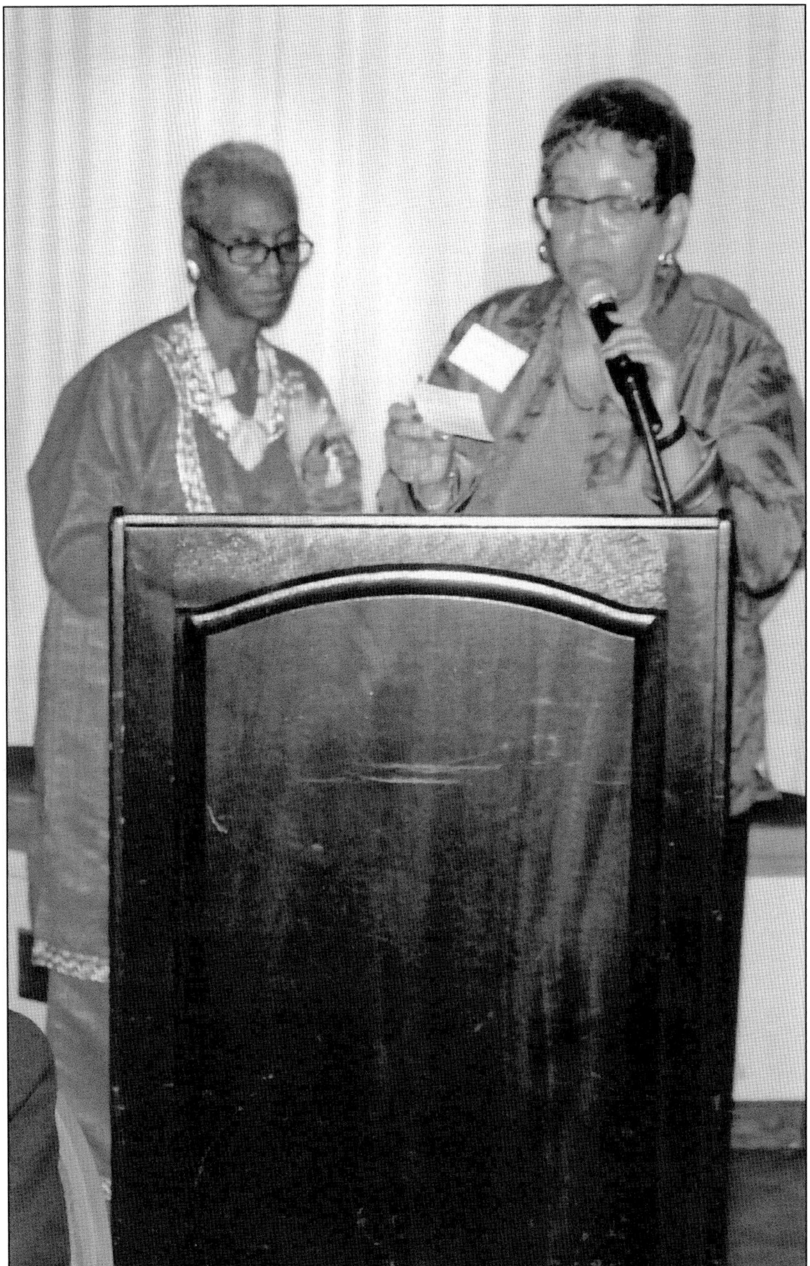

Eunice Peele (right) and Catherine Howard (left) are past and present chairs of the annual Black History Programs hosted by the Aberdeen Gardens Historic and Civic Association, Inc. Howard has been chair since 2004. She lives on Randal Court in Granger Court East, south of Aberdeen Gardens Historic District. Howard does much of the research to bring speakers who had a direct influence on Aberdeen. Peele, the secretary and former chair, lives in a partner neighborhood of the Aberdeen Gardens Historic and Civic Association, Inc. She is the neighborhood contact realtor. These program chairs work enthusiastically to select individual speakers who have impacted the Aberdeen Gardens neighborhoods. (Courtesy of Aberdeen Gardens Historic and Civic Association, Inc.)

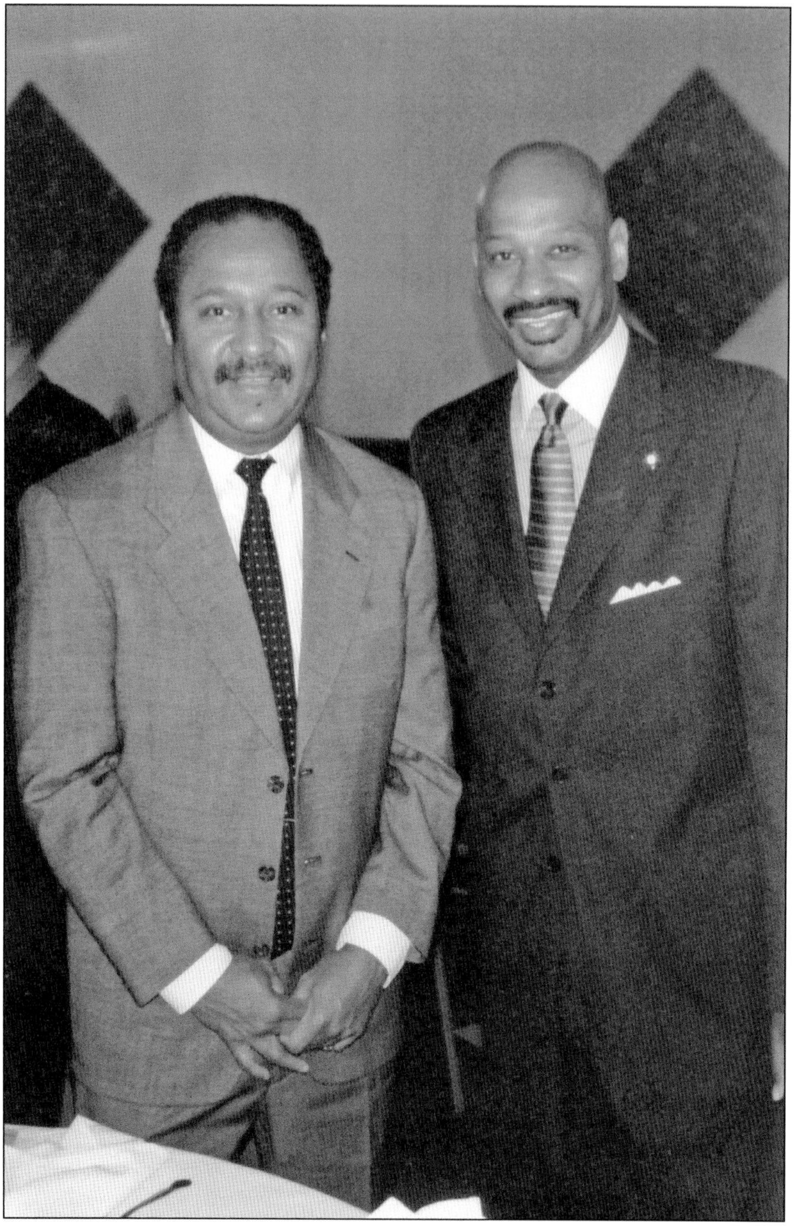

Judge Wilford Taylor Jr. (left) was the keynote speaker at the Aberdeen Gardens Historic and Civic Association Annual Black History Program in 2005. He was raised in East Aberdeen, a partner neighborhood of the Aberdeen Gardens Historic and Civic Association. He started at Aberdeen Elementary School and attended Hampton schools. After 10 years as a general district court judge for the City of Hampton, he was elected a circuit court judge by the general assembly. B. J. Roberts (right), the sheriff of the city of Hamtpon, received the Aberdeen Gardens Historic and Civic Association's Historic Recogniation Award. He attended the police academy in 1972 and was the first African American elected as a state constitutional officer and sheriff in 1992. Under Roberts's leadership, the Hampton sheriff's community relations unit runs programs such as Ident-A-Kid, Adopt-A-Senoir, and many more. (Courtesy of Aberdeen Gardens Historic and Civic Association, Inc.)

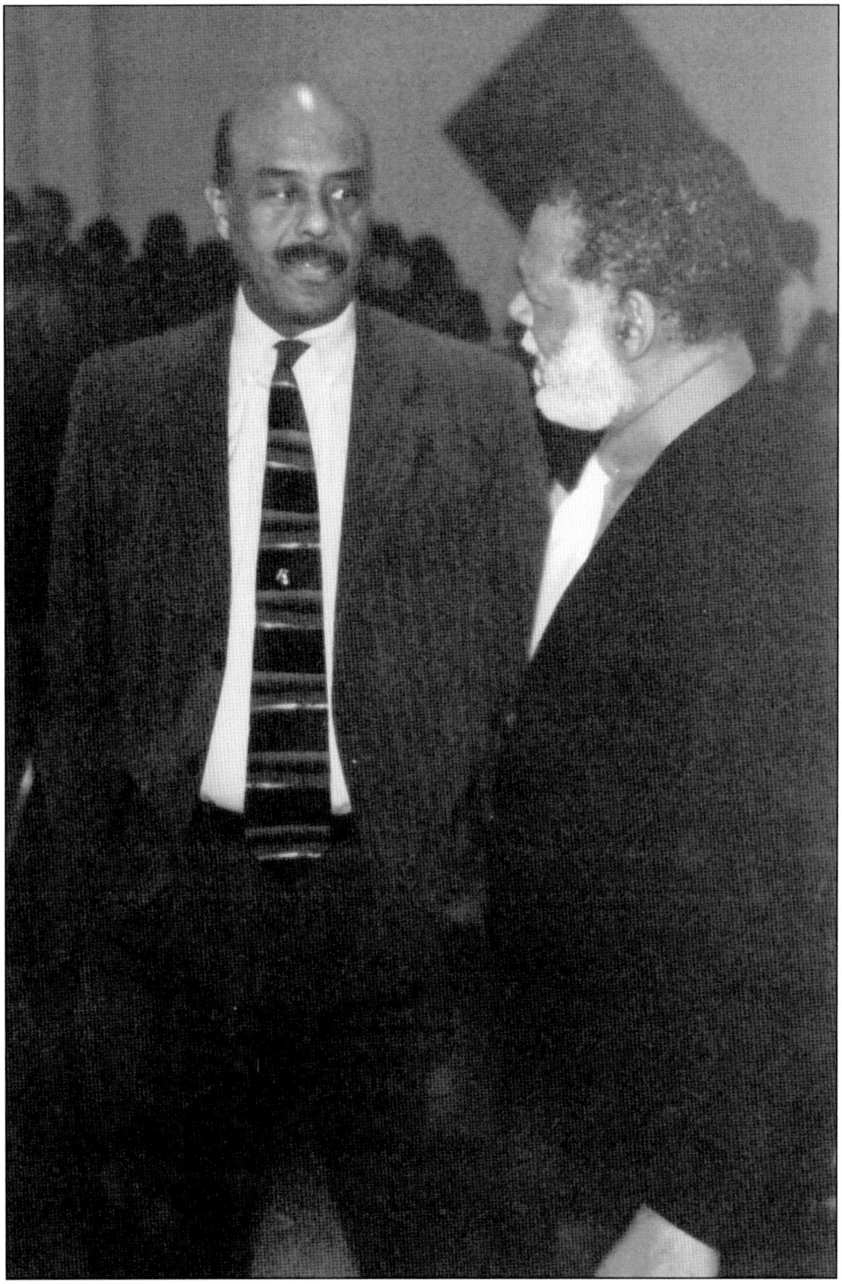

George E. Wallace (left) is shown here speaking with Burt Williams of the Aberdeen Gardens Historic District at the Aberdeen Gardens Historic and Civic Association's Black History Breakfast in 2005. Wallace became the city manager of Hampton on August 4, 1997, replacing Robert J. O'Neill Jr. He earned degrees from North Carolina Central University in Durham and Golden Gate University. A native of Williamsburg, Wallace currently lives in the Farmington neighborhood of Hampton. In 2002, Wallace received the Program Excellence Award for Innovations in Local Government. Before leaving the office of city manager in 2005, the city of Hampton had collectively received 17 national awards for its youth initiatives, its 311 call center, and its diversity and neighborhood programs. (Courtesy of Aberdeen Gardens Historic and Civic Association, Inc.)

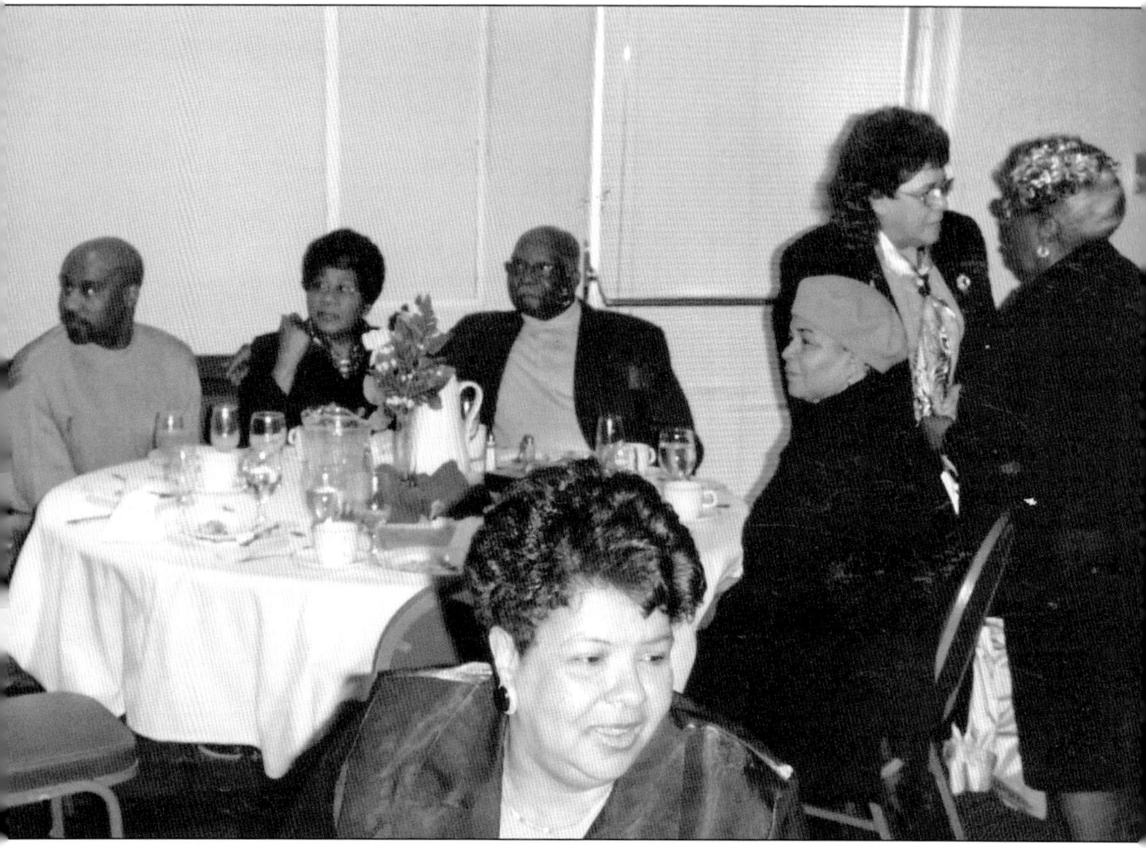

Shellae Blackwell, seen clearly at the bottom of the page, is Hampton's District 10 facilitator. She has received the Aberdeen Gardens Historic and Civic Association Historic Recognition Award. She works with all Hampton City District 10 neighborhoods, including the Aberdeen Gardens Historic District, by providing technical assistance to neighborhood leaders and organizations in the area of neighborhood development. Her 25 years with the City of Hampton has given her vital experience from the positions she has held, including employment specialist, assistant director of developmental programs, grants administrator, and senior facilitator with the neighborhood department. She has received numerous awards and certificates from organizations throughout the Hampton Roads community. She has served as president of the Hampton Roads chapter of the Conference of Minority Public Administrators and the Hampton Coalition for Youth. In 1984, she was listed in Outstanding Young Women of America and appointed to the Virginia Council on Vocational Education. (Courtesy of Aberdeen Gardens Historic and Civic Association, Inc.)

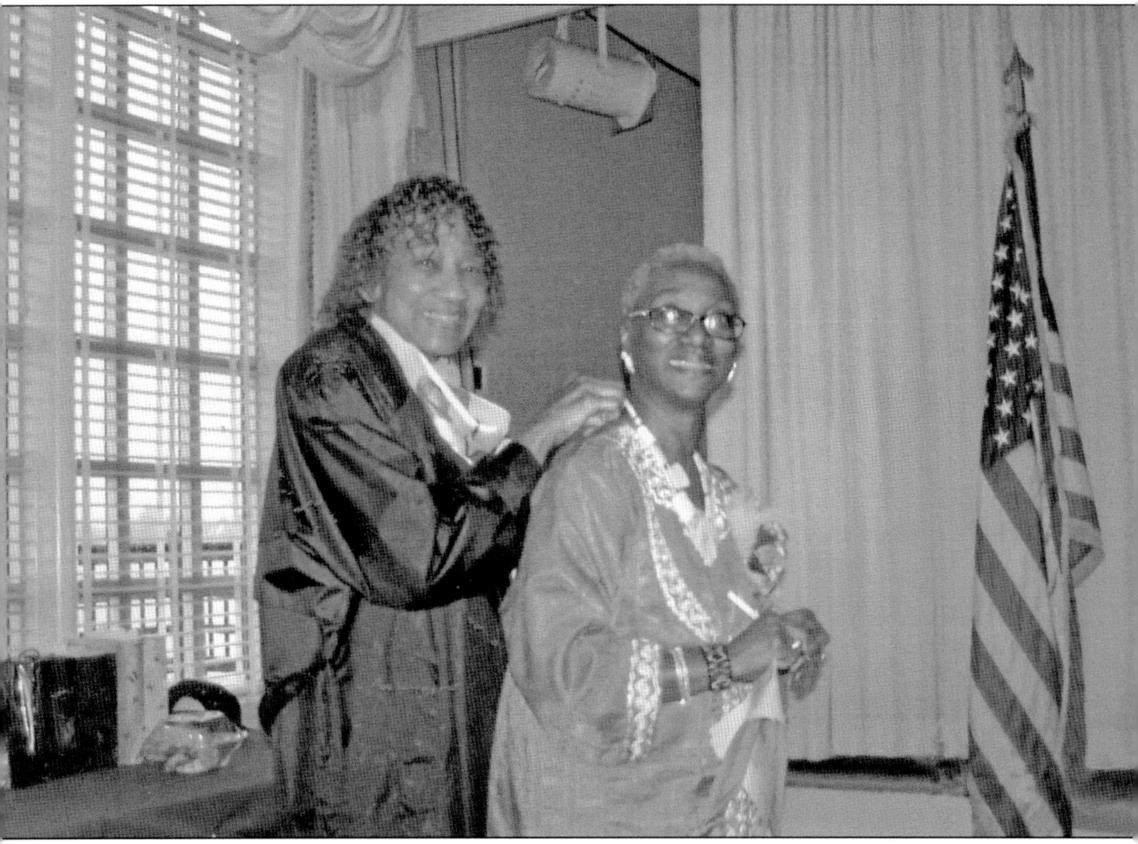

Addie D. Threatt (left) received the Aberdeen Gardens Historic and Civic Association Historic Recognition Award in 2002. She resides on East Walker Road in the Aberdeen Gardens Historic District. She has served the association as president, treasurer, and secretary. Here Threatt is helping Catherine Howard (right) with a last-minute attire check. (Courtesy of Aberdeen Gardens Historic and Civic Association, Inc.)

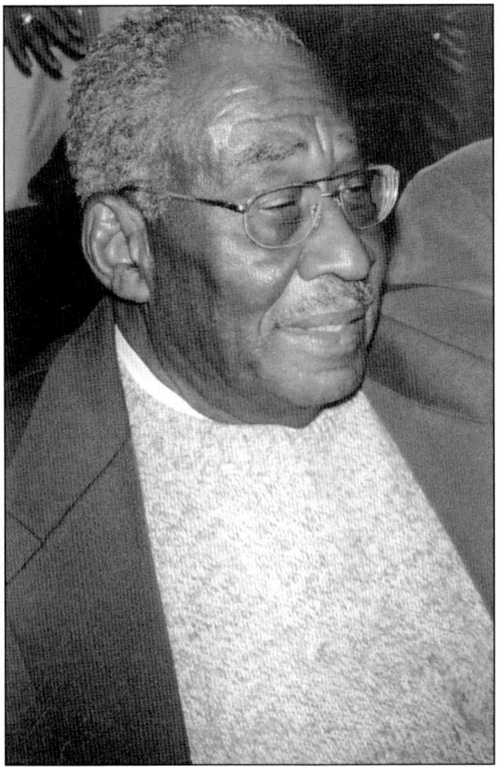

Harmon F. Stokes received the Aberdeen Gardens Historic and Civic Association Historic Recognition Award in 2002. He is married, has one son, and resides on Micott Drive in Granger Court East. He is the safety officer for the association and provides the neighborhood with safety resources and safety guidelines as communicated from the Hampton Police Department. (Courtesy of Aberdeen Gardens Historic and Civic Association, Inc.)

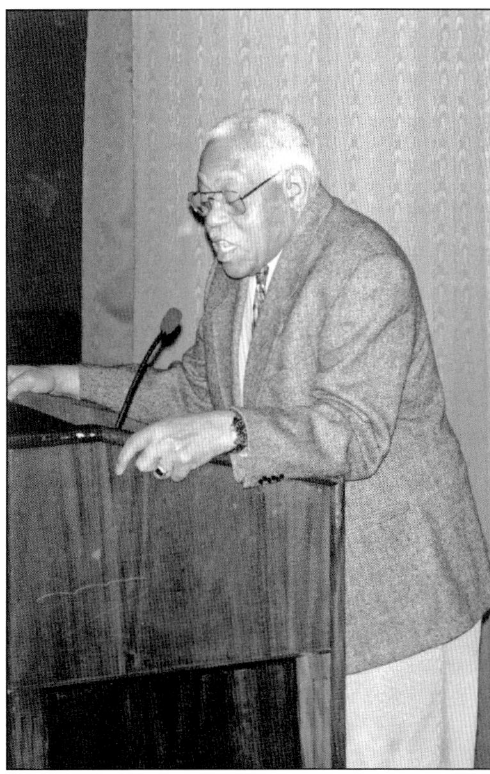

Samuel Daniel is the chaplain and family services chairman for the Aberdeen Gardens Historic and Civic Association. He is a deacon in First Baptist Church East End. Chaplain Daniel received the Aberdeen Gardens Historic and Civic Association Historical Recognition Award in 2003. (Courtesy of Aberdeen Gardens Historic and Civic Association, Inc.)

Agnes Stokes Chisman (left), who resided on Langston Boulevard in the Aberdeen Gardens Historic District, received the Special Black History Recognition Award in 2003 along with two other nurses, Mildred Smith (right) and Patricia McKenzie (not pictured), for their simple act against segregation by demonstrating a freedom sit-in in the cafeteria at the local Hampton Dixie Hospital in 1963. Senator Mamie Locke is pictured center. (Courtesy of Aberdeen Gardens Historic and Civic Association, Inc.)

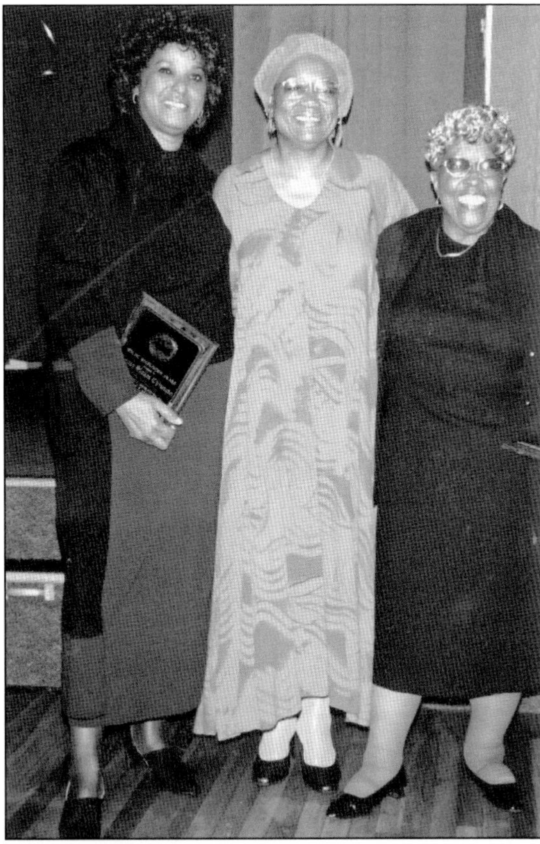

In 2004, Champ Morgan received the Aberdeen Gardens Historic and Civic Association Historic Recognition Award. Pictured from left to right are Shirley G. Morgan, Champ Morgan Jr., and a European student that resided with the Morgans during his exchange program. Champ operated a business providing plastering and stucco services throughout the Hampton Roads area. He was married and had three sons: Champ III, Jonathan, and Jason. (Courtesy of Shirley G. Morgan.)

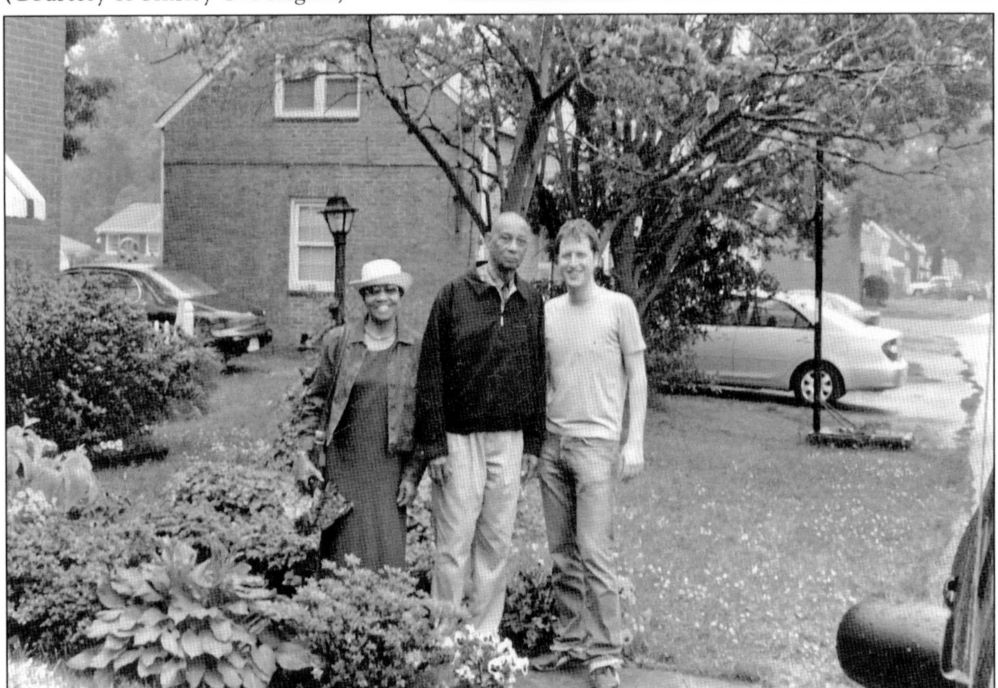

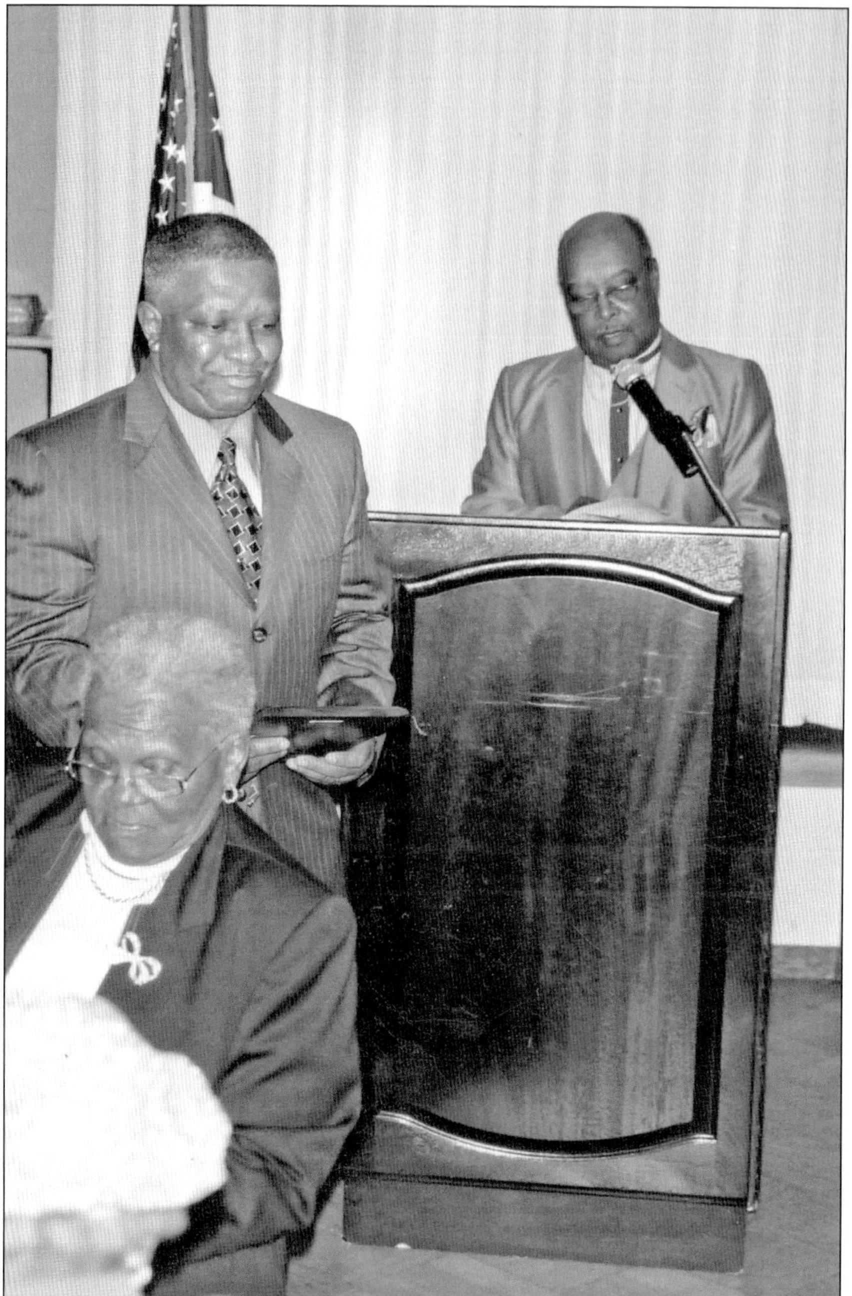

Aberdeen Gardens Historic and Civic Association vice president Howard Cary is at the podium. Curtis Lee Franklin received the Aberdeen Gardens Historic and Civic Association Special Recognition Award in 2006 for the replica of the Aberdeen Gardens Historic Museum he built. The museum replica is used for the Hampton parade display and neighborhood history display. He lives on Sharon Court in Prestige Park, adjacent to East Aberdeen Gardens, a partner neighborhood of the Aberdeen Gardens Historic and Civic Association. He is married to Electra Mitchell Franklin and has two daughters. (Courtesy of Aberdeen Gardens Historic and Civic Association, Inc.)

Leon Gerald Kerry is commissioner and chief executive officer of the Central Intercollegiate Athletic Association (CIAA), which is headquartered in Hampton. He was raised in the Aberdeen Gardens Historic District on Langston Boulevard. He was a guest speaker at the 2007 Aberdeen Gardens Historic and Civic Association Black History Program. He is married to Angela Kerry and has two daughters, Leeann and Lisa. (Courtesy of Aberdeen Gardens Historic and Civic Association, Inc.)

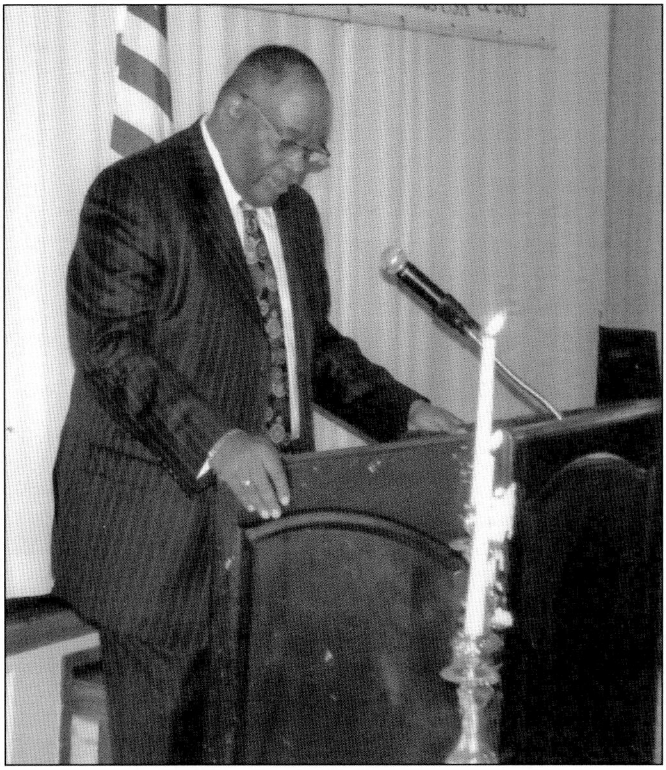

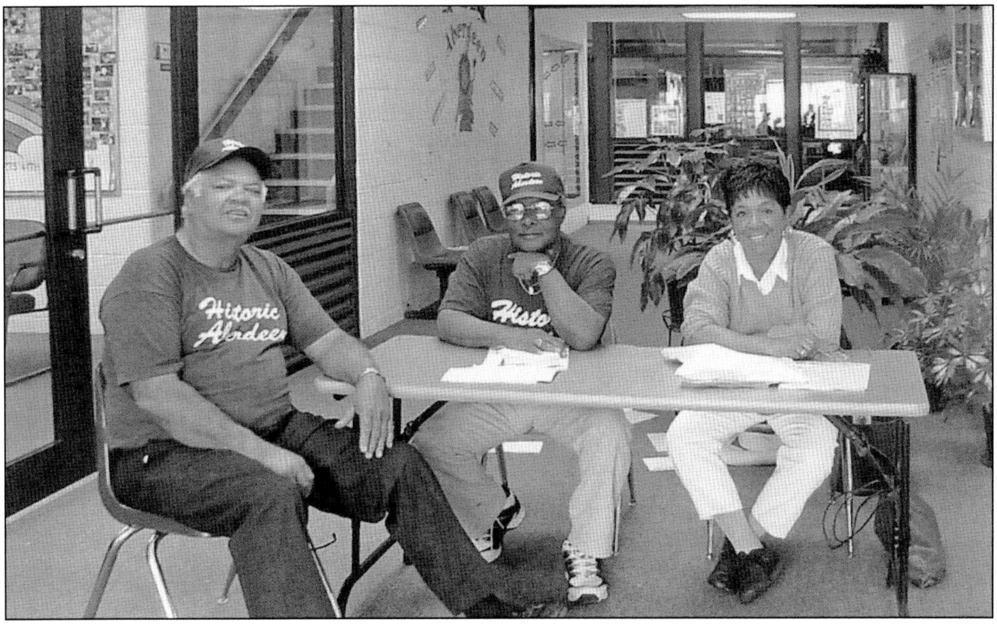

Dorothy Milo Smith (right) is the hospitality chair for the Aberdeen Gardens Historic and Civic Association. She lives in her family home on Langston Boulevard in Aberdeen Gardens Historic District. "Dot," as she is called, has traveled extensively in Europe. She is a true greeter. She has three daughters: Teneane, Tonya, and Terrena. Also pictured are Claude Vann Sr. (left) and Howard Cary (center) (Courtesy of Aberdeen Gardens Historic and Civic Association, Inc.)

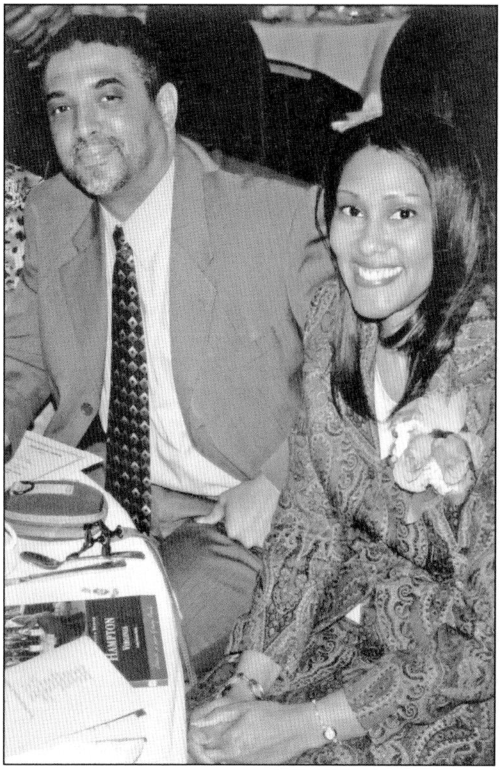

Colita Nichols Fairfax and her husband attended the 2006 Aberdeen Gardens Historic and Civic Association Black History Program where she was the guest speaker. She has ties with Aberdeen Gardens in that she coauthored an article about Maggie Walker, after whom Walker Road in the Aberdeen Gardens Historic District was named. Colita hopes that her contributions to history and social policies will provide alternative insights into the strength of black culture. She has been an inspiration to the Aberdeen Gardens community. (Courtesy of Catherine Howard.)

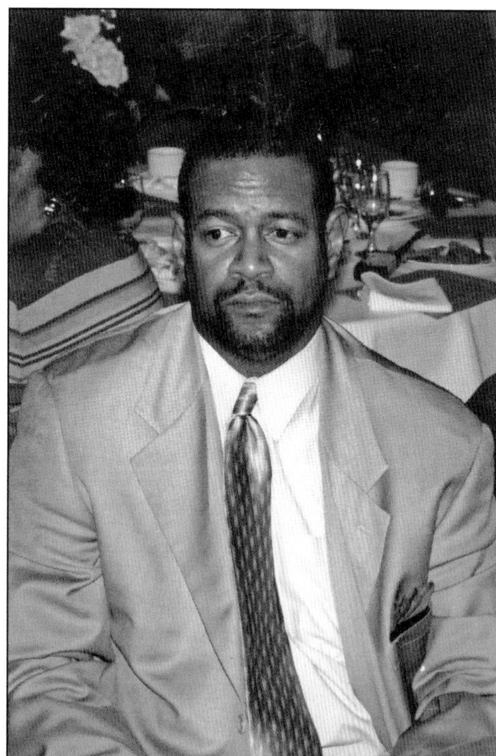

Evelyn Daniels Chandler, as history program coordinator and mistress of ceremony, was successful in getting Salim Khalfani as guest speaker for the Aberdeen Gardens Historic and Civic Association Black History Program in 2003. Khalfani is the executive director of the Virginia State Conference of the NAACP. "You Must Return to the Past before You Move Forward" was his topic. (Courtesy of Catherine Howard.)

Mary Belle Pittman Johnson was inducted into the Aberdeen Gardens Historic and Civic Association Historic Recognition Award in 2007. She lived on Langston Boulevard in the Aberdeen Gardens Historic District. She was married to the late Thomas F. Johnson and has one daughter and one son: Carolyn (deceased) and Joseph. Pictured with Johnson is Joseph Holland of the Historic Foundation of Aberdeen Gardens. (Courtesy of Catherine Howard.)

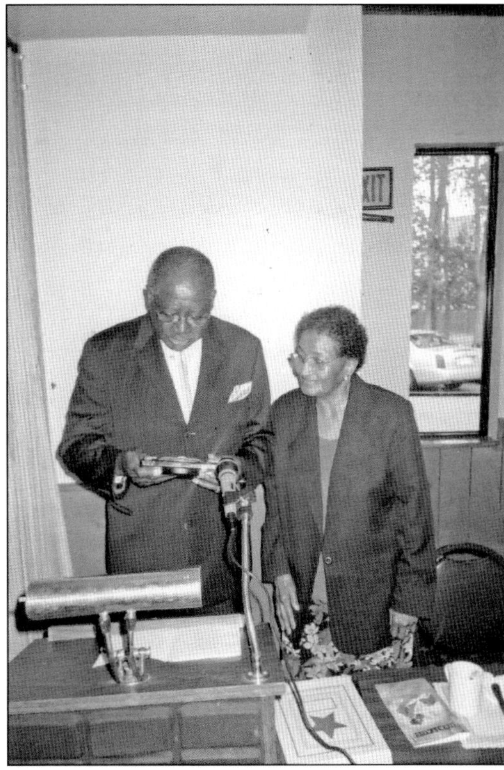

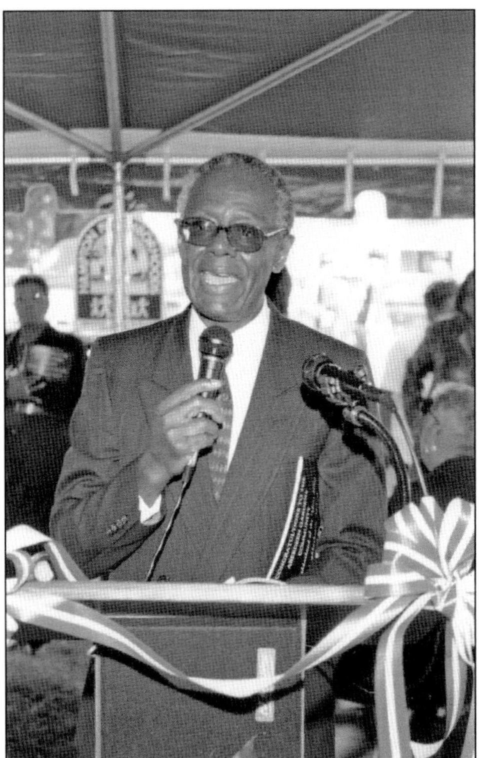

Allen Houston was the recipient of the Historical Recognition Award in 2003. He is the government affairs chairman for the Aberdeen Gardens Historic and Civic Association. He lives on East Weaver Road in Aberdeen Gardens. Houston has attended NUSA conferences and state conferences. He plans public forums to bring awareness to issues in the neighborhoods. (Courtesy of Catherine Howard.)

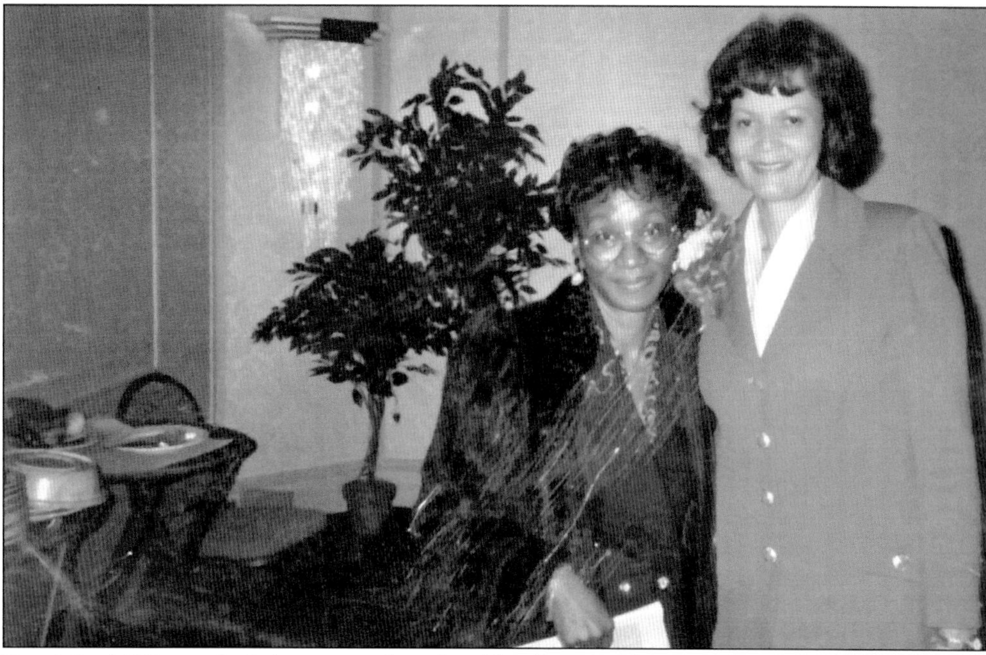

Hazel Reid O'Leary (right) was raised in the Aberdeen Gardens Historic District on Langston Boulevard. She was Pres. Bill Clinton's secretary of energy. O'Leary attended the annual Black History Program in 2006. Here she poses with Catherine Howard (left), a historian and program chair. (Courtesy of Catherine Howard.)

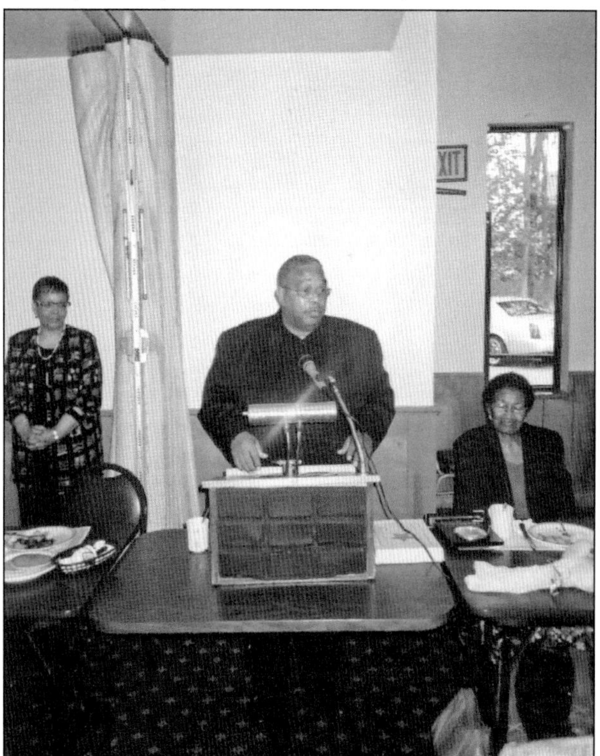

Paul Gillis, a former state NAACP president, was a speaker at the Historic Foundation of Aberdeen Gardens and presented the 2006 Longevity Award to Mary Johnson (seated). He is a resident of Langston Boulevard in the Aberdeen Gardens Historic District. (Courtesy of Aberdeen Gardens Historic and Civic Association, Inc.)

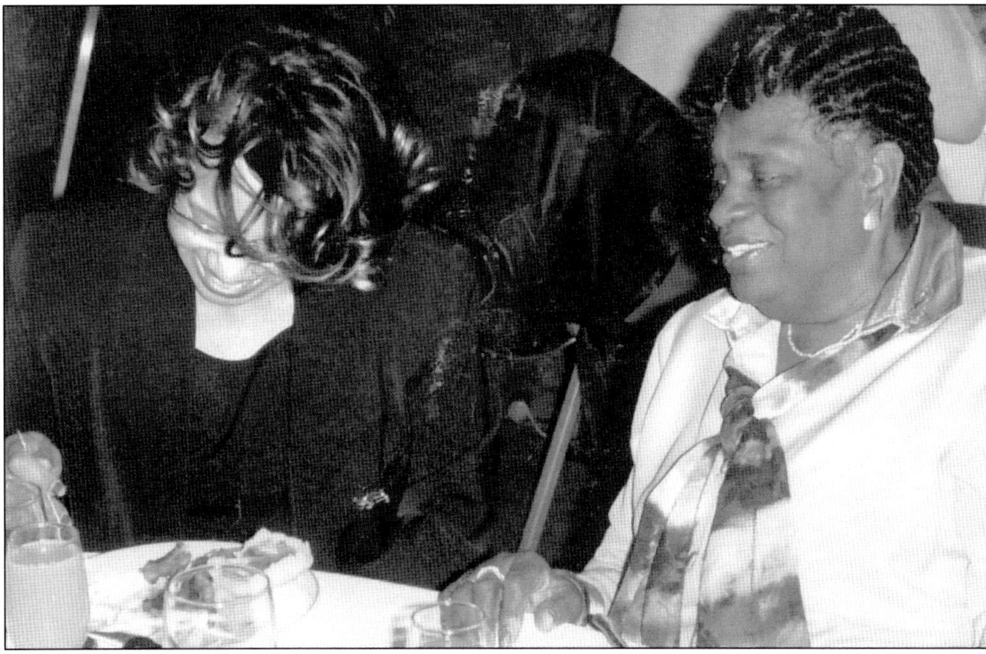

Agnes Gatling (right) lived in the Aberdeen Gardens Historic and Civic Association partner neighborhood of Joynes Road for many years. She is a pianist for First Baptist Church East End in Newport News. Gatling attended the 2002 Black History Program hosted by the Aberdeen Gardens Historic and Civic Association. (Courtesy of Aberdeen Gardens Historic and Civic Association, Inc.)

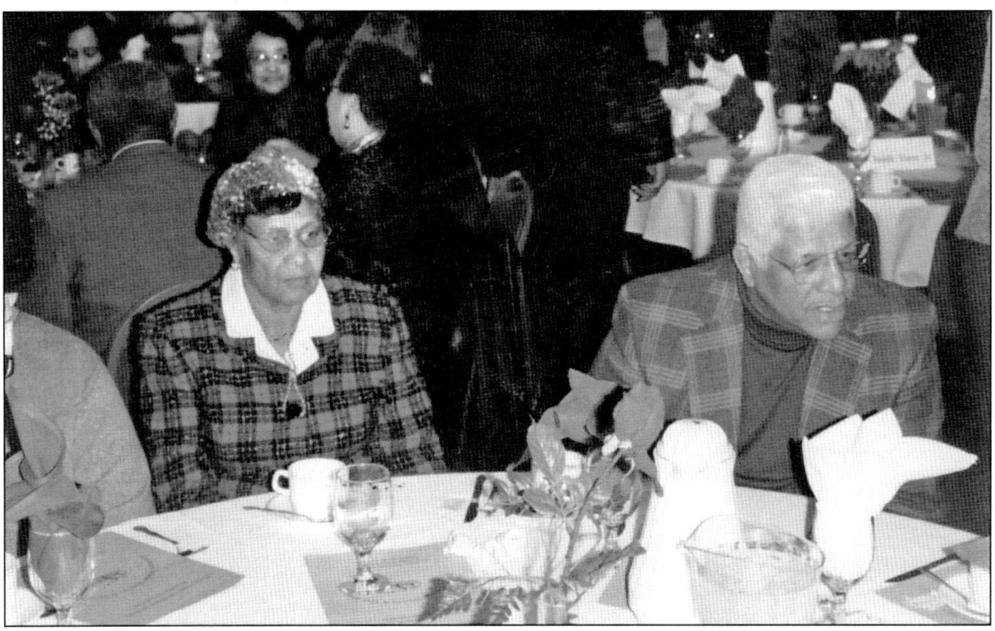

Richard and Addie Hall are supporters and members of the Aberdeen Gardens Historic and Civic Association. They reside on North Walker Road in North Aberdeen, north of the Aberdeen Gardens Historic District. Addie is on the hospitality committee and is a greeter for various functions. (Courtesy of Aberdeen Gardens Historic and Civic Association, Inc.)

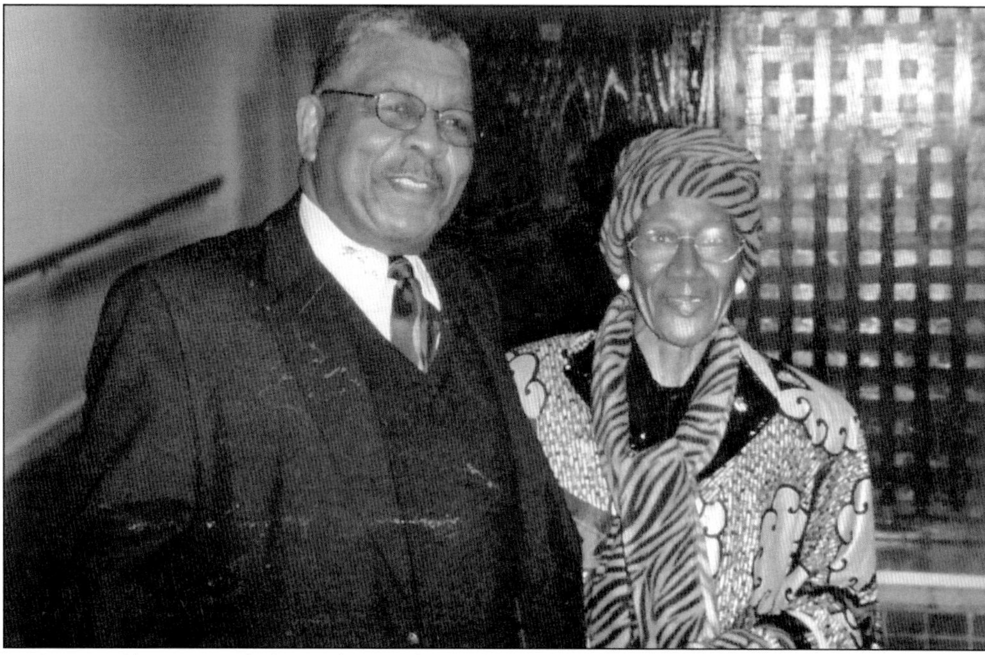

Pauline Williams stands by Walter Jackson; both are Aberdeen Gardens Historic and Civic Association members. Williams lives on East Weaver Road east of the Aberdeen Gardens Historic District. She keeps the Aberdeen Gardens Historic and Civic Association informed of senior citizen activities and safety. (Courtesy of Catherine Howard.)

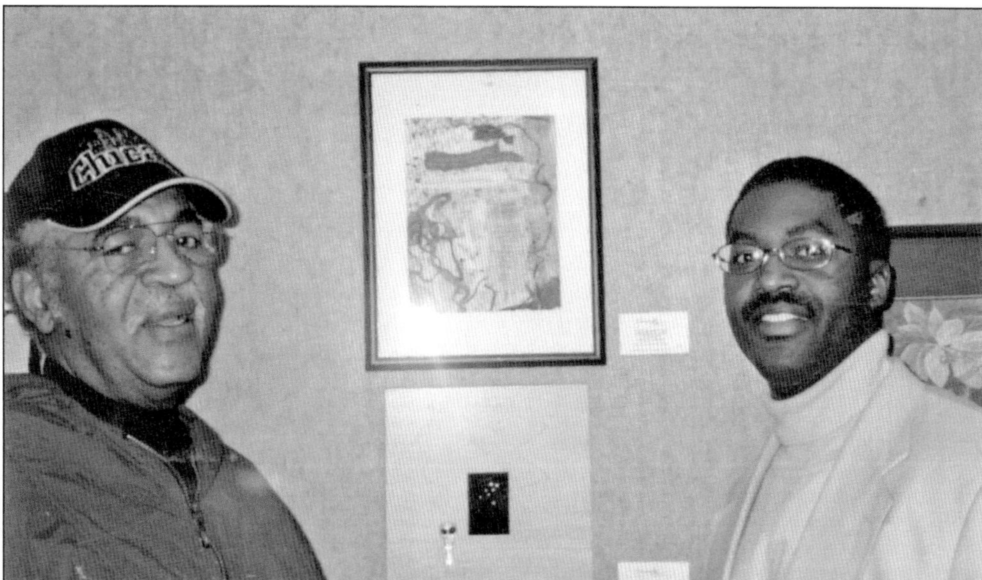

Harold Johns (left) and his son Reginald Johns stand by Reginald's drawing in the museum. Harold was one of the first Aberdeen Gardens Historic District members to serve on the Hampton Planning Commission and on the board of Hampton's District 10 commissioners that included Aberdeen Gardens neighborhoods. Reginald is an author, artist, and a teacher in the Hampton school system. The Johns family lives on Mary Peake Boulevard in the Aberdeen Gardens Historic District. (Courtesy of Harold Johns.)

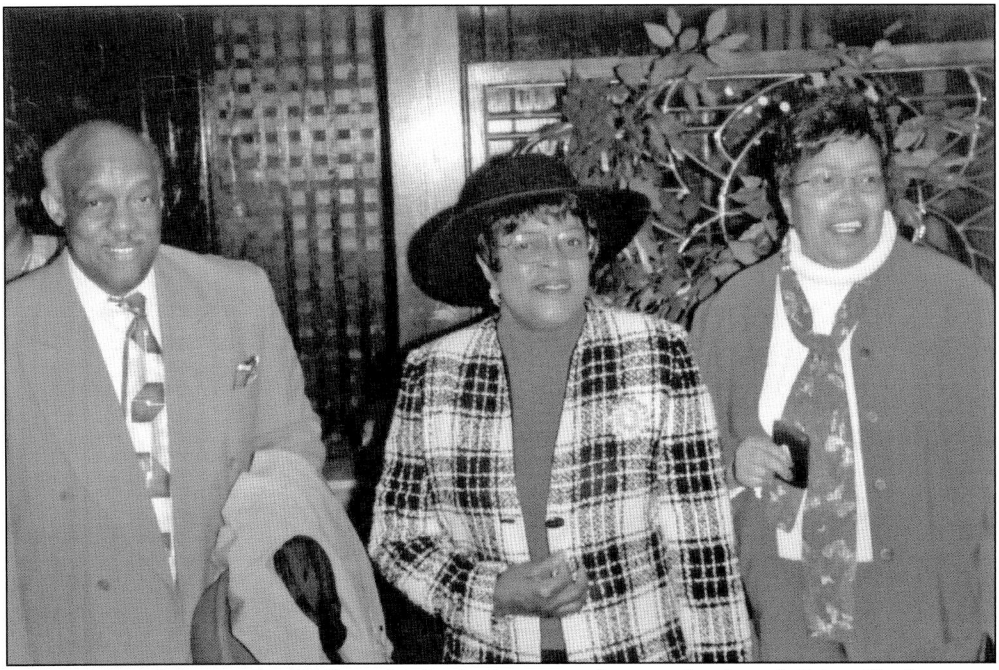

Pictured from left to right, William Taylor Jr.; his sister, Lois; and a friend, Sylvia Tonkins; are all Aberdeen Gardens Historic and Civic Association supporters. Lois and Sylvia lived in the Aberdeen Gardens Historic District. They all grew up and attended school together. (Courtesy of Aberdeen Gardens Historic and Civic Association, Inc.)

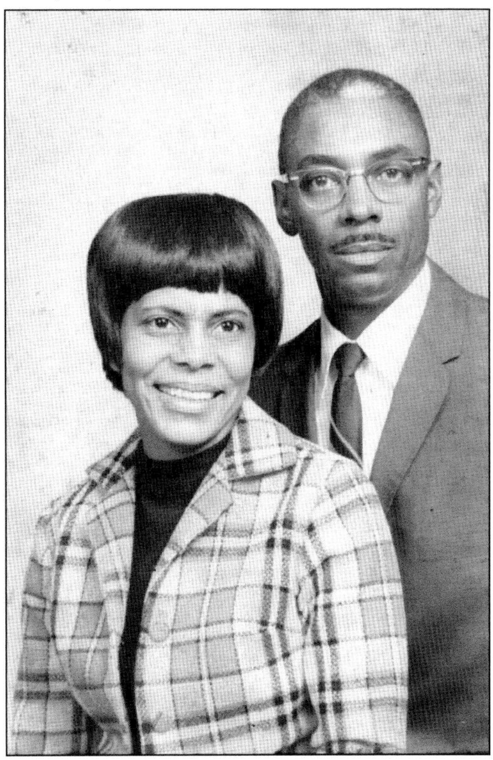

Charles and Annie Cook are faithful members and workers in the Aberdeen Gardens Historic and Civic Association. Annie, a librarian, is happiest amongst books and assisting children with reading. Charles was a mailman for 30 years. They reside on North Walker Road in North Aberdeen. Their daughters' names are Sharon and Silvia. (Courtesy of Charles and Annie Cook.)

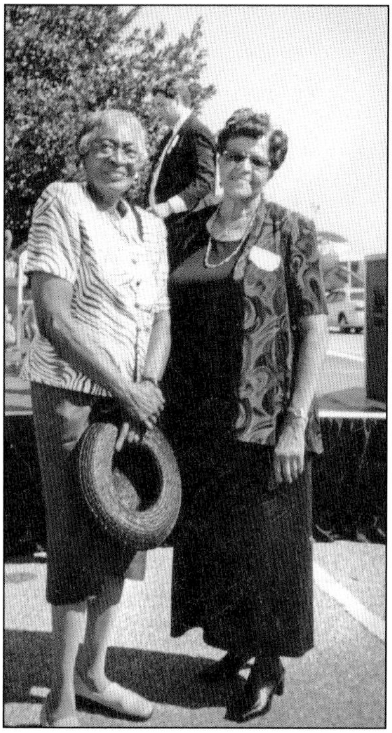

Myrtle Taylor (left) was a Yard of the Month recipient. Clara Sargent Challenger (right) had a brother, Ruppert Leon Sargent, whose name was etched on one of Hampton City's administration buildings on October 5, 2002. Sargent was the first African American officer to be awarded the nation's highest award for valor in combat: the Medal of Honor. Both ladies live in East Aberdeen, a partner neighborhood of Aberdeen Gardens Historic and Civic Association. (Courtesy of Catherine Howard.)

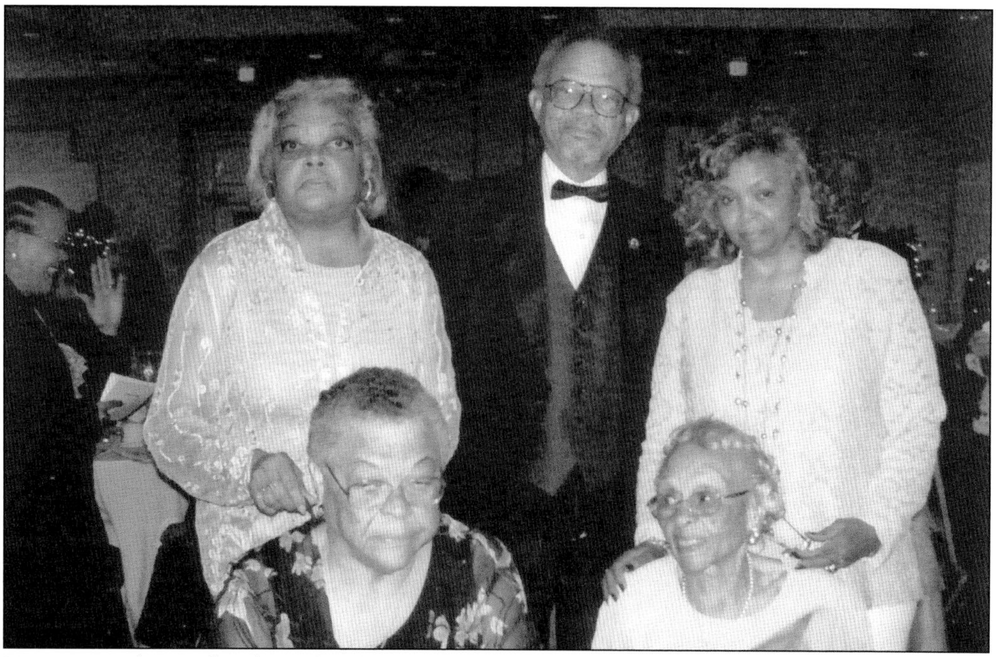

Margaret Colvert Allen (seated, right) received the Pioneer Award at the Historical Foundation of Aberdeen Gardens Gala 2007. Allen is the mother of Vice Mayor Charles C. Allen (standing, center) of Newport News. The Allen family lived on Langston Boulevard in the Aberdeen Gardens Historic District. Pictured with Allen are, from left to right, (standing) Lynn Allen, one of Margaret's daughters; Charles C. Allen; and Marion Christian; (seated) Beverly Henderson, also Margaret's daughter. (Courtesy of Catherine Howard.)

Celestine W. Carter and Antonio Hinton Sr. are NAACP Hampton Chapter presidents and Historic Foundation of Aberdeen Gardens Gala guests. They are supporters of the Aberdeen Gardens Association's activities. Carter lives on Mary Peake Boulevard in Granger Court, west of the Aberdeen Gardens Historic District. (Courtesy of Aberdeen Gardens Historic and Civic Association, Inc.)

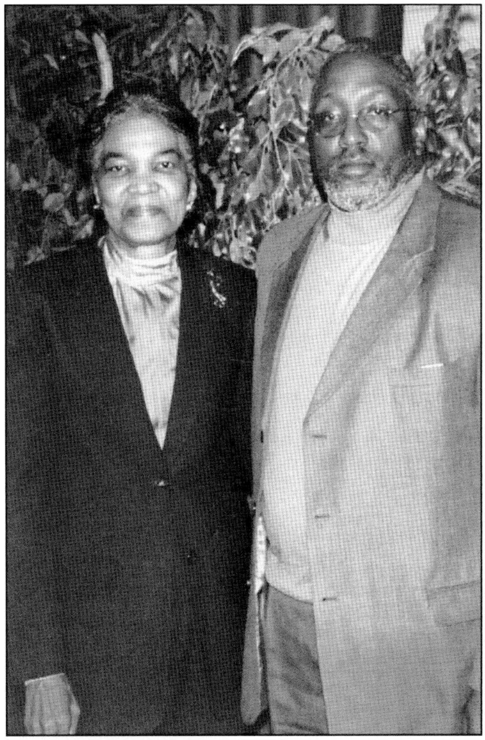

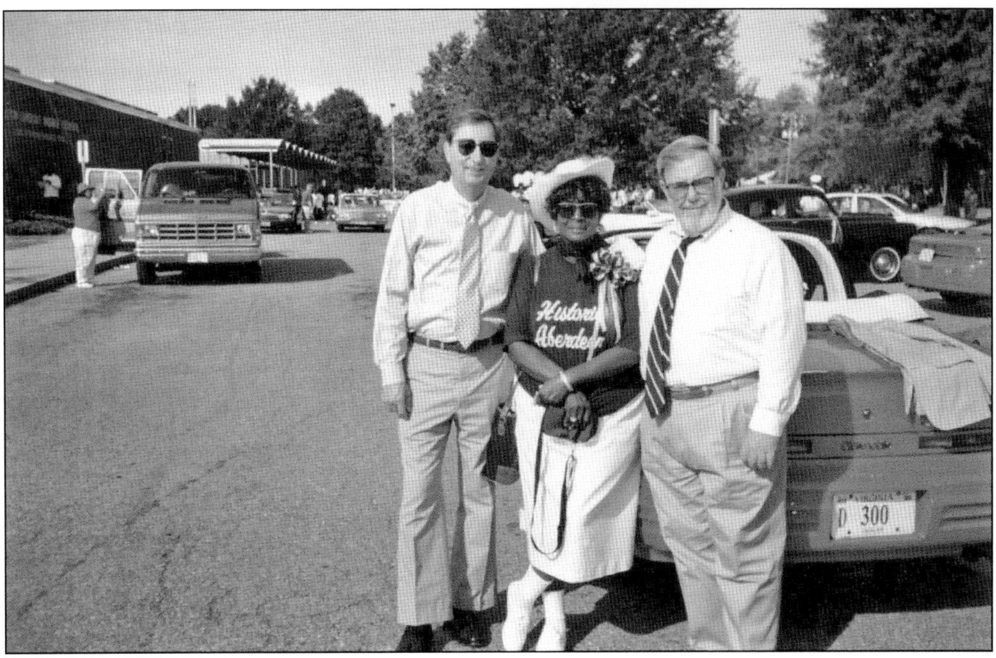

Pictured from left to right are Hampton city councilman Joseph H. Spencer, Evelyn Daniel Chandler, and Hampton mayor Ross A. Kearney II (mayor since 2004) at Aberdeen Elementary School after the Aberdeen Gardens Deen's Day parade. Hampton government officials support Aberdeen Gardens in its endeavors. Chandler was raised in the Aberdeen Gardens Historic District on Langston Boulevard. (Courtesy of Aberdeen Gardens Historic and Civic Association, Inc.)

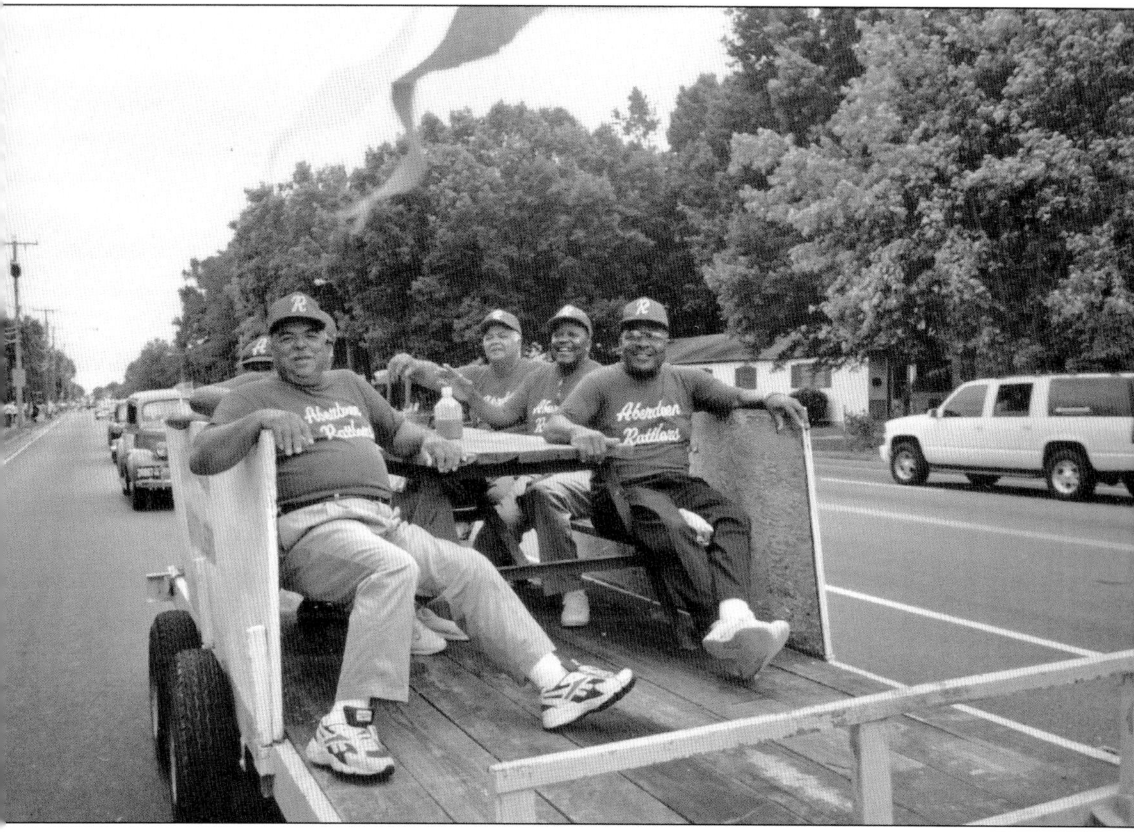

Andre McCoy Vann Sr. (left in truck) was among the first residents of Aberdeen Gardens. As a child, he, his brothers, and his sister were tasked by his parents with gardening and raising chickens. He moved from the family home on Langston Boulevard to East Davis Road in the Aberdeen Gardens Historic District, thus putting him among a few residents that has lived, married (Bernadine Brown Vann), raised children (Andre Jr., John, and Terry), and remained residents in Aberdeen to the present. He retired from the Newport News Shipbuilding and Dry Dock Company after 37 years. Service to the community is done in his leisure time by busily assisting with the Aberdeen Gardens Historic Museum and grounds maintenance projects, transporting the elderly, gathering support for worthy causes, and helping the Aberdeen Rattlers deliver seasonal baskets to the team's widows. Andre Vann Sr. was awarded the Historic Recognition Award from the Aberdeen Gardens Historic and Civic Association in February 2006. Claude Vann Jr., Roland A. Gatling, and Walter P. Jackson are seated on the right side of the table in the truck. The two men seated behind Andre Vann Sr. are unidentified. (Courtesy of Aberdeen Gardens Historic and Civic Association, Inc.)

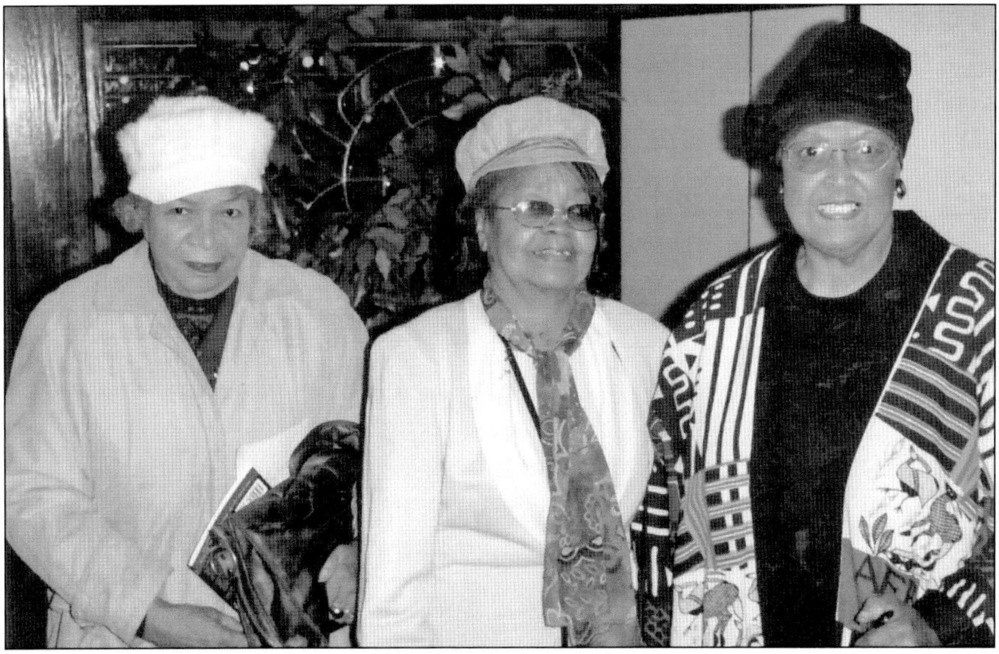

Pictured from left to right are Irene McCadden Brooks, Novella Green, and Mary Holloman Kelly attending the Aberdeen Gardens Historic and Civic Association Black History Program in 2006. They are supporters of the Aberdeen Gardens Historic and Civic Association. (Courtesy of Aberdeen Gardens Historic and Civic Association, Inc.)

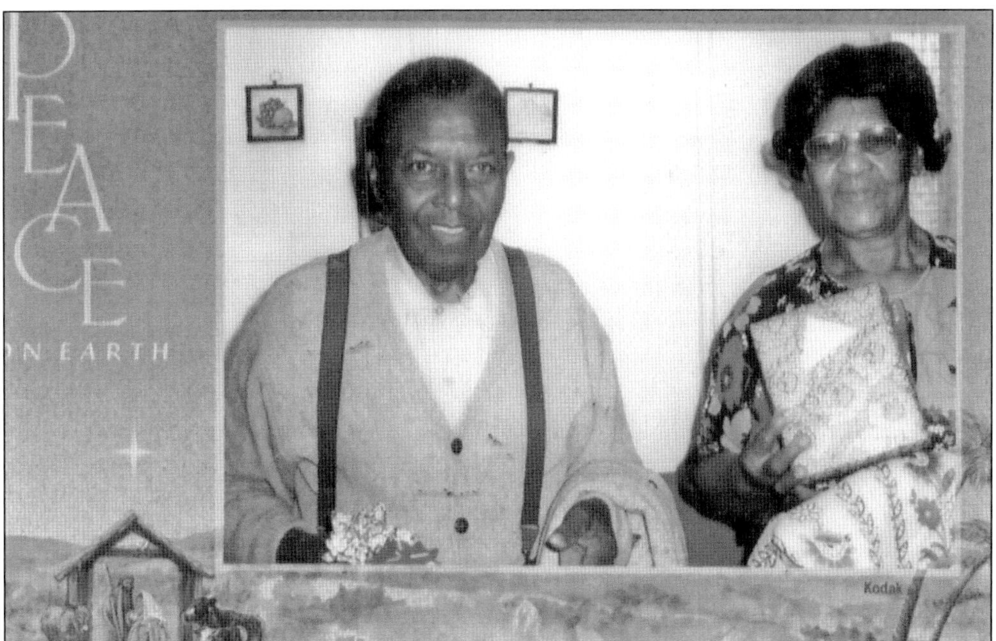

Joseph and Sarah Moore lived on East David Road in the Aberdeen Gardens Historic District. Joseph was a Newport News Building Shipbuilding and Dry Dock worker, and Sarah was a stay-at-home mom who took care of their only daughter, Louise. Alfreda M. Ward, their granddaughter, presently lives in the family home. (Courtesy of Alfreda M. Ward.)

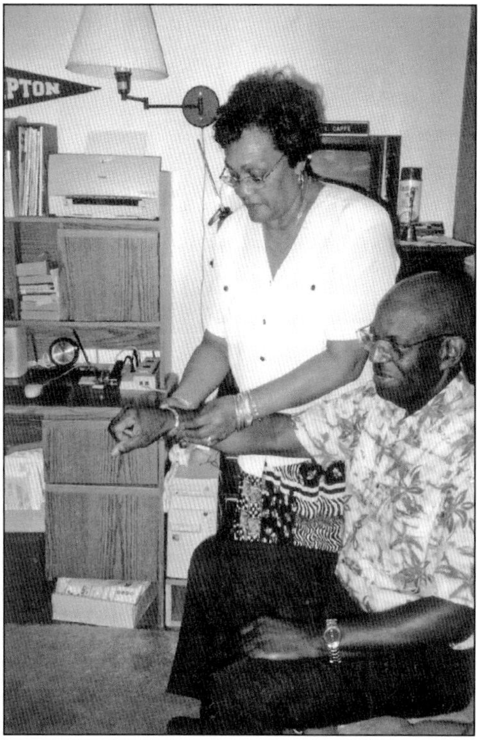

Frank Cappe receives a watch from his wife, Luvenia, on his 70th birthday. He was the chairman of the wetlands committee of the Aberdeen Gardens Historic and Civic Association. He lived on Micott Drive of Granger Court East. (Courtesy of Aberdeen Gardens Historic and Civic Association, Inc.)

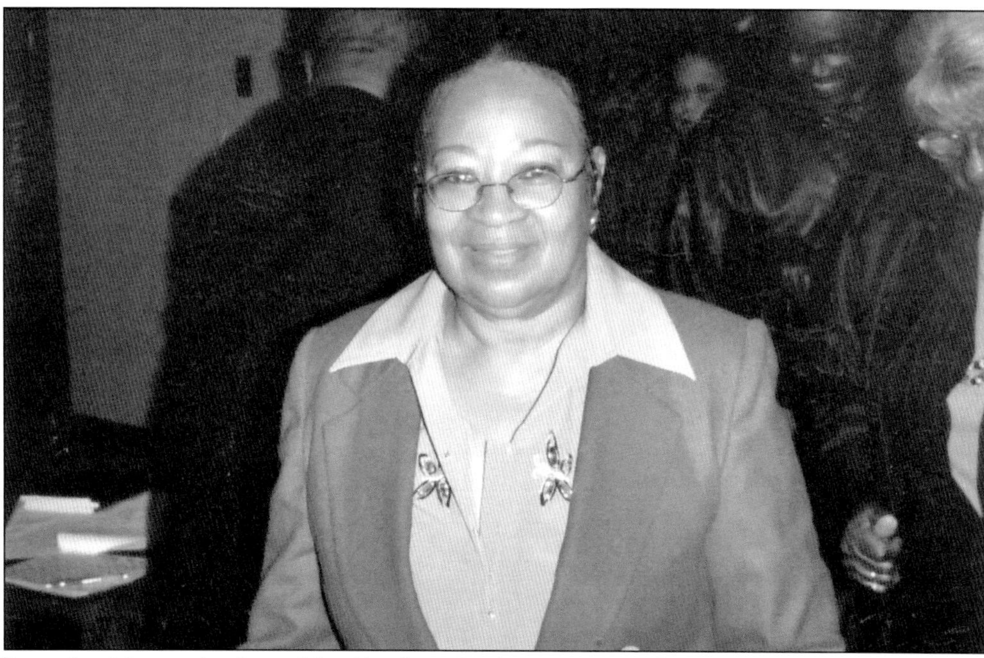

Bernadine Vann is the chair of the Aberdeen Gardens Historic and Civic Association Beautification Committee. Her original committee members were Lenrow Milo Jr., Cora Johnson, Earline William, Adell Morgan, Anna Jones, and Lillian Gist. The committee selected the most beautiful yard of the month by awarding a decorated yard plaque. At Christmastime, a certificate is given to the most decorated yard. (Courtesy of Aberdeen Gardens Historic and Civic Association, Inc.)

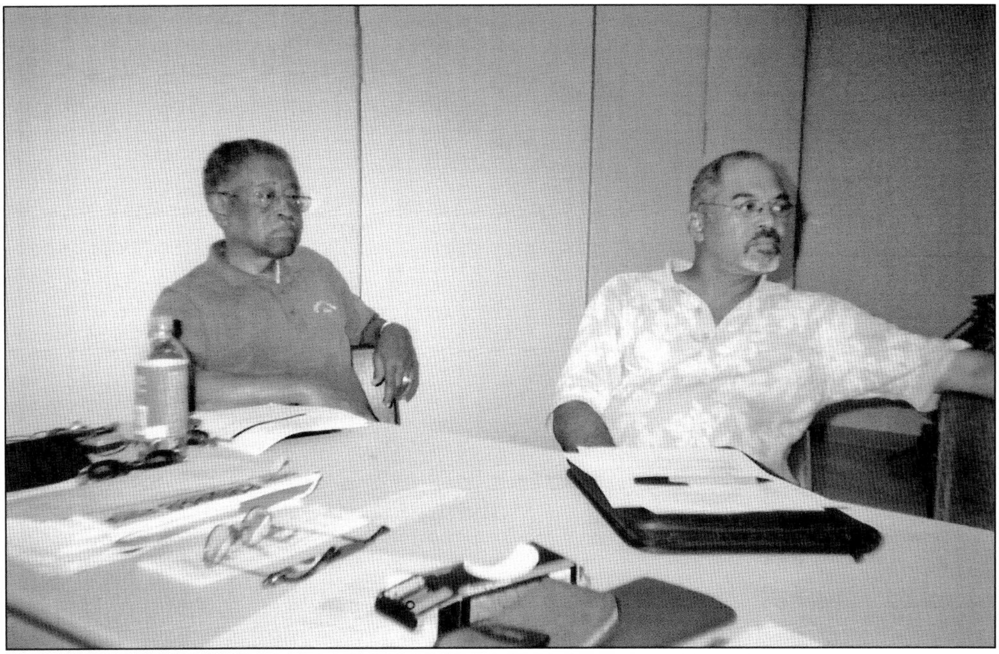

Robert Ayers (left) and Troy Smith Jr. attend the first organized golf challenge meeting sponsored by the Historic Foundation of Aberdeen Gardens. These golfers decided the who, what, when, why, and where. As a result, the golf challenge has been successful for two years. (Courtesy of Aberdeen Gardens Historic and Civic Association, Inc.)

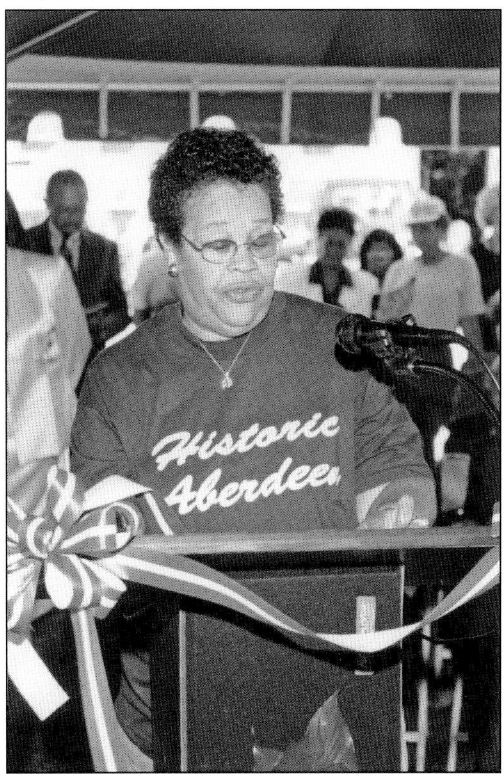

Joyce Wilkins grew up in the Aberdeen Gardens Historic District and truly supports the Aberdeen Gardens Historic and Civic Association in its endeavors. She composed a poem titled "Aberdeen Kids." It starts, "When we were kids in Aberdeen," and 45 lines down ends, "Yes, it still takes a whole village to raise a child!" (Courtesy of Aberdeen Gardens Historic and Civic Association, Inc.)

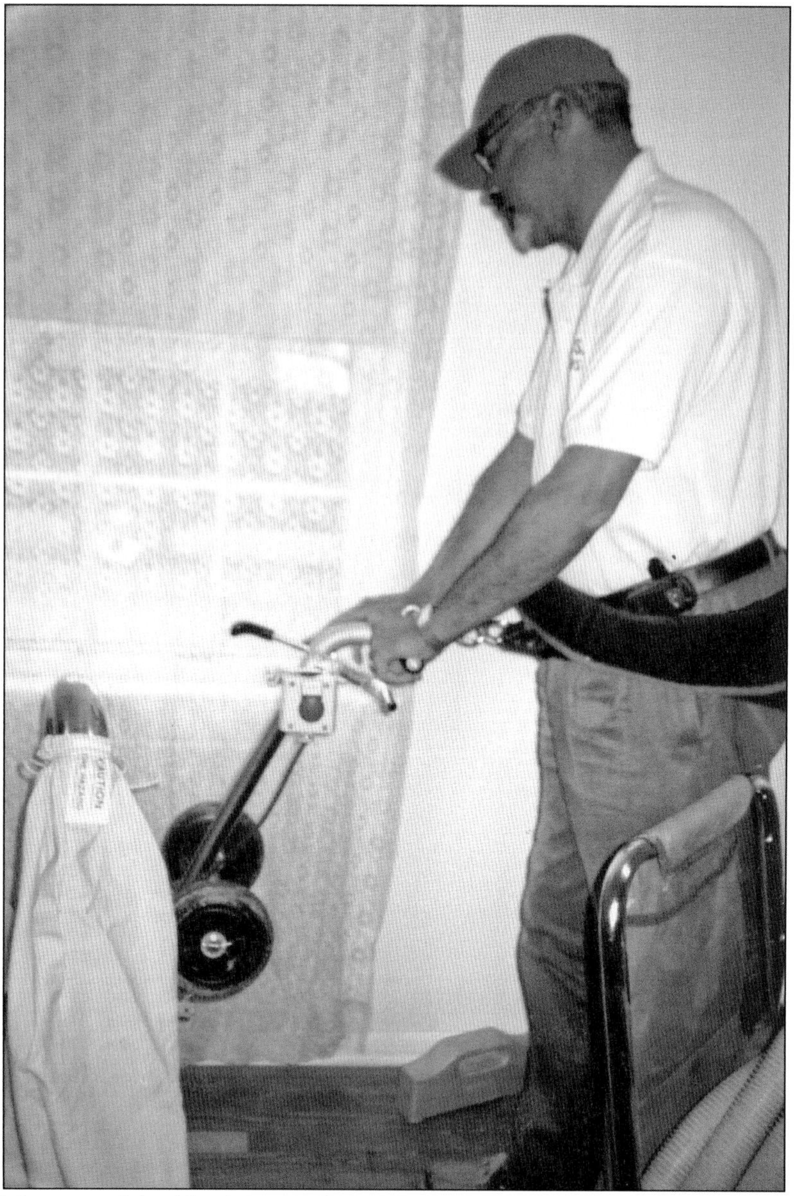

Troy Smith Jr. received the Aberdeen Gardens Historic and Civic Association Special Recognition Award in 2007. He works in the family-owned business, Smith Brothers Enterprises, which specializes in the installation and finishing of new wood floors, as well as refinishing old floors. He assumed daily management of Smith Brothers Enterprises in 1980, and under his guidance, the business remains a well-known and thriving black business celebrating 61 years of service to the Peninsula and Tidewater area. Troy Jr. is married to Treganza Wiggins-Smith and has five children: Troy III, Loren, L'Allegro, Helena, and Autumn. He is active as a board member of the Historical Foundation of Aberdeen Gardens; vice and former president of Friends of the Homeless, Inc.; commissioner of the Virginia Board of Contractors (appointed by former governor Mark Warner); and a member and former board member of the Peninsula Home Builders Association and Peninsula Remodelers Council. He is shown using the skills of his trade. (Courtesy of Aberdeen Gardens Historic and Civic Association, Inc.)

Lt. Col. Jesse J. Johnson (in wheelchair) was a multilingual individual and a distinguished author. He wrote eight books about black men and women in the military. He donated many of his books to universities, colleges, organization, and libraries. Lieutenant Colonel Johnson (retired) was the recipient of the Aberdeen Gardens Historic and Civic Association Historical Recognition Award in 2004. (Courtesy of Aberdeen Gardens Historic and Civic Association, Inc.)

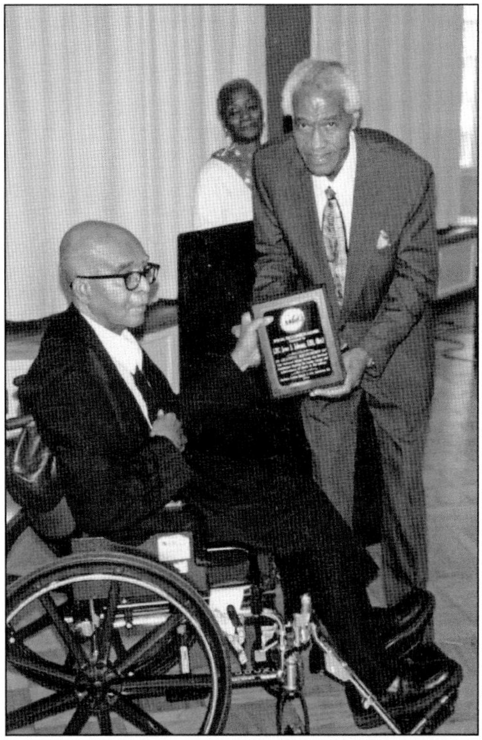

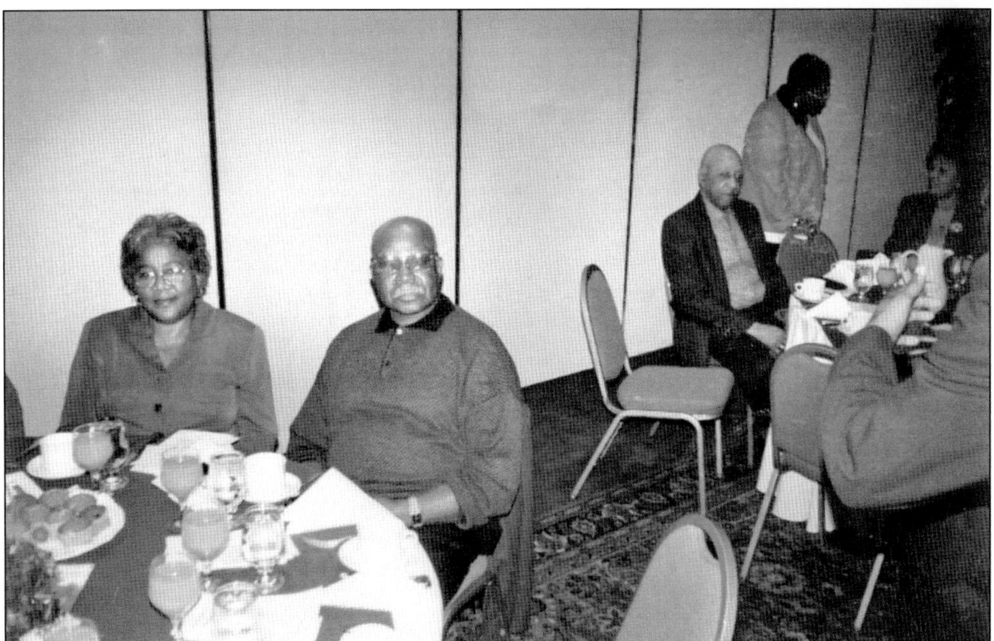

Arthur McRae and his wife, Dorothy, attend the Aberdeen Gardens Historic and Civic Association Black History Program. Arthur received the Historical Recognition Award in 2003. He is a member of the Aberdeen Gardens Historic and Civic Association Wetland Committee. He lives in Briarwood Terrace, a partner neighborhood with the association. (Courtesy of Aberdeen Gardens Historic and Civic Association, Inc.)

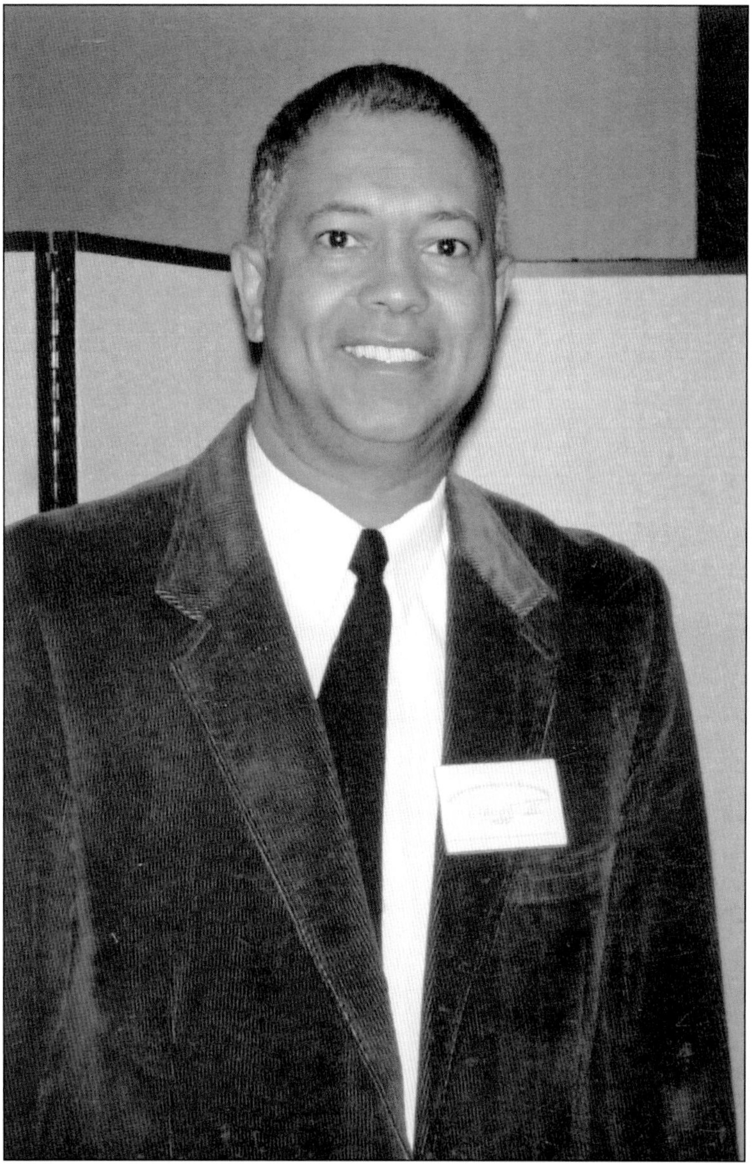

Claude Vann III is a second-generation Aberdeener. Lieutenant Colonel Vann was recognized by Hampton University president William R. Harvey as an outstanding Alumnus at Large. Harvey said, "He [Vann] was recognized for his involvement in the community as well as his continued support toward the university. Lt. Colonel Vann is the president of the Hampton University Military Alumni Association. While serving on the board of directors for the Hampton Roads Chapter of the American Red Cross, he has worked to improve support resources to assist residents of Hampton, Newport News, and Isle of Wight County." Lieutenant Colonel Vann is supportive of his father's and grandparents' Aberdeen Gardens Historic District neighborhood. He is attentive to activities of the Aberdeen Gardens Historic and Civic Association, as well as the Historic Foundation of Aberdeen Gardens. He truly takes time out of his busy schedule to lead a hand in whatever the need maybe. He introduced the guest speaker, Brig. Gen. Bettye H. Simmons (U.S. Army retired), for the 2004 Black History Program. (Courtesy of Aberdeen Gardens Historic and Civic Association, Inc.)

Rodney Ballard Jr., a Norfolk State University student, was awarded the Aberdeen Gardens Historic and Civic Association Youth Leadership Award in 2001. He had been active in the Aberdeen Gardens Historic and Civic Association for three years, participating in needs assessment to help bring about the West Hampton Community Center, which is being built in the Neighborhood District 10 area of Hampton. (Courtesy of Aberdeen Gardens Historic and Civic Association, Inc.)

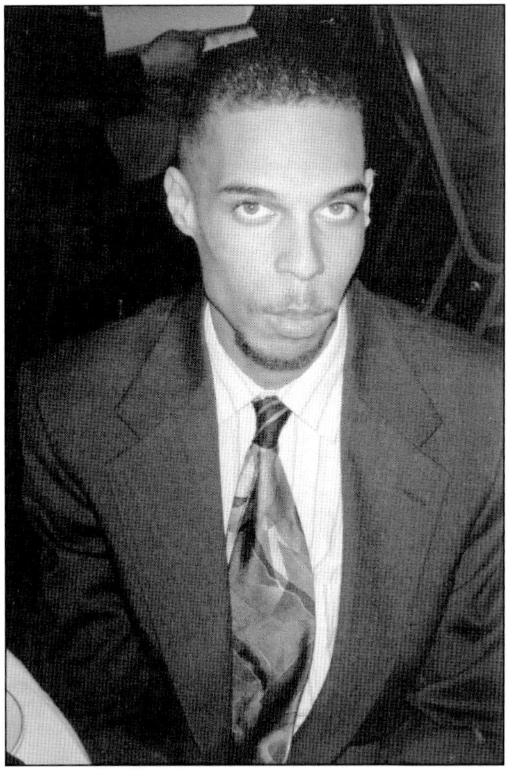

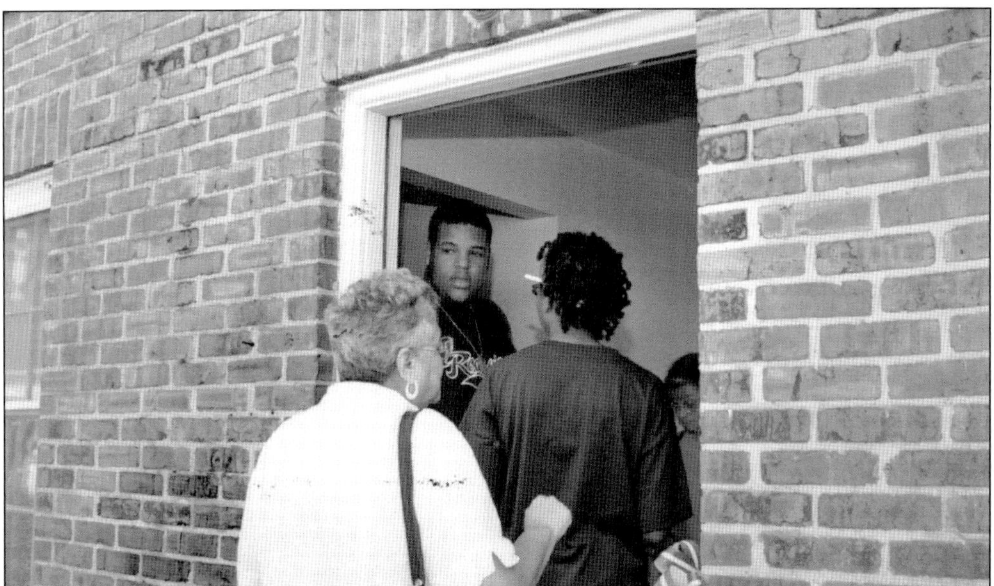

Gaselle H. Saleem (standing in back) received the Youth Leadership Award in 2003. In this image, he is one of the youth docents. Youth docents guided guests through the Historic Aberdeen Gardens Museum on Dedication Day 2002. He resides on West Queen Street east of Aberdeen Gardens Historic District. Gaselle has been very active in Youth Alternatives. (Courtesy of Aberdeen Gardens Historic and Civic Association, Inc.)

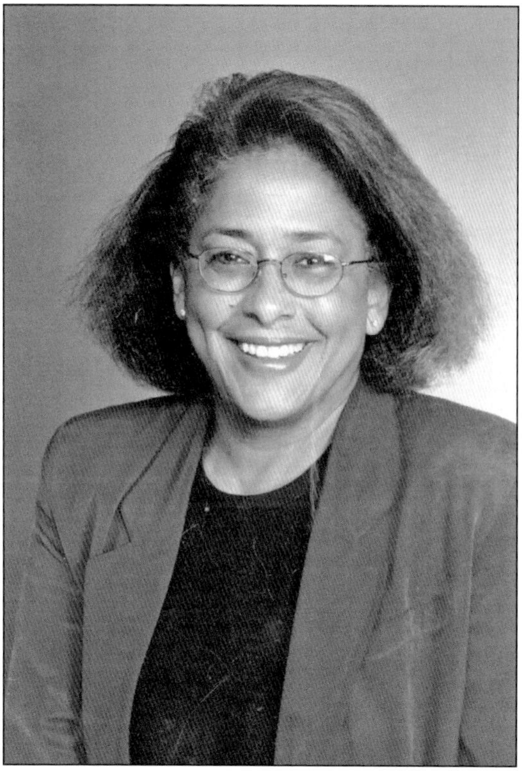

Brig. Gen. Bettye H. Simmons (U.S. Army retired) directs the Leadership Institute at Hampton University and was the Aberdeen Gardens Historic and Civic Association guest speaker at the 2004 Black History Program. She is actively involved in community-based organizations and serves on the board of directors of the Hampton Roads Chapter of the American Red Cross. (Courtesy of Aberdeen Gardens Historic and Civic Association, Inc.)

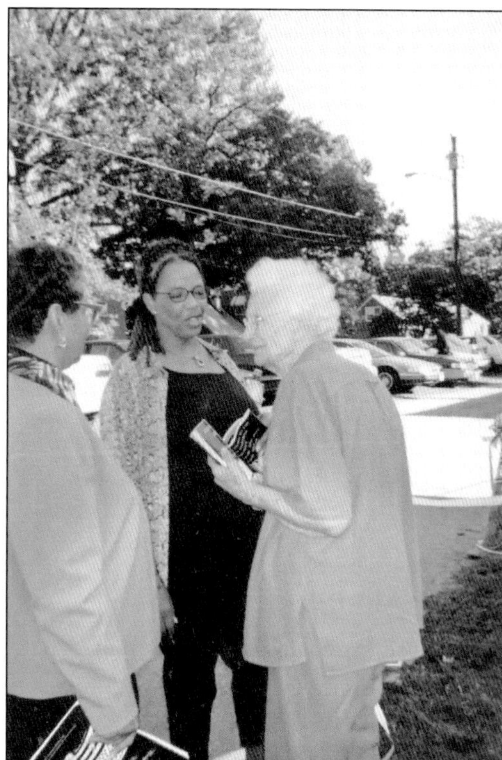

Brenda Frazier (center) speaks with Beulah Hunter (right) and Eunice Peele (left). Frazier is a second-generation Aberdeener. The Heritage Day celebration brings out residents of the Aberdeen Gardens Historic District. Frazier lived on West Walker Road in Aberdeen Gardens Historic District. (Courtesy of Aberdeen Gardens Historic and Civic Association, Inc.)

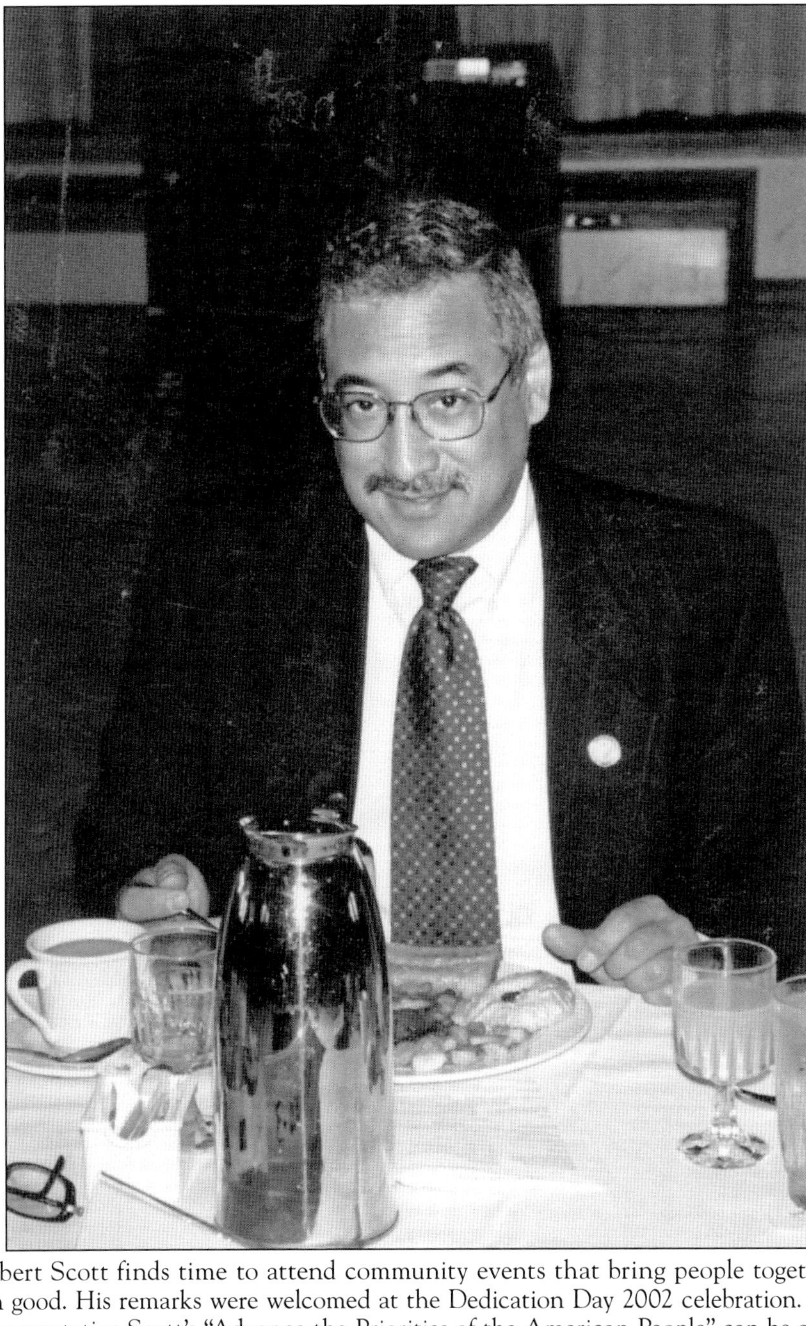

Rep. Robert Scott finds time to attend community events that bring people together for a common good. His remarks were welcomed at the Dedication Day 2002 celebration. Excerpts from Representative Scott's "Advance the Priorities of the American People" can be a message to a neighborhood's awareness priorities as well: "Children's Health: Provide every child in the United Stated with health insurance. Education: Ensure no child is left behind. Veterans: Honor them by increasing funding for health care and benefits. Justice: Make local communities more secure by funding juvenile justice, gang prevention, prisoner re-entry and local law enforcement programs and ensure that every voice counts. Communities: provide our communities with support: Diplomacy: contribute to the global community by investing in child survival and health." (Courtesy of Aberdeen Gardens Historic and Civic Association, Inc.)

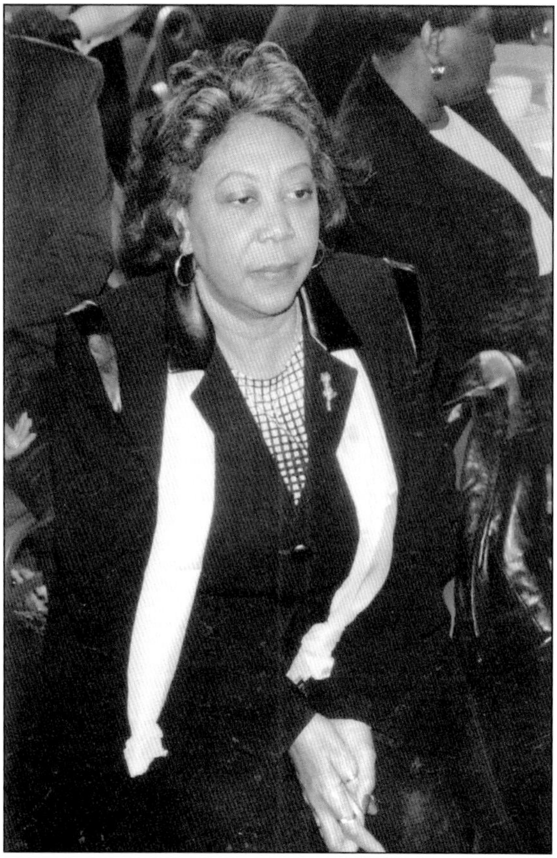

Doris Dancey was a resident of Granger Court, south of the Aberdeen Gardens Historic District. The Praise Dancers of St. Paul AME Church were organized in 2000. The dance movement's purpose was to instill ladylike qualities; thus, the attire for young girls consisted of long white shirts, white tights/leotards, white gloves, and blue shoulder sashes with St. Paul's Praise Dancers (SPPD) on it. The dancers are from 7 to 18 years of age. (Courtesy of Aberdeen Gardens Historic and Civic Association, Inc.)

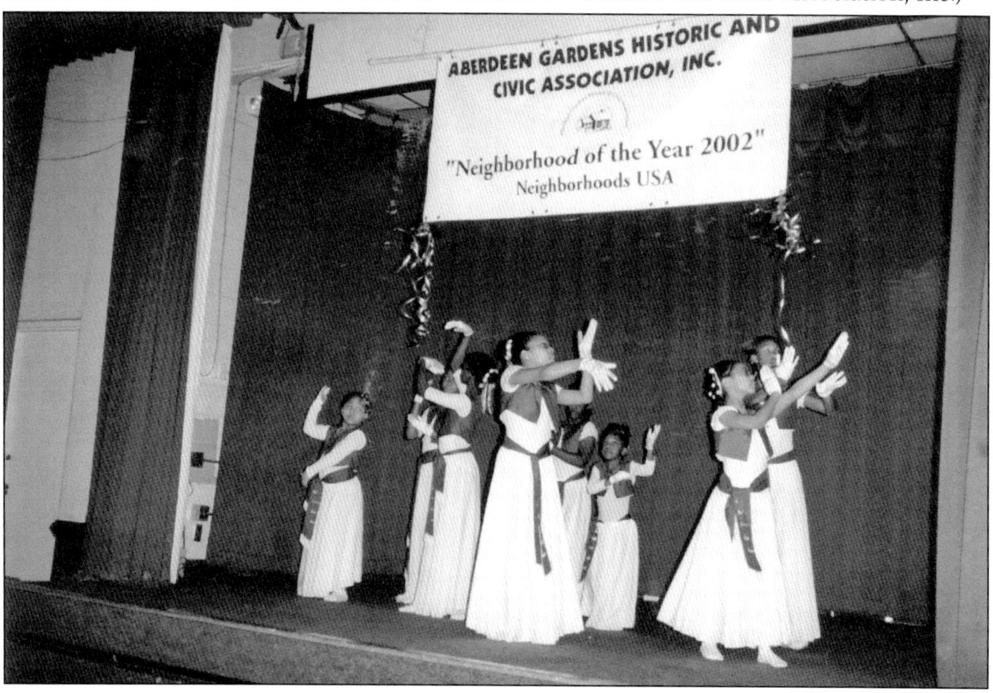

Hampton NAACP president Carmen Taylor supports community endeavors. Many Aberdeen Gardens Historic District residents are members of the NAACP. One of the NAACP socials encourages the Aberdeen Gardens Historic District to maintain the values set forth by the organization or community's elders. (Courtesy of Aberdeen Gardens Historic and Civic Association, Inc.)

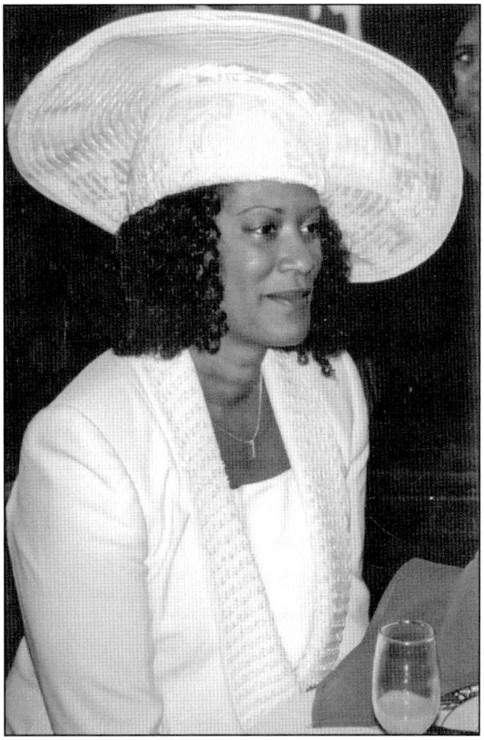

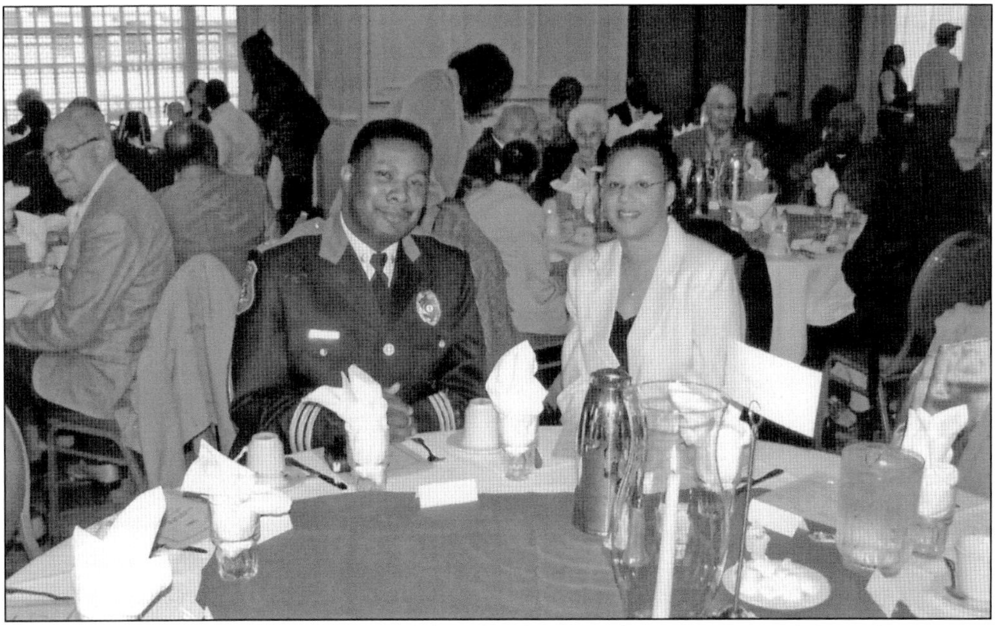

Maj. Ronald and Helen Davis attended the Aberdeen Gardens Historic and Civic Association Black History Program. Ronald is a member of the Aberdeen Gardens Historic and Civic Association and the heritage committee. Major Davis, a member of Hampton Virginia Police Department since January 1977, became the police department operations officer in December 2005. He donated items for the winners of the 2005 Student Essay Contest and the first annual Heritage Day celebration in June 2005. (Courtesy of Catherine Howard.)

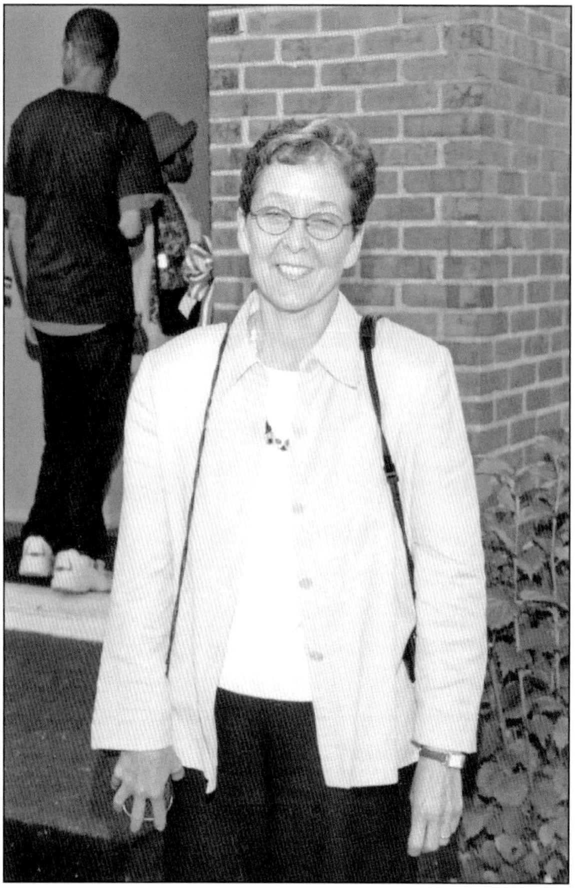

Kathleen Kilpatrick (below, seated third from right in first row) was grand marshal at the 2002 Deen's Day parade, and Ann Andrus (left) was very significant in the distribution of the $100,000 grant for the Aberdeen Gardens Historic Museum. Kilpatrick and Andrus were very important in obtaining preservation assistance for Aberdeen Gardens. They attended this 2002 dedication to view the results of all of the work it took to achieve such a massive job and overcome challenges. The Aberdeen Gardens Historic and Civic Association matched the grant. (Courtesy of Aberdeen Gardens Historic and Civic Association, Inc.)

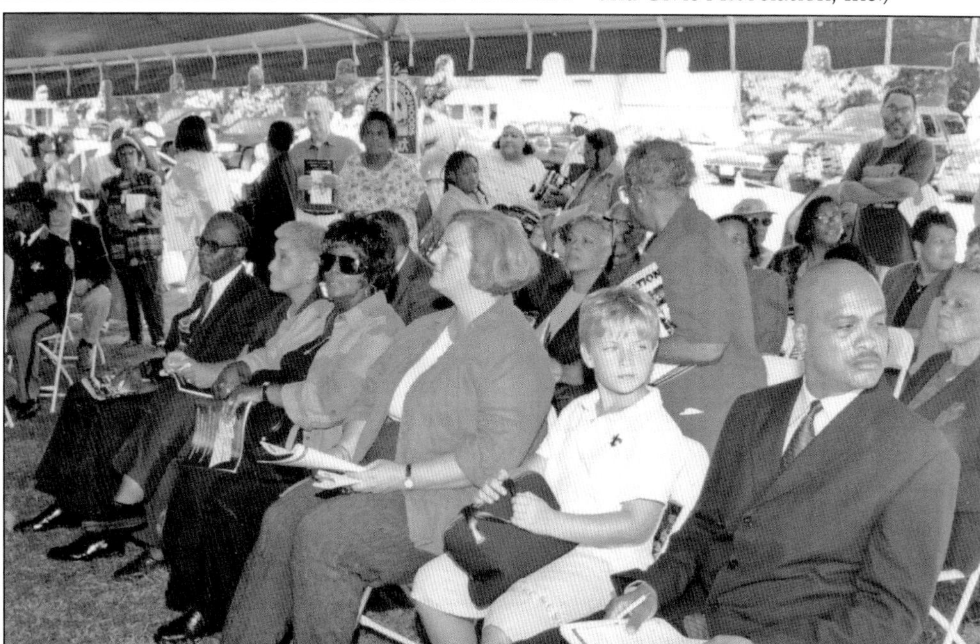

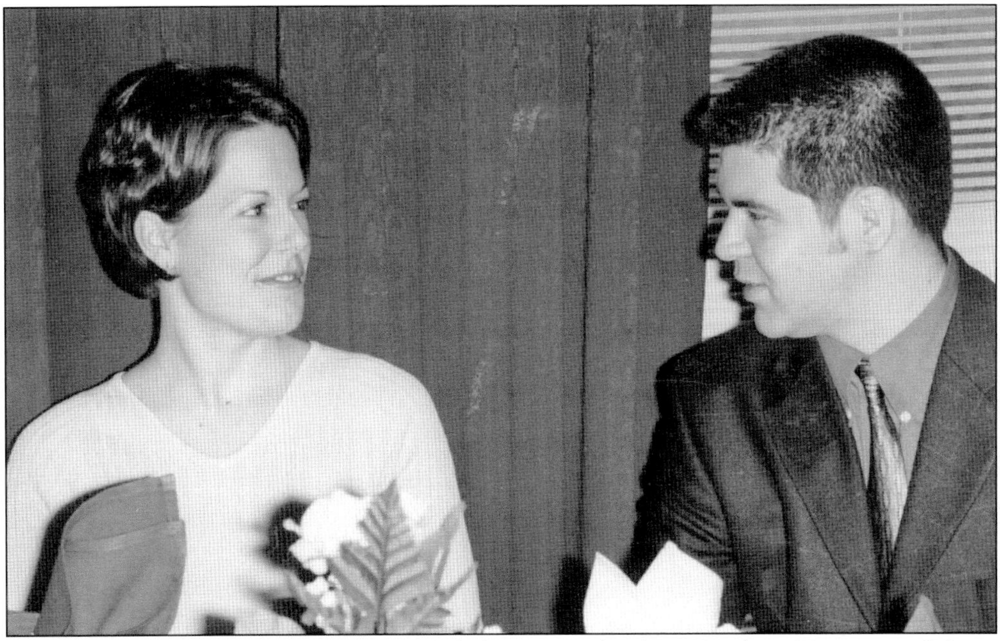

Mr. and Mrs. Jonathan McBride attended the 2006 Aberdeen Gardens Historic and Civic Association Black History Program. Jonathan McBride was in Youth Alternatives prior to accepting a position at the neighborhood office as District 10 facilitator for 2008. He was a member of the Aberdeen Gardens Historic and Civic Association and bridged gaps between the elderly and the youth. (Courtesy of Catherine Howard.)

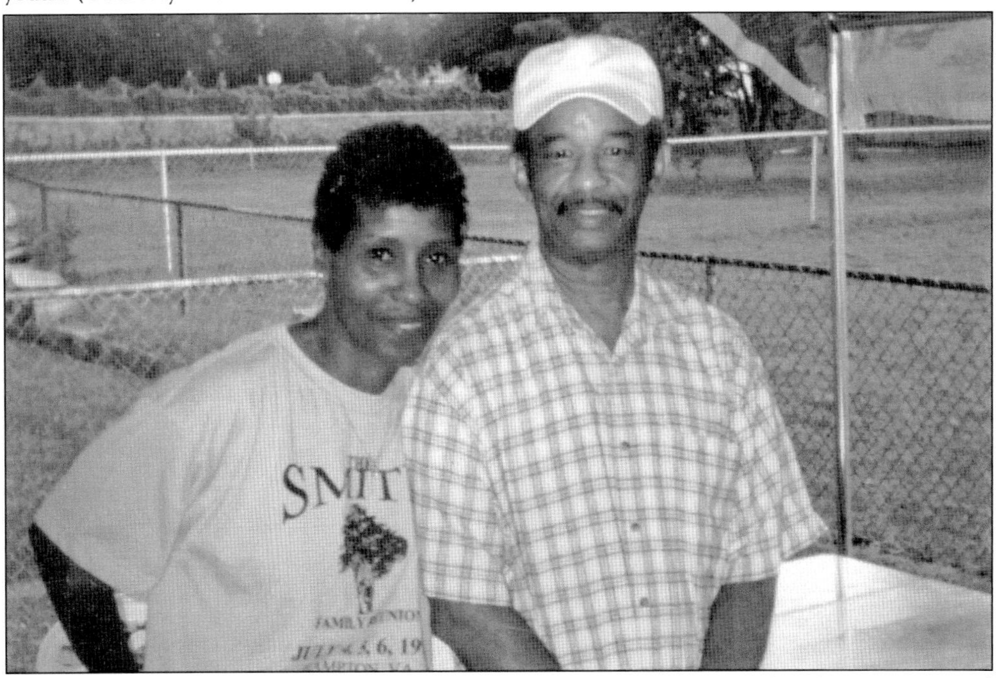

Milton and Ruth Anthony live in Granger Court East on East Davis Road. Milton was a retired postman in Hampton. His assignment was not routinely Aberdeen. He enjoys working in his yard and flowerbeds. (Courtesy of Milton Anthony.)

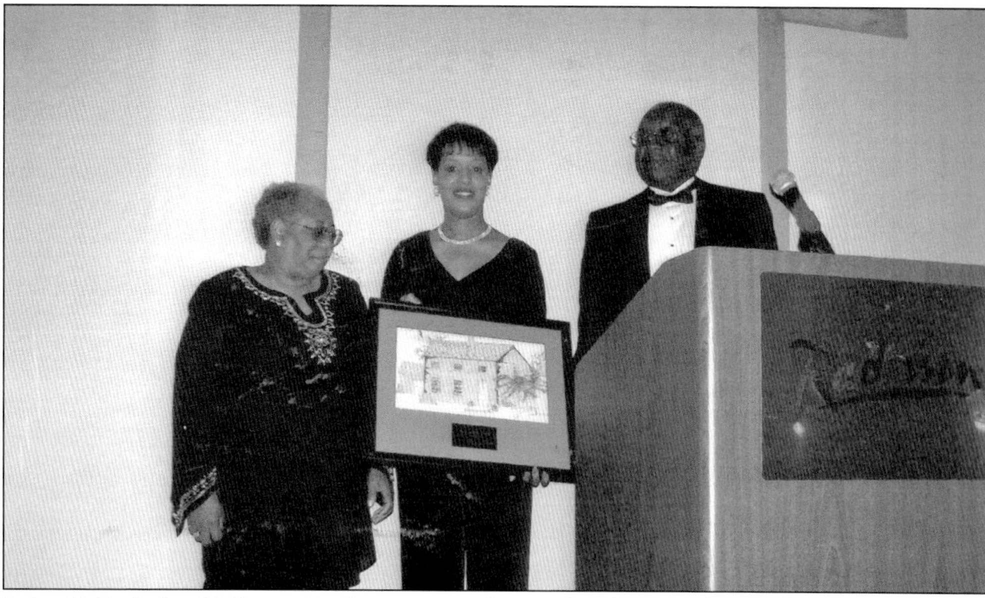

Judge Belinda Joy Hill was the keynote speaker at the Historical Foundation of Aberdeen Gardens' First Annual Harvest Fest Gala in 2006. Judge Hill spoke at National College of District Attorneys–sponsored criminal prosecution courses throughout the country. In 1997, Gov. George W. Bush appointed her to the 230th District Court of Harris County, Texas. Judge Hill was selected as one of Houston's 1997 Women on the Move and a 1999 Houston Newspages Woman of Distinction. In 2002, she received Judge of the Year Awards from the Texas Gang Investigators Association and the Criminal Justice Section of the State Bar of Texas. (Courtesy of Catherine Howard.)

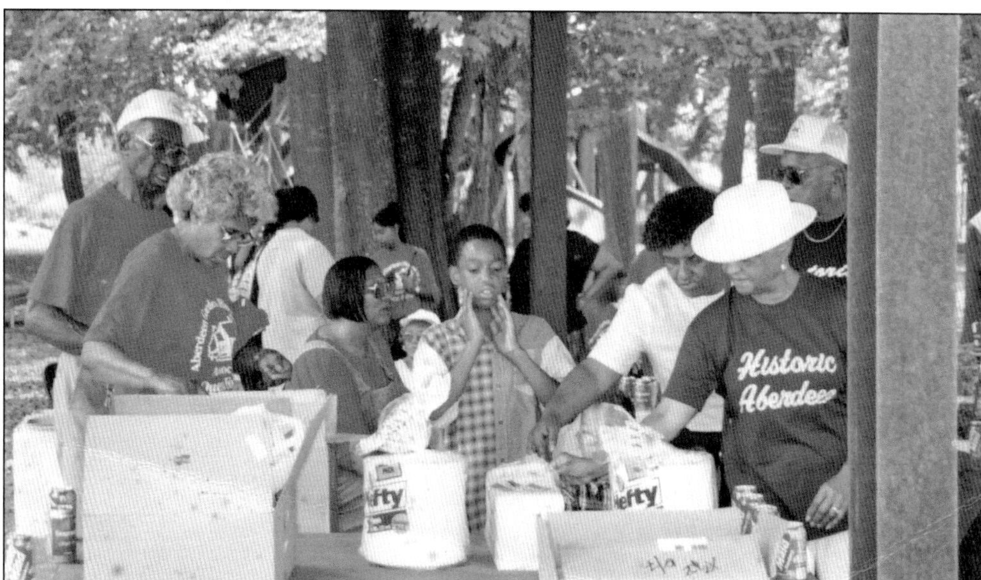

John Henry and Hester Mae Epps were residents of Langston Boulevard in the Aberdeen Gardens Historic District. Their sons are residents of the family home. John was the local car mechanic. If anyone had a problem, he could more than likely help. (Courtesy of Aberdeen Gardens Historic and Civic Association, Inc.)

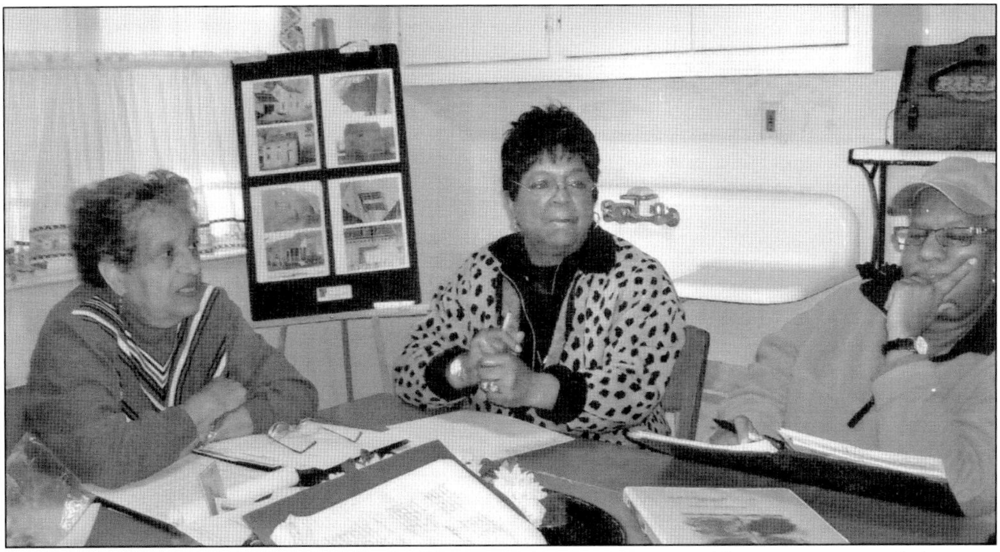

Lillian Lovett (left), director of the Newsome House in Newport News, gave a workshop on caring for a museum. She was invited because the Newsome House is similar in purpose to the Aberdeen Gardens Historic Museum. It is the hub of the local black community and is listed on the Virginia Landmarks Register and the National Register of Historic Places; the house museum focuses on black cultural and historical themes. Also pictured are Dorothy Milo Smith (center) and Clarice Hughes (right). (Courtesy of Catherine Howard.)

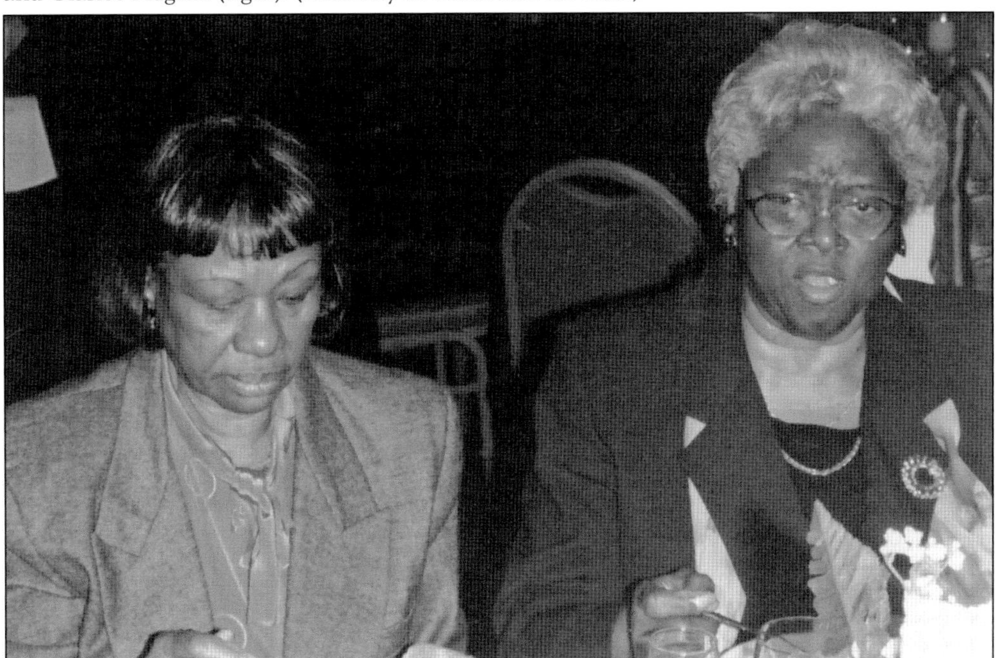

Vertie Porter (left) lives on Ethel Drive in Briarwood Terrace, a partner neighborhood to the Aberdeen Gardens Historic and Civic Association. Porter and Annie Thomas (right) are nurses. They are at the 2003 Aberdeen Gardens Historic and Civic Association Black History Program, where three nurses received Special Recognition Awards for their courage in the advancement of civil rights. (Courtesy of Catherine Howard.)

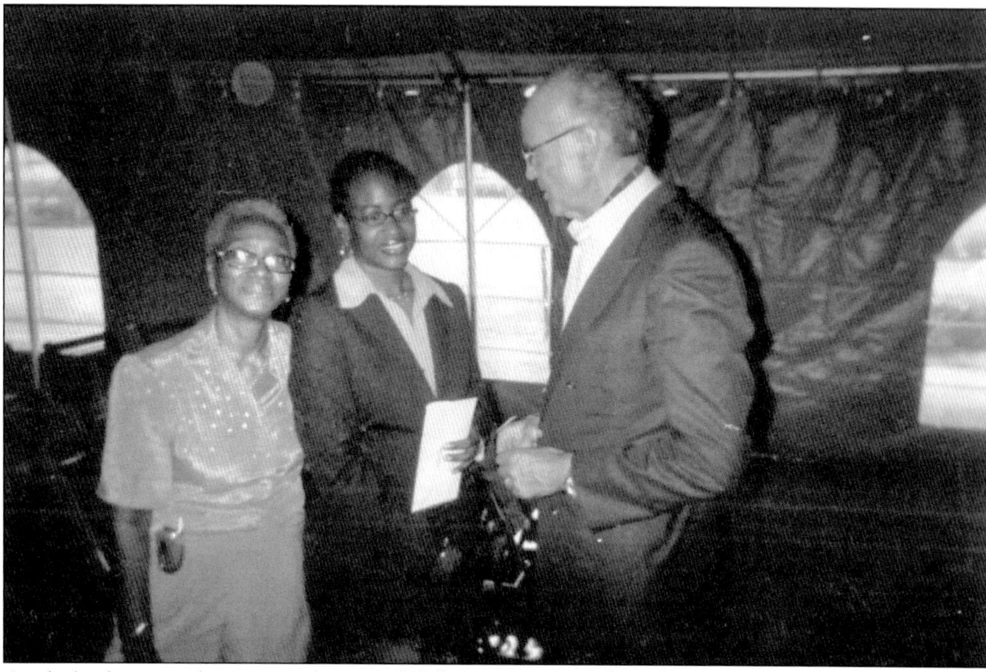

A scholarship award is given in honor of William Roscoe Walker, the resident manager of Aberdeen Gardens in 1936, and his wife, Jean, a community activist. From left to right are Catherine Howard, Jametta Davis, and William Walker. Davis was a recipient of William and Jean Walker Scholarship. Her research was on the development of the New Deal resettlement community of Aberdeen Gardens. (Courtesy of Aberdeen Gardens Historic and Civic Association, Inc.)

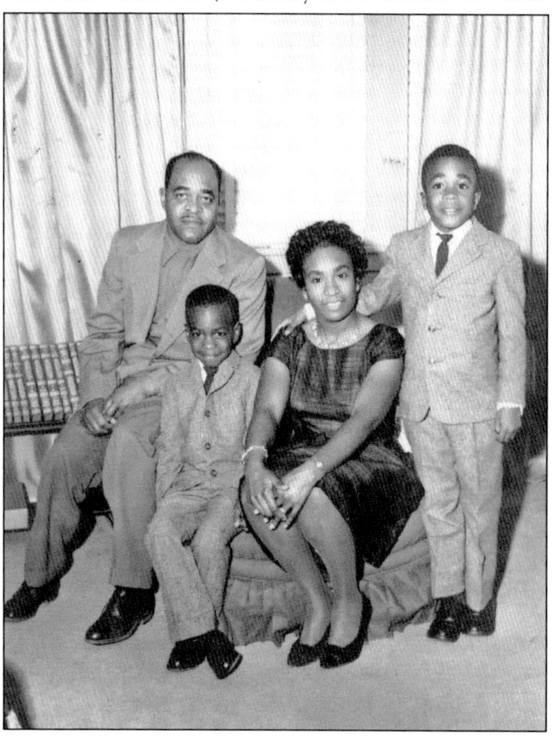

Edward and Almeda McDonald and their family first lived in an Aberdeen Gardens Historic District home on West Lewis Road. Edward McDonald is a retired instructor from the Deaf and Blind Virginia State School. Almeda McDonald is a retired Hampton schoolteacher. (Courtesy of Almeda McDonald.)

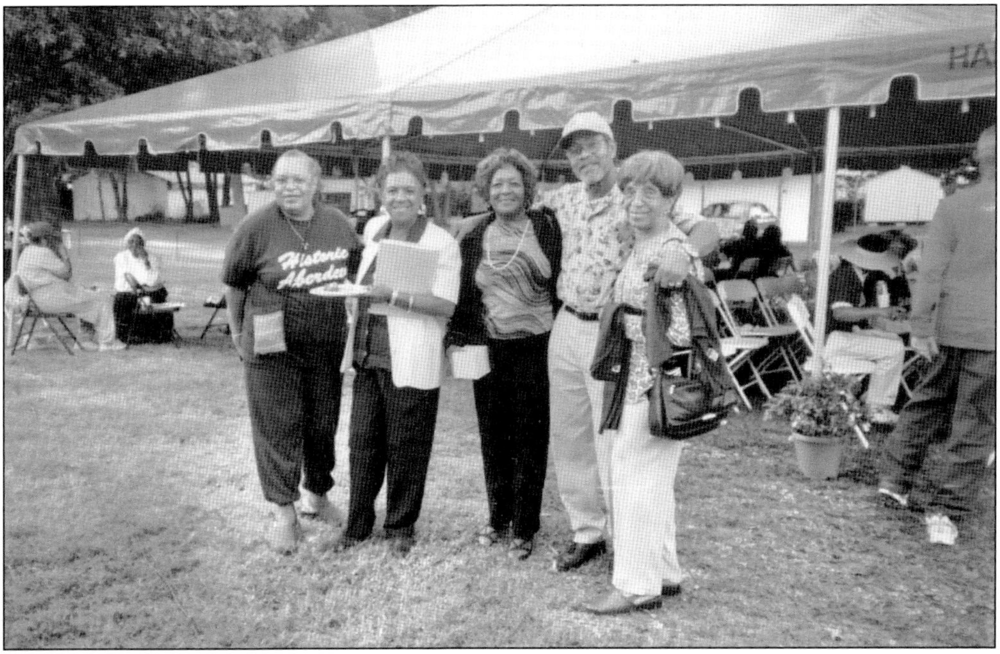

Pictured from left to right are Ellen Clark Jenkins, Dorothy Milo Smith, Dorothy Washington White, Tommy Brown, and Bernice Brown (Tommy's wife). These ladies enjoyed reuniting and talking about old times at the Heritage Day 2005 celebration. They were buddies growing up in the Aberdeen Gardens Historic District. (Courtesy of Joyce Brown Wilkins.)

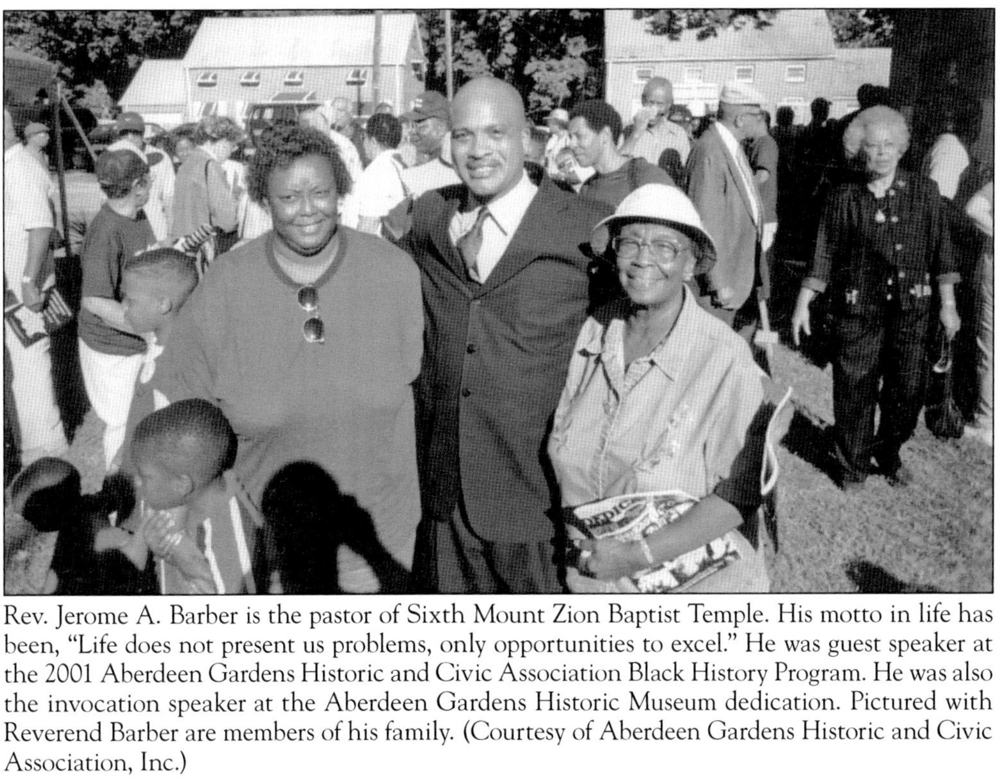

Rev. Jerome A. Barber is the pastor of Sixth Mount Zion Baptist Temple. His motto in life has been, "Life does not present us problems, only opportunities to excel." He was guest speaker at the 2001 Aberdeen Gardens Historic and Civic Association Black History Program. He was also the invocation speaker at the Aberdeen Gardens Historic Museum dedication. Pictured with Reverend Barber are members of his family. (Courtesy of Aberdeen Gardens Historic and Civic Association, Inc.)

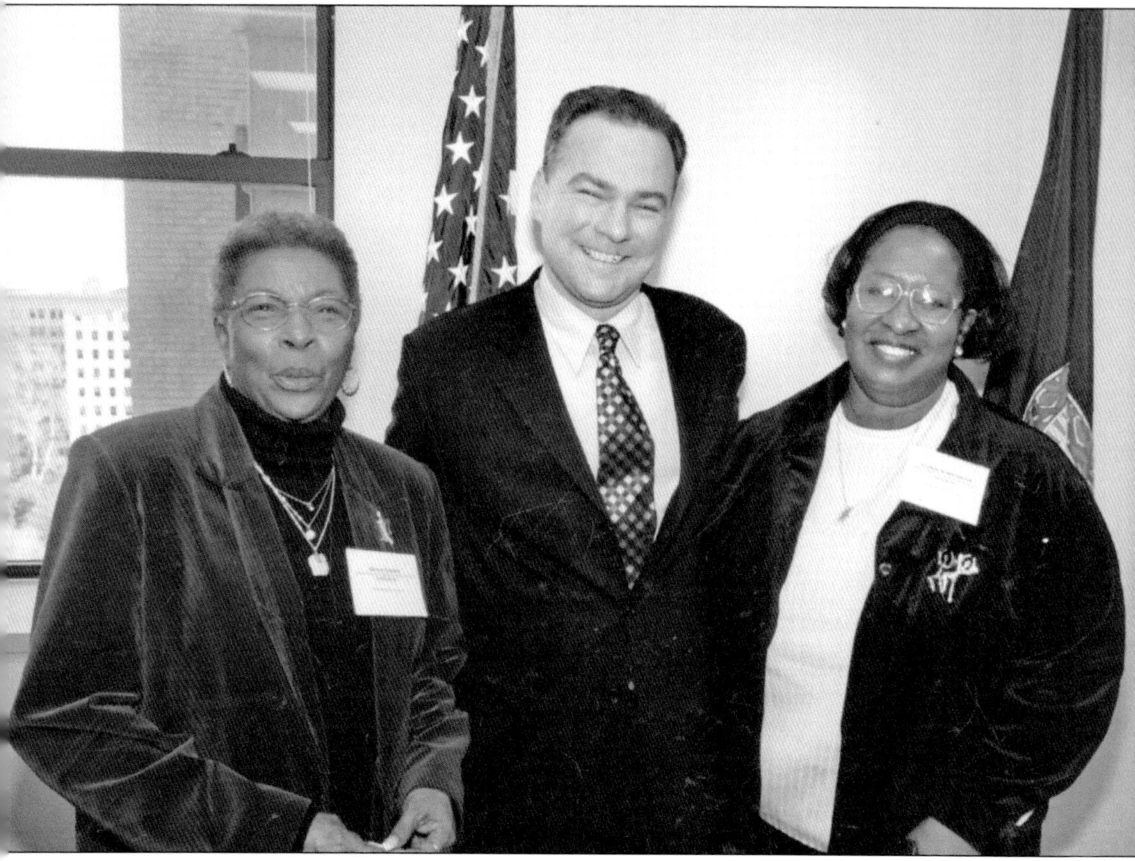

Attending the Preservation of Virginia Conference in Richmond in 2003 are, from left to right, Geneva Cooper, treasurer and editor of the newsletter *Rattler Chronicles*; Timothy Kaine, then lieutenant governor; and Jacqueline Arrington, secretary of the Aberdeen Gardens Historic and Civic Association. The women were honored to be photographed with Kaine, elected the 70th governor of Virginia in 2006. Kaine was elected lieutenant governor in 2001. He was the first Virginia governor to be inaugurated at the Colonial Capitol in Williamsburg since Thomas Jefferson. In 2007, based largely on the commonwealth's strong educational performance, Education Week ranked Virginia as the state where "a child is most likely to have a successful life." The governor has worked with the legislature to make record investments in cleaning Virginia's rivers and the Chesapeake Bay. (Courtesy of the Preservation Alliance of Virginia.)

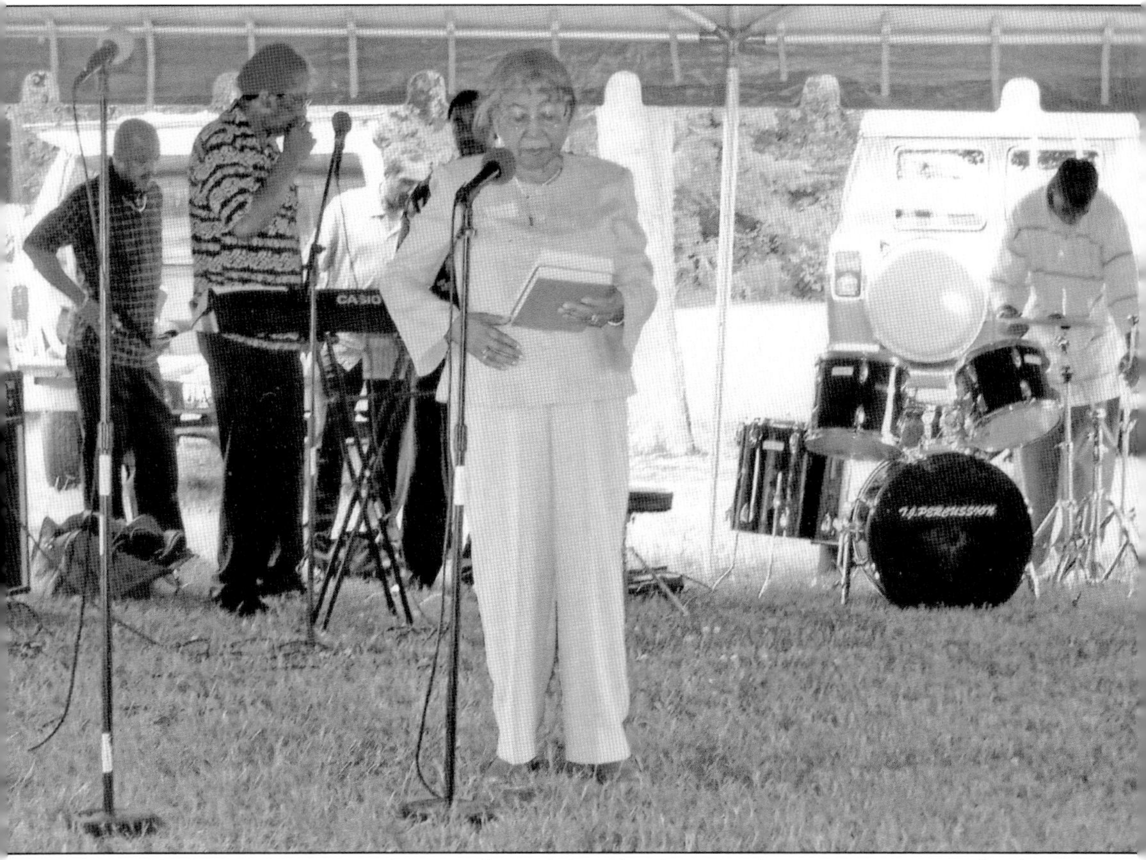

Author Alfreda L. A. Drummond is a resident of the Aberdeen Gardens community. Her book *The Hands of a Teacher: The Alfreda Drummond Story* was published in 1998. The book records the tragedies and triumphs of her journey to become a teacher and tells a story that spans 60 years. Drummond has been a motivational speaker and continues to be a philanthropist, assisting in the furthering of education for teachers. She was one of the speakers at the Heritage Day 2006 celebration. She shared the ups and downs of writing a book but found it to be delightful. In the background, the Little Zion Baptist musical group is preparing to perform. (Courtesy of Catherine Howard.)

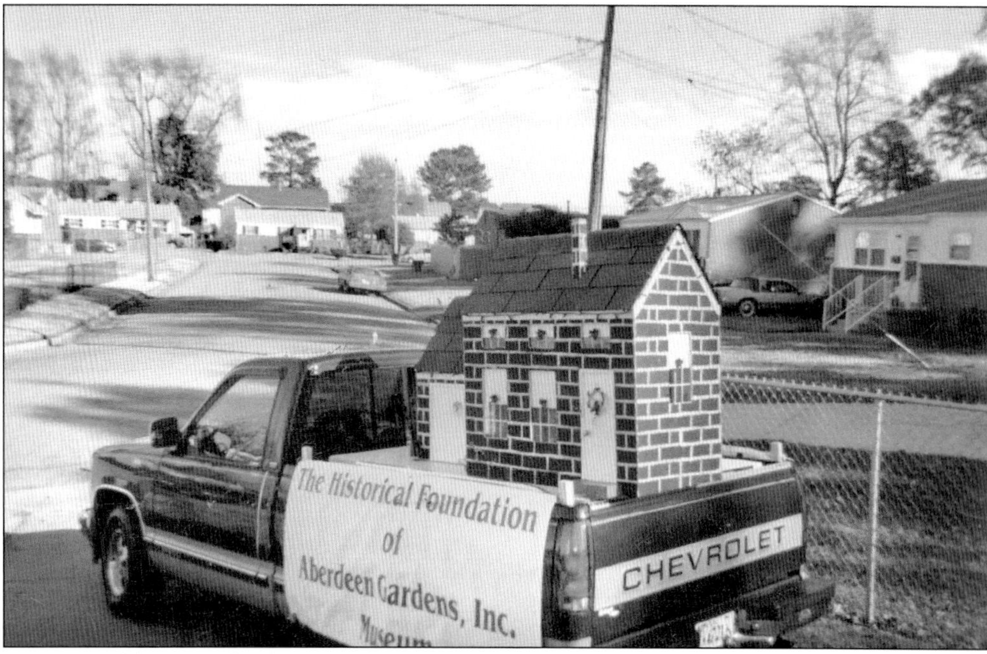

Curtis Franklin, an Aberdeen Gardens Historic and Civic Association member and craftsman, built this replica of the Aberdeen Gardens Historic Museum. The house is used in parades and displays. Recently it was used in the Hunt for Hampton's History event at the newly built 2006 Hampton Conference Center. (Courtesy of Curtis Franklin.)

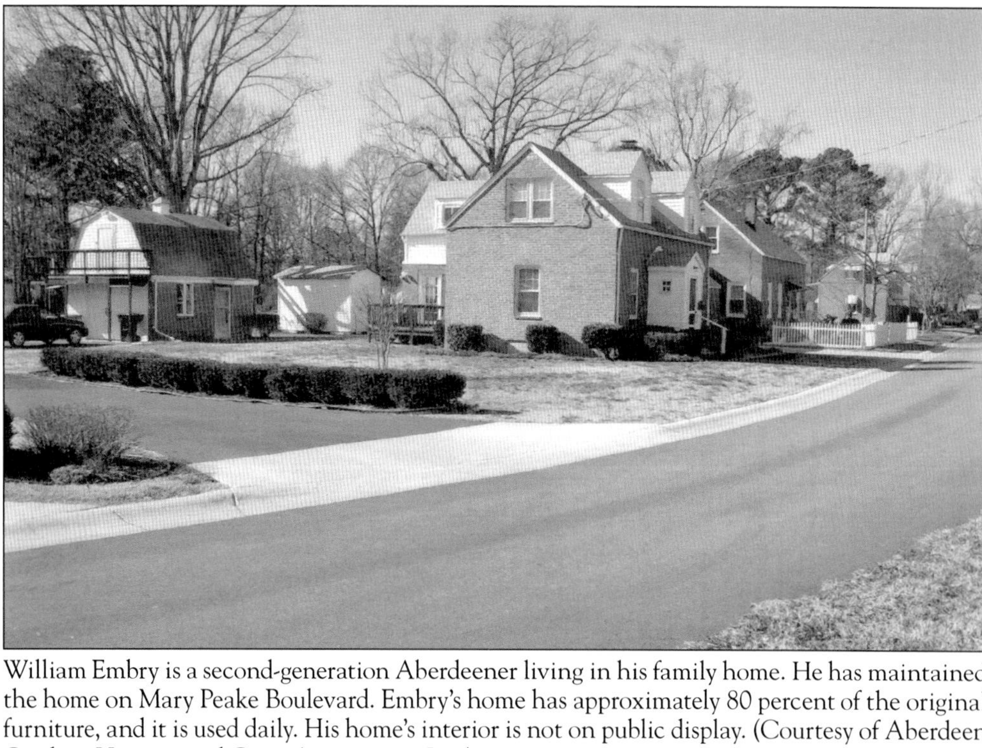

William Embry is a second-generation Aberdeener living in his family home. He has maintained the home on Mary Peake Boulevard. Embry's home has approximately 80 percent of the original furniture, and it is used daily. His home's interior is not on public display. (Courtesy of Aberdeen Gardens Historic and Civic Association, Inc.)

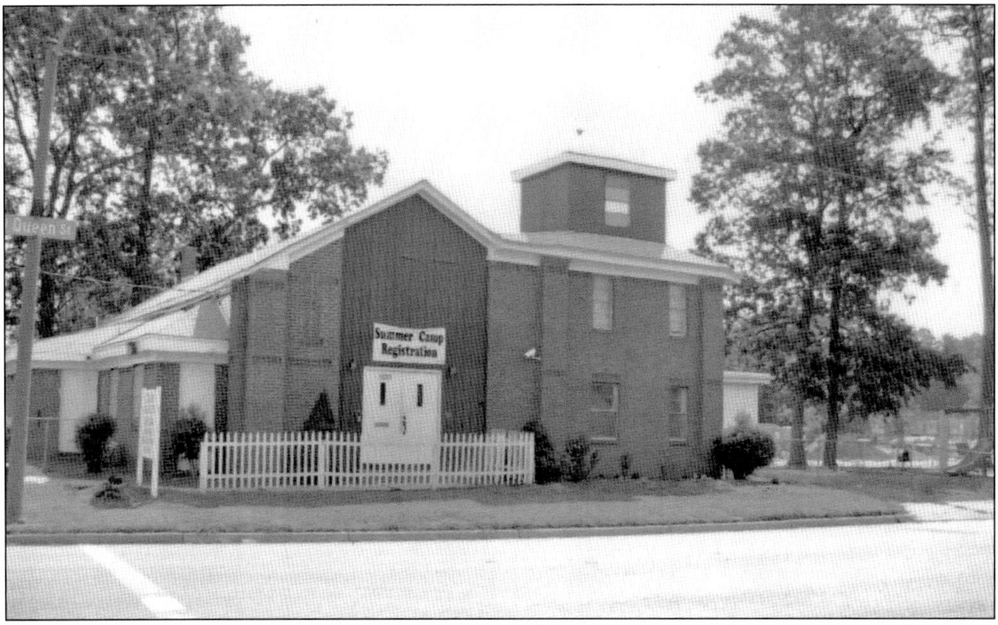

The original Little Zion Baptist Church was established in 1885 under Rev. G. W. Thornton. The church was 26 feet by 36 feet in 1885, and in 1962, after renovations under pastor James Walter Dodd, the church measured 44 feet by 69 feet. In 1981, under Pastor Dodd, a new edifice was begun (below). The old church has now become a daycare center (above). (Courtesy of Jacqueline Baker Roundtree.)

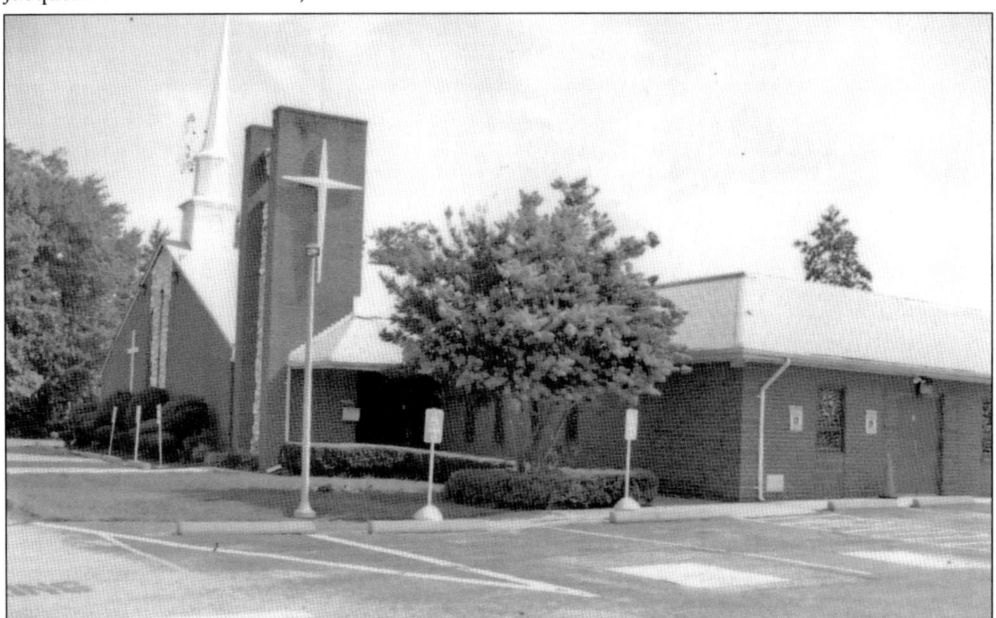

The current Little Zion Baptist Church is located on West Queen Street in Hampton, with Rev. Hallie Richardson Jr. as pastor. The church today is enveloped by hotel construction in the background, but that doesn't deter the members. Church services are at 8:00 a.m. and 11:00 a.m. every Sunday. (Courtesy of Jacqueline Baker Roundtree.)

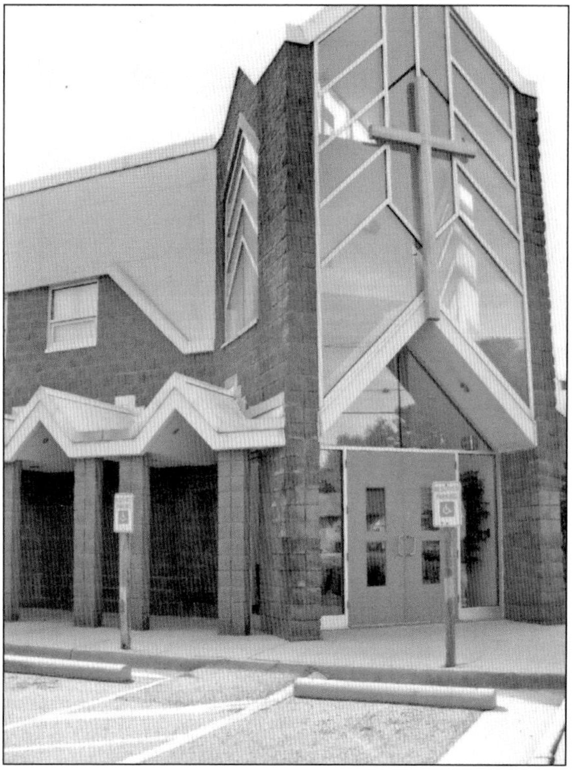

Mount Olive Baptist, one of the early historical churches in the area of Aberdeen Gardens, was built around 1872 and is located on Big Bethel Road in Hampton. The original edifice was a small white building with steps. Rev. W. Randolph Rylander is the pastor. The church and parishioners thrive today in this new edifice on the same acreage. (Courtesy of Jacqueline Baker Roundtree.)

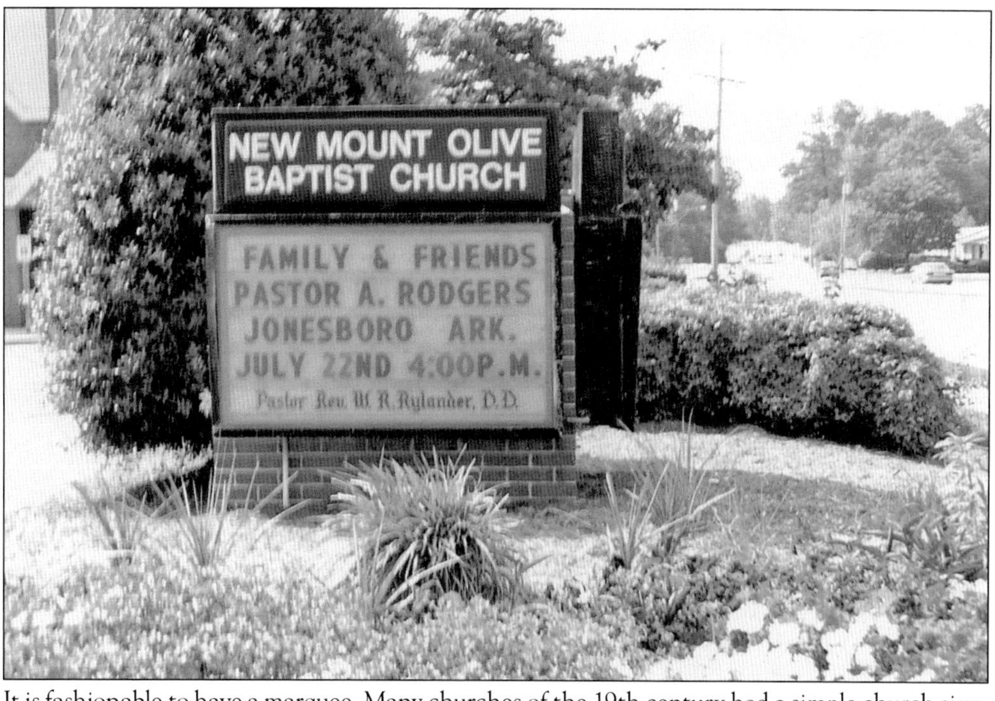

It is fashionable to have a marquee. Many churches of the 19th century had a simple church sign. Today the sign's letters are arranged manually, lighted or unlighted, digital, and big. This marquee's message indicates an upcoming program. (Courtesy of Jacqueline Baker Roundtree.)

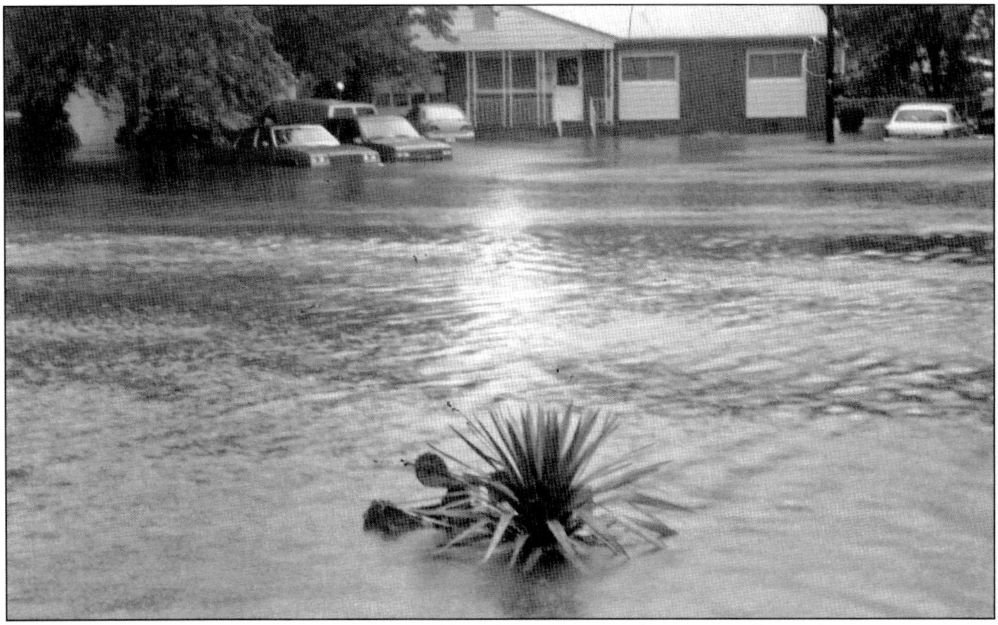

Hurricane Isabel was the costliest and deadliest hurricane in the 2003 Atlantic hurricane season. The Aberdeen Gardens Historic District and surrounding neighborhoods are approximately five miles from the James River and within less than one mile in some areas and two in others from the Newmarket Creek. Flooding does occur during extreme downpours. (Courtesy of Catherine Howard.)

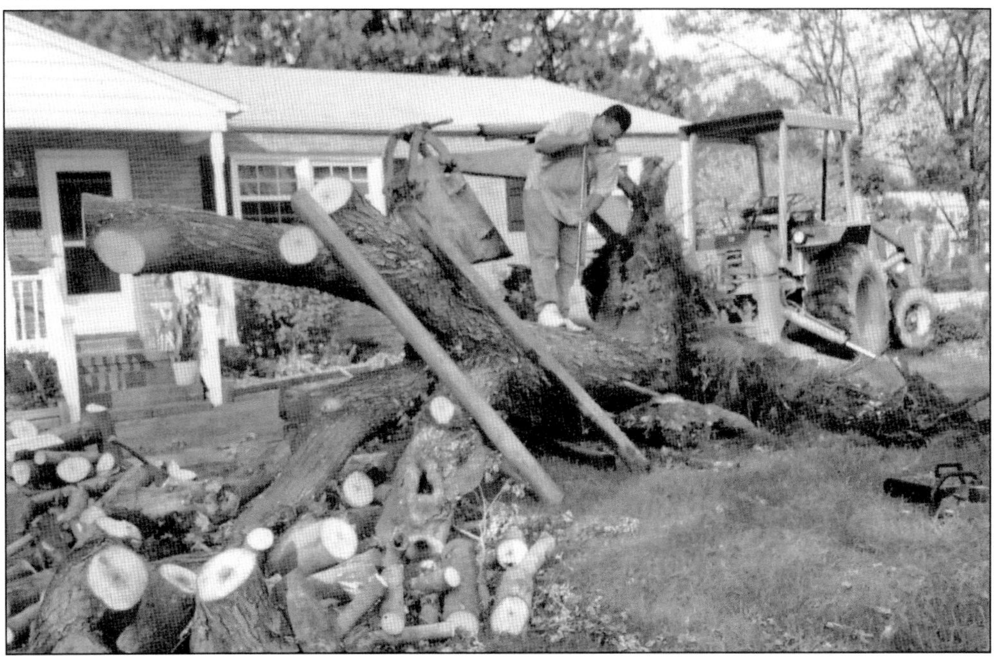

Hurricane Isabel was the ninth tropical storm and fifth hurricane of the 2003 season, and it played havoc. Rainy days for two or three weeks weakened long standing and heavy trees. This was a scene in Granger Court East, south of the Aberdeen Gardens Historic District. (Courtesy of Catherine Howard.)

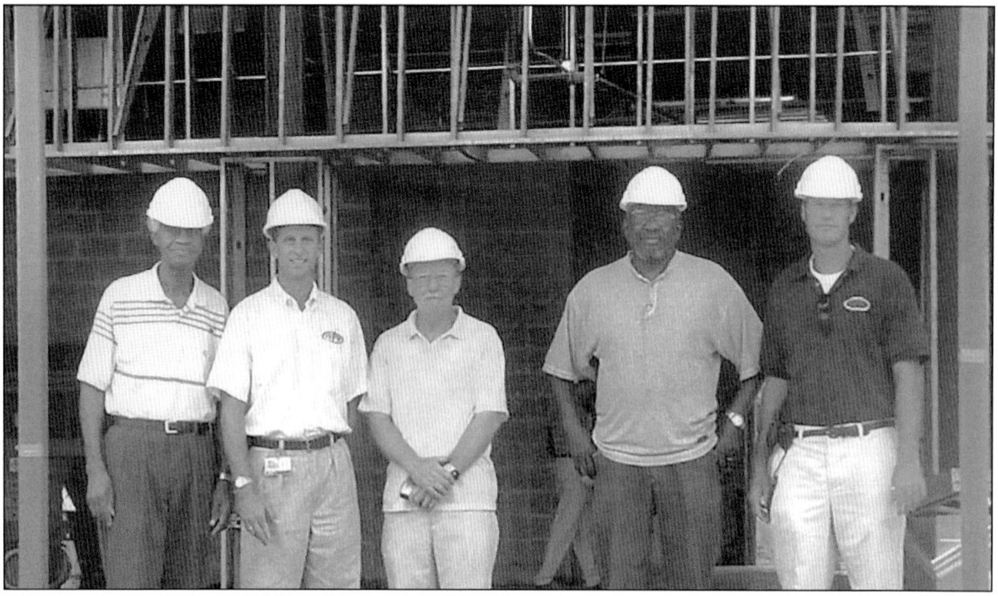

The C. Alton Lindsay Middle School ground-breaking took place on August 13, 2002. Community partners instrumental in the development of West Hampton Community Center were the Aberdeen Gardens Historic and Civic Association neighborhood development committee; Hampton City Parks and Recreation Department neighborhood office; and the Coalition for Youth Alternatives. The architects, engineers, and planners were Hayes, Seay, Mattern, and Mattern, Inc.; the construction company was Sun Bay. (Courtesy of Hampton Neighborhood Office.)

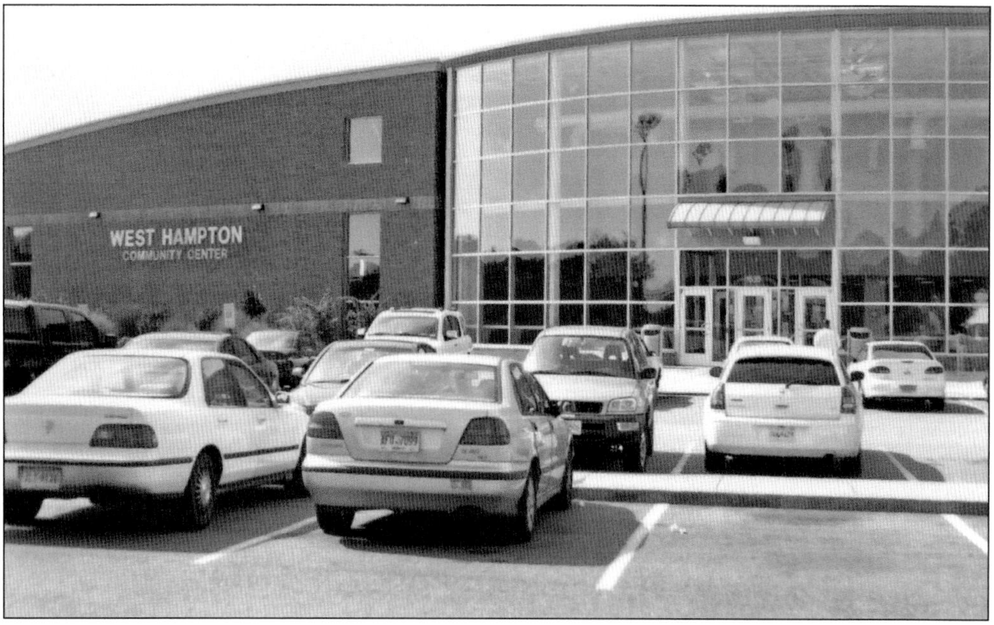

The West Hampton Community Center is a beautiful 24,000-square-foot building. The Aberdeen Gardens Historic and Civic Association was honored to be a part of the reason for its existence. The building was built in 2004 next to the C. Alton Lindsay Middle School at 1636 Briarfield Road in Hampton. There is an outside track that the public has been using for years. Now when it rains, the inside track is available. (Courtesy of Jacqueline Baker Roundtree.)

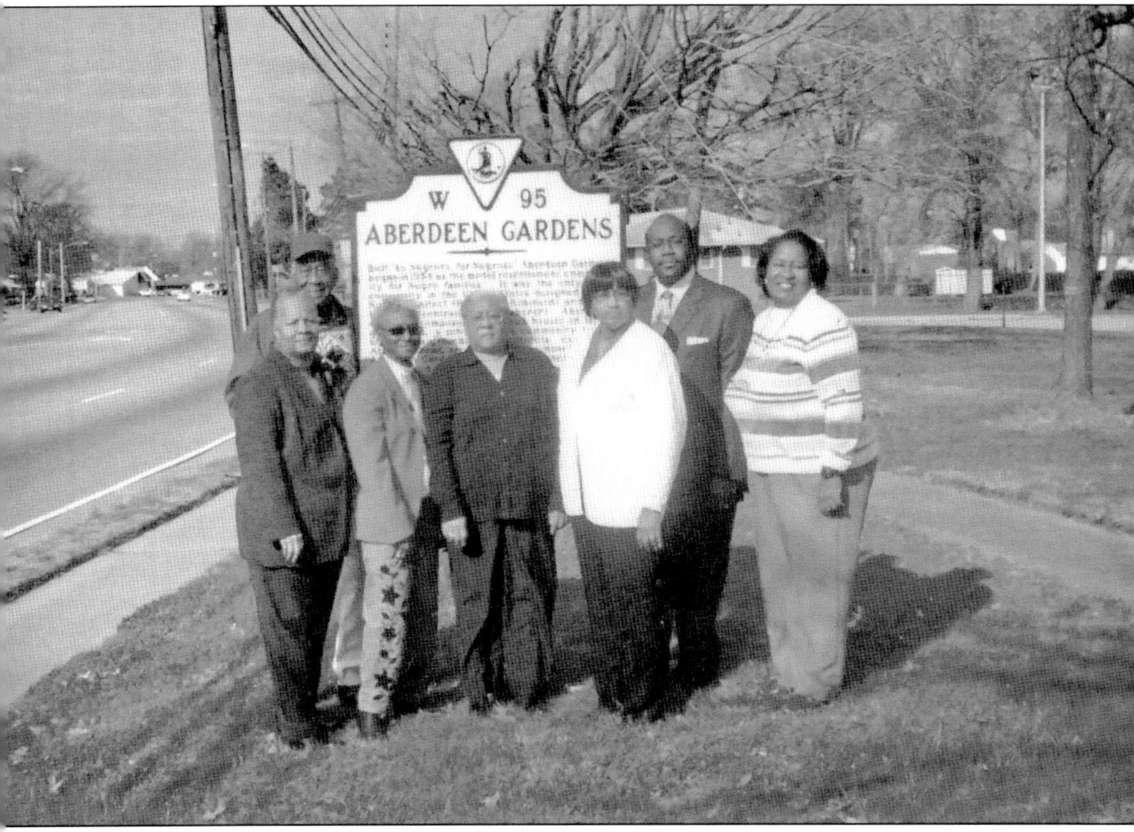

The heritage committee was appointed by the Aberdeen Gardens Historic and Civic Association in 2004 to represent Aberdeen neighborhoods on the City of Hampton's 2007–2010 Implementation Committee, which is in partnership with the overall Jamestown community theme Come Back to Virginia for the Jamestown 400th Anniversary Celebration. The heritage committee uses the theme Come Back to Aberdeen. This committee has been successful in operating the Aberdeen Gardens Historic Museum three days a week: Monday, Wednesday, and Friday from 10:00 a.m. to 2:00 p.m. The heritage committee stands in front of the Aberdeen Gardens marker W95, which rests in the front of the Aberdeen Elementary School. Pictured from left to right are Harmon Stokes, Clarice Burwell Hughes, Catherine Howard, Margaret Jones Wilson, Jacqueline Baker Roundtree, Rev. Hallie Richardson Jr., and Jacqueline Arrington. Members not in this picture are Maj. Ronald Davis and Del. Jeion A. Ward. (Courtesy of Jacqueline Arrington.)